# THE INFERNO OF DANTE

LONDON: HUMPHREY MILFORD
OXFORD UNIVERSITY PRESS

# THE
# INFERNO
# OF DANTE

TRANSLATED INTO ENGLISH TERZA RIMA VERSE
WITH INTRODUCTION AND NOTES BY

## LACY LOCKERT

A.M., PH.D.  FORMERLY ASSISTANT PROFESSOR OF ENGLISH
AT KENYON COLLEGE

*PRINCETON*
PRINCETON UNIVERSITY PRESS
1931

COPYRIGHT, 1931, PRINCETON UNIVERSITY PRESS

PRINTED AT THE PRINCETON UNIVERSITY PRESS
PRINCETON, NEW JERSEY, U.S.A.

*To the Memory of*
*My Dear Aunt*
*Margaret S. Rhodes*

## TRANSLATOR'S PREFACE

*TO compare my own rendering of Dante's* Inferno *with the versions of other translators, would be most unbecoming; it is surely legitimate, however, to explain what sense of lack prompted me, and what I have attempted to do.*

*Translations of the* Divine Comedy *into prose and blank verse have been numerous, and some of them are excellent of their kind. But blank verse can give little idea of the intricately rhymed original, and prose can give little idea of any poetry whatsoever. Renderings which employ the terza rima of Dante himself*[1] *have been, in the main, unsatisfactory; yet difficult as this medium is in English with our paucity of rhymes, it is the only one in which a really adequate version is even possible. The metrical form of the* Divine Comedy *is too distinctive, and too striking in aesthetic effect, to be properly separable from it.*

*A terza rima translation obviously entails certain sacrifices. Even with so flexible a medium as blank verse, the exact word or the definitive phrase must sometimes yield before the demands of metre. Such compromises with perfection are, necessarily, far more frequent when one has to meet the additional requirements of rhyme. The best conceivable terza rima translation of Dante cannot hope to better or to equal a blank verse one in every line. But I do believe that it is possible to render Dante into terza rima with lines of a higher average of excellence, so that the translation is better as a whole, than any existent in blank verse, and with a fair percentage of individual lines and passages not infrequently even*

[1] I mean, of course, its English equivalent; the precise Italian form with hendecasyllabic lines is quite impracticable in our language.

*superior to all previous renderings of them. For Rossetti, in his fragment of Francesca da Rimini, has done exactly this.*

*By far the best terza rima version of the* Divine Comedy *which has yet appeared is that of Melville Best Anderson. Indeed, I doubt whether any considerable improvement upon his (save in respect to a certain coldness of temper which it possesses in sharp contrast to the burning intensity of the original) would be humanly practicable with no greater licence of rhyme than he allows himself. But just such greater licence—at times the most extreme—is in my opinion entirely legitimate in a terza rima translation; for with the additional latitude of phrasing thus gained, hitherto unexploited possibilities of rendering are created, while at the same time the effect of the verse is not seriously impaired. The terza rima form is so close-knit, its rhymes are so numerous beyond the wont of English verse, that the employment of half rhymes, of bare suggestions of rhyme, or even occasionally of mere assonance does not destroy the reader's impression of a continuity of medium. And, moreover, in a language so much richer in rhymes than our own as is the Italian, the ear is less sensitive to the clash of recurrent sounds (as witness our avoidance of verbal repetitions in contrast to the usage in highly inflected languages); so that to us partial rhymes are probably as noticeable correspondences as are perfect rhymes to the countrymen of Dante.*

*With these considerations in mind—their theory vindicated by the illustrious practice of Rossetti and of such translators of* Faust *as Bayard Taylor and Latham—I have permitted myself a degree of licence generally proportionate in each instance to the gain in effectiveness of phrasing which it would secure. In a few cases (e.g. v, 29, 31, 33; xxxiii, 71, 73, 75) where the precisely desired rendering of an especially fine passage would otherwise be lost, I have been content with little more than assonance. Occasionally I have disregarded a final r-sound, since this in correct English pronunciation is not rolled but is almost inaudible. And here and there throughout the poem (perhaps a score of times in all) I have counted as a rhyme the correspondence of the final, unaccented syllable of a hendecasyllabic line with the final, accented syllable of normal decasyllabic lines (e.g. "visage" with "rage" and "sage"). Such a hendecasyllabic line should be read naturally, without distortion of accent to force a rhyme; and the ear will accept it—so actual experiment has demonstrated—without a sense of interruption of the rhyme scheme. And this, I repeat, is the one essential point; these and the other licences are not genuine rhymes—of course not—but* they are substitutes for rhyme *which in their infrequent occurrence are assimilable*[2] *by the terza rima verse to maintain satisfactorily its characteristic flow and thus the general effect of the medium of Dante. The employment of them is a stratagem to secure more effective phrasing without apparent sacrifice of form; all translation is largely a matter of stratagems.*

*Vocally perfect rhymes on which the voice cannot pause, as when a line ends with a preposition or a conjunction (which most terza rima translations now and then admit) are really, unless the verses are read improperly, not so acceptable to the ear as are the licences mentioned above; but because they are impeccable to the eye they are less likely to be cavilled at, and are equally justified, when used sparingly, for the sake of some compensatory advantage.*

*In the matter of literalness, as in the matter of precise rhyme, I have been governed by what could, in each instance, be gained by departing from it. At times I have boldly paraphrased the letter of the original; at other times I have spared no effort to render Dante exactly. Here I have put abstruse Italian into plain English; there I have been careful to preserve the dubiety of an obscure or doubtful text. In this passage the correspondence of sentence-ending with tercet-*

[2] This applies especially to reading aloud; the ear, not the eye, is the real test of verse.

*ending has been maintained; in that one, quite disregarded. I have tried scrupulously to avoid close or frequent repetition of word or sound, a matter generally neglected by translators of Dante (save Cary). The poet's own practice in this respect should no more justify its reproduction in defiance of English usage than a reproduction of his exact syntax or word order would be justified; a good English translation must first of all be good English, conformative to English usage and pleasing to the English ear.*

*Proper names are kept in the Italian form when they are themselves originally Italian; otherwise the customary English form is used. The only exception to this rule is "Beatrice," which I have Anglicized for convenience and because it is a familiar name to us, also.*

*The number of English versions of the* Inferno *almost precludes any originality of phrasing. Therefore I have not hesitated to use the language of previous prose or blank verse translations; indeed, I have at times deliberately appropriated whole lines—have even been at some pains to preserve them intact—when their felicity has made them definitive renderings (e.g. "All hope abandon, ye who enter here"); for I believe that to fit them into the terza rima is a task and achievement arduous enough to be properly considered legitimate and independent work. On the other hand, I have scrupulously avoided indebtedness to any rhymed version. The only exceptions to this rule are a few borrowings from Plumptre and Byron in the latter half of Canto v and from Plumptre in the first half of Canto xxxiii—passages which I did for my own diversion before I had contemplated a translation of the whole poem; and iv, 8 and 9, where an accidental acquaintance with Anderson's splendid lines:*

> *Above the valley of the abyss of woe*
> *Which gathers roar of wailings infinite*

*so impressed them on my mind as to obstruct my own efforts.*

## TRANSLATOR'S PREFACE

*In no other instance did I ever read a word of Mr. Anderson's translation before completing my own, so any other parallels —and there are some striking ones, as instance a whole sequence of identical rhymes in the final canto—between my version and his (or any other rhymed one) are purely fortuitous and simply show that two people have independently solved the same problem in the same way.*

*I have taken over complete and incorporated in my text Dante Gabriel Rossetti's matchless fragment, the last thirty-one lines of the Francesca episode; emulation here would be presumptuous and futile.*

*The Notes pretend to no original research or fresh insight; their substance is eclectic, drawn variously from previous commentators. They attempt to give only such information as one coming to Dante for the first time would need for a proper understanding and appreciation of the poem. Similarly, the Introduction is written for the uninitiated reader, to place before him in brief compass those facts of history and of the poet's life which throw light upon the* Divine Comedy, *and to indicate what, precisely, are the distinctive qualities which make it one of the great masterpieces of the world's literature, and which uniquely characterize it among those masterpieces.*

*In the preparation of this volume, many friends have helped me with criticism, information, or advice. My thanks are especially due to Dr. Orville E. Watson of Bexley Theological Seminary, Dr. and Mrs. Charles Kelsey Gaines of Saint Lawrence University, Mrs. William Foster Peirce, and Dr. Philip W. Timberlake of Kenyon College. There is a great deal in my translation with which they may reasonably be dissatisfied; I have not always followed their suggestions; some may have doubted the wisdom or the value of my ambitious attempt; but, even so, I trust that none of them would wish to forbid me the pleasure of thus making grateful acknowledgment of their unfailing kindness.*

*To Miss Louise Allen my indebtedness is different and far greater. Nearly every tercet of the translation has been submitted to her patient criticism, amounting almost to collaboration; for though she has not infused merit where merit was none, perhaps fully half of the lines have taken their final form in accordance with her judgments, reached frequently after extended debate over the respective advantages of several different renderings. Whatever may be the shortcomings and whatever the excellences of this version of Dante's* Inferno, *it would assuredly have been a much feebler and faultier thing without the aid of her sensitiveness of ear and her discriminating taste.*

LACY LOCKERT

# INTRODUCTION

THE *Inferno* has been selected for translation in this new attempt to convey an understanding and appreciation of Dante to the English reader, because, being the first part of the *Divine Comedy*, it can better be read alone than the *Purgatorio* or the *Paradiso*; because there is no version of it in our language as well done as Melville Best Anderson's rendering of the other two parts[1]; because it is more interesting and appealing to most people than they are; and because (let the truth be plainly told) it is a greater poem than the rest.

This last fact will be vehemently protested by the more extreme devotees of Dante; but it is a logical inference from the one immediately preceding it. For, though in every great work of art there is much of beauty and subtlety that escapes the average reader and is perceived only by those of exceptional taste and insight, it is none the less true that the greatest art is broadly universal in its appeal—that it contains something for every one and not only for the superior few, though these of course will get more from it than will others. If, beginning with Dante's own day, the first part of the *Divine Comedy* has always been the most celebrated and popular, so that, as Mr. Anderson deplores, it "has perhaps a hundred readers where the *Purgatorio* has a score and the *Paradiso* one or two," we may be fairly certain that this

---

[1] Mr. Anderson's hand, as he himself recognized, gained in skill during the course of his translation of the *Divine Comedy*. His *Purgatorio* is in parts much better than his *Inferno*; his *Paradiso* better almost throughout and really very fine. I should as soon think of trying to rival Rossetti's translations as to vie with Mr. Anderson's rendering of Cantos i, ix, and xii of the *Purgatorio* or Cantos xxiii and xxxi of the *Paradiso*—especially these last two; they are definitive achievements, not to be improved upon.

state of affairs is not unwarranted by the relative merits of the three divisions. The fad or prejudice of a single generation does indeed result sometimes in strange temporary errors of appraisal; but the consistent "verdict of the centuries" is not to be gainsaid or reasonably disputed.

Not only is the *Inferno* the highest achievement of Dante, but it does not, as some have asserted, reveal only one side of him. Though it does not emphasize equally all aspects of his mind and genius, in some measure it exhibits most of them. Nothing could be further from the truth than the statement of Dr. Edward Moore that "any one familiar with the *Purgatorio* only, would form a conception of the Poet and of the man Dante so totally different from that formed by a reader of the *Inferno* only, that it would seem inconceivable that both portraits could possibly belong to the same individual." Because of its theme, the first third of the *Divine Comedy* naturally is more concerned with sin and pain and ugliness and acrimony, and less with things benign and beautiful, than are the other two thirds; but the difference is one of proportion alone. The same savage indignation towards his unworthy countrymen which animates so much of the *Inferno* reappears in at least a dozen cantos after Hell is left behind, notably in *Purgatorio* iv and xiv and in *Paradiso* ix; and the very last words that the poet hears from the lips of his adored Beatrice, in the actual presence of God, are a reference to the wickedness of Italy and her Popes. The ingenious and symbolically appropriate tortures of the *Inferno* are paralleled by the ingenious and symbolically appropriate tortures of the *Purgatorio*. The cruel theology which doomed the best of virtuous pagans, like Virgil himself, to Hell's Limbo is dialectically examined and reiterated in the courts of Heaven; the exceptions of Trajan and Rhipeus are of such a nature as but to confirm the rule. On the other hand, even while Dante is depicting the horrors

# INTRODUCTION

of the abyss, he indulges in brief touches which unmistakably indicate his potentialities as a poet of light and not only of darkness—the coming of dawn after his night in the gloomy wood, the fall of twilight at the opening of the second canto, the thirsty Capocchio's vision of the water springs of the Casentine, the brief simile of the chilled flowers reviving beneath the rays of the morning sun and the extended ones of the peasant beholding his fields white with hoarfrost and of the fireflies spangling the summer dusk of a peaceful vale, and the many comparisons drawn from a close observation of bird life. Beatrice is seldom so gracious and attractive a figure in her actual presence as in Virgil's story of her appearance before him. What is indeed unique in the *Inferno* is such grasp of human drama and pathos as the episodes of Francesca and Ugolino display; what one indeed might not anticipate of Dante from a perusal of the *Inferno* alone, is that he was capable of such grotesquely fantastic allegory as characterizes the mystical procession in the *Purgatorio*, or of the tedious philosophical and theological disquisitions which occupy so many pages both of it and of the *Paradiso*. And to say this, is but to repeat what was said at the outset: that the *Inferno* is a greater work than the other parts of the *Divine Comedy*.

## BIOGRAPHY

To a real understanding either of this poet or of his poem, some knowledge of his life and times is essential, for scarcely any other man has so woven these things into his writings.

By all odds the most important fact of Dante's environment was the civil strife by which the Italy of his day was torn. This strife began with the historic feud between the Guelfs and the Ghibellines, the supporters respectively of the Pope and the German Emperor in their conflicting claims to authority. The two factions represented a social as well as a political division. The Ghibelline party was that of the nobles, haughty and irreligious—a military aristocracy of Teutonic strain who were prone to set themselves above the law. The Guelfs, on the other hand, were the popular party; their chief adherents were wealthy burghers, pious and stout champions of civic freedom against the oppressive sway of the Empire; they bore certain resemblances to the English Puritans of a later age. The discord engendered by this cleavage was established in almost every city of northern Italy, in each instance coloured by local quarrels which it absorbed and deriving from them special features peculiar to that place alone. Houses were converted into strongholds, streets were barricaded, and there were frequent reversals of fortune, now one side and now the other temporarily gaining the upper hand, expelling the leaders of the opposing faction from the town, and destroying or confiscating their property.

The Guelf-Ghibelline feud raged at its height during the latter part of the life of the Emperor Frederick II (1194-1250). After the passing of that great monarch the defeat of his successors, Manfred and Conradin, and the extermination of his line dealt a death blow to the Ghibelline cause. The era of comparative tranquillity which followed was for the Italian cities one comparable to that enjoyed by Greece between the Persian and Peloponnesian wars; and among them the rôle most similar to that of Athens was played by Florence. A virtually independent municipality like many of her neighbours, this city grew so rapidly in wealth and magnificence that within the space of forty years she was almost completely transformed. Manufactures and commerce prospered; ancient ways of simplicity were exchanged for luxurious living; art dawned with the paintings of Cimabue, and then came Giotto; and literature, no longer couched in dead Latin but in the native tongue—the amatory poetry of

## INTRODUCTION

Provence with all the artificial conventions and idealizations of the medieval love code, but with a graver note and a more metaphysical turn—now first flourished. Toward the end of the century buildings of hitherto unexampled splendour began to be erected. Power was vested in the hands of the trades' guilds, and a complicated system of government was designed to protect the populace from the machinations of nobles or merchant princes. Throughout this time there was indeed no lack of wars, just as in the case of the Athens of Cimon and Pericles; but they were not of an exhausting sort, and were in the main successful.

It was in this city of Florence and immediately on the eve of this fortunate period, in the year 1265, that Dante Alighieri was born. His family were well-to-do Guelfs, of a station not the highest yet sufficiently high to open to him the best circles of Florentine society. He early showed an aptitude for studies and letters, came at least in some measure under the influence of Brunetto Latini, the most notable scholar of the day, and won the friendship of Guido Cavalcanti, the greatest poet who had yet arisen in Italy, and of other lyrists. He appears to have served in the campaign of 1289, taking part in the defeat of the Tuscan Ghibellines at Campaldino and in the siege and capture of the Pisan fortress of Caprona. But by all means the most important event of his boyhood and youth was a love comprehended with difficulty by the modern mind, but so strong as to colour and shape all his life.

Dante was only nine years old when he first met Beatrice Portinari, herself a child of eight. He declares that even then he felt her compelling influence. Certainly at eighteen, on his next recorded sight of her, she utterly possessed his heart. The passion which he conceived for her was one wholly engendered by idealizing fancy. He appears to have seen her but a few times in all, and may never really have talked with her. He could have had no genuine comprehension of her mind and character. She very possibly was never aware of his feelings. But to his brooding imagination she seemed the epitome of all grace and goodness, and the inspiration and source of all good in him. There was never any hope of possession—she presently married some one else—nor the slightest trace of illicit sensual desire mingled with his worship.

We must understand that this passion, so strange and even absurd to our habits of thought, was not at all strange or unique in that day. It was precisely in accord with the current philosophy of the "courts of love" and the traditions of chivalry, was exactly the emotion which the ideal lover and poet was supposed to have for his lady; and as people in every age generally manage to pour their feelings into the mould prescribed by dominant convention, similar artificial and high-flown sentiments were professed alike by spiritual, imaginative souls who more or less thoroughly convinced themselves of possessing them, and by the carnally minded who made of them the cloak for their amours. What was indeed unusual in Dante's love for Beatrice was its intensity, an intensity which was the result of the man's fervent heart and vivid imagination, so that what for many others was a delicate plaything became for him a consuming fire and a master passion.

Beatrice died in 1290, and at some unknown date thereafter appeared Dante's first volume, the *Vita Nuova,* or "New Life," consisting of various sonnets and canzoni which he had written on the subject of his love during her lifetime and of his sorrow after her death, connected by commentary and explanation in prose. Many of these poems had been circulated separately, when they were first written. Almost prostrated with grief for a time, he at length found absorption in study, particularly of philosophy. He presently married one Gemma Donati—they had perhaps been contracted to each other in childhood—who bore him at least three children. And in view of numerous plain statements in the *Divine Comedy*, it is impossible not to ascribe also to these concluding years of the thirteenth century a certain amount of unworthy and dissolute conduct from which he was eventually turned by some inner experience closely resembling the phenomenon of religious conversion.

In about 1295 Dante entered politics. The clouds of factional strife were again lowering darkly over Florence. Dissension had long been gathering head in the ranks of the victorious Guelfs. The new Guelf aristocracy, composed of the greater magnates, was arrayed against the middle-class burghers. The former party, called the Neri or Blacks, represented the extreme Guelf position; their opponents, the Bianchi or Whites, were the moderates; and paradoxically it was now the ultra-Guelfs who were in a position analogous to that of the Ghibellines formerly, for just as the Ghibellines had sought to impose the authority of the Emperor on Florence, so now did the Neri, as the extreme partisans of his adversary, the Pope, seek similarly to impose the authority of the Pope, whereas the Bianchi, now as always, stood for local autonomy.

Himself numbered among the Whites, and his wife a kinswoman of Corso Donati, head of the Blacks, Dante's part in this turmoiled situation appears to have been that of a sensible and patriotic citizen. He stoutly resisted all papal encroachments upon the liberties of Florence. After the riots and bloodshed of May 1, 1300, being elected one of the six priors or governors of the city for the prescribed term of two months, he and his colleagues enacted a decree of banishment against the leaders of both parties, as a last desperate measure to preserve the peace, though this decree affected his own dearest friend, Guido Cavalcanti. Had the sentence been impartially sustained, Florence might even yet have been saved. But on account of the unhealthiness of their place of exile (which cost Guido his life) the Bianchi were permitted by the next Priorate to return, soon became all-powerful, and proceeded to persecution and expulsion of their enemies. A break with the Pope followed, a French army was summoned to reduce the "rebels," Charles of Valois entered Florence in November, 1301, with the exiled Neri at his heels, the city was given over to massacre and rapine, and wholesale banishment was visited upon the hapless Whites.

Dante was at that time absent on an embassy to Rome, in a futile effort to come to terms with Pope Boniface. He never saw again the place of his birth. Early in 1302, on the trumped-up charge of peculation and corrupt practices while in office, he was sentenced to exile and the payment of a heavy fine. A little later all his property was confiscated and he himself was condemned to be burned alive if he should ever come within the territories of Florence.

The rest is but a confused record of wanderings, of temporary sojourn at the court of this or that petty ruler, while his proud, sensitive spirit learned "how salt is the taste of another's bread, and how hard a path it is to ascend and descend another's stairs." He is thought to have visited Paris, and possibly even England. His wife did not share his exile; her connection with the chief family of the Neri insured her and their children against want if she remained in Florence. He for a time made common cause with the other banished Whites, but at length, disgusted by their folly, withdrew himself from them and became "a party of his own." His political creed was a sort of ideal Ghibellinism, a belief that both Pope and Emperor were equally ordained by God to rule the world—the one in the religious, the other in the temporal sphere—and that any invasion of the mutually exclusive prerogatives of either was a usurpation and a crime.

## INTRODUCTION

On the appearance in Italy of the new Emperor, Henry of Luxemburg, in 1310 he was thrown into a state of feverish anticipation, but Henry's untimely death left his prospects more hopeless than ever. Finally, in 1315, he was offered an opportunity to return to Florence, on condition of submitting to a nominal fine and penance. The letter is still preserved in which he indignantly refuses to accept the stigma of a crime of which he was innocent, and declares that he will never enter Florence save with honour, and if not thus, then elsewhere he can still contemplate nature and truth, assured that his bread will not fail. And so this great, lonely, embittered man, whose best beloved were dead, who had left behind him whatever was yet dear, and who saw his aims and ideals frustrate throughout the world, moved on his austere path —to Verona, and later to Ravenna.

But meanwhile, through all these years, a marvellous poem had been taking shape under his hands. At the end of the *Vita Nuova* he had spoken of a wonderful vision that was granted him, after which he had resolved to celebrate Beatrice no further till he could do so more worthily. Since that time he had written, besides various lyrics, an unfinished volume called the *Convito,* or "Banquet," of mingled poems and prose commentary like the *Vita Nuova* but abstrusely philosophical, and two imposing Latin works, one, the *Monarchia,* setting forth his political theories, the other an unfinished treatise in favour of the vernacular Italian as the language for literary composition. At what date he finally commenced the discharge of his vow to say of Beatrice what had never before been said of any woman—presumably by developing the theme of his "vision"—is unknown. The task may have been begun prior to his banishment and then been interrupted by the loss of the manuscript, which he left behind him in Florence, until, after some years, this was restored to him—such is the legend transmitted by Boccaccio, and if it is true, we should infer that the *Convito* was undertaken in the interval and then abandoned when he found himself able to resume the other work. Be that as it may, nothing could have been more humanly natural than that, amid the isolation and defeat and sorrows of his exile, his heart should return to the love dream of his youth, from which it had fallen away by reason of his engrossment in the studies and pursuits of life; that through the desolate blackness which enveloped him, the gracious memory of that long-lost, worshipped one, with all the associations of the old untroubled days that could never be again, should rise before him like a shining star; and that he should passionately rededicate to her his genius and its master work. Nor is it unlikely that at that indeterminate but doubtless earlier time when he abandoned the evil ways into which he had strayed, it was indeed his thought of the dead Beatrice which furnished the initial or decisive impulse toward rectitude; so that in a real sense, if not in the sense that his adoring fancy conceived, he owed to her the regeneration of his soul.

His great poem was finished at Ravenna, where he spent the last years of his life in comparative peace and happiness. Fame was his: the *Inferno* and the *Purgatorio* were already circulated when he went there; and folk used to look with awe, as he passed them, at the man who had walked in Hell. Bologna desired his presence, and offered the laurel crown if he would come. His two sons and perhaps his daughter were with him, and he did not lack congenial associates; especially strong was his friendship for Dino Perini, a younger Florentine. But it was as though the prayer with which he had ended the *Vita Nuova*, that he might be permitted to follow his lady when he had fitly celebrated her, had been heard, and his vital forces had sustained him but for the achievement of that task. The *Paradiso* was scarce completed and the great work of his life accomplished

# INTRODUCTION

when, in 1321, he undertook a diplomatic mission to Venice in the service of his host, Guido da Polenta, from which he returned unsuccessful, and, contracting a fever, died soon afterwards, at the age of fifty-six.

He died; but with an immediacy and a fervour which have rarely been equalled and never surpassed, his poem was universally recognized as a classic. He had called it a "Comedy," both because it begins in gloom and ends in bliss and because it was written in the Italian vernacular and not in time-honoured Latin like Virgil's stately epic, which he calls a "lofty tragedy" in the twentieth canto of the *Inferno*; later generations affixed to his noun the adjective "Divine," and as the "Divine Comedy" it is still known. Lectures upon it were endowed at Florence, and the first lecturer was Boccaccio himself. During the darkest days of Italian servitude in the sixteenth, seventeenth, and eighteenth centuries, its repute indeed suffered a decline, but thereafter waxed again and for the last one hundred and fifty years has grown apace until to-day the danger is actually not of insufficient appreciation, but rather of unmeasured and undiscriminating worship. Enthusiasts have maintained that "this medieval miracle of song" is the greatest single work, and its author the greatest poet, in the literature of the world; few competent judges would deny that it stands with the *Iliad* and the *Odyssey* above all other examples of non-dramatic poetry.

### CRITICAL APPRAISAL

The most obvious gift possessed by the author of the *Divine Comedy*—for it strikes at once upon the attention of every reader, whether scholarly or unlettered—is that of telling a story. In view of the difficulty of his theme, which deals with things outside of human experience and encountered nowhere in mortal life or on the face of the earth, it is doubtful if any other writer has ever equalled Dante in this respect. Considered simply as a story, how marvellous his poem is, alike for imaginative invention and sheer narrative power! Save perhaps in its latter portions, where symbolism and didacticism have too large a place, it will hold the absorbed attention of any one who yields himself to its flow of fancy—even to-day when its theological and cosmological ideas have long been obsolete. We can somewhat imagine how gripping must have been its spell when it was thoroughly in line with current conceptions. The variety of incident is inexhaustible, the choice of figures and scenes shrewdly effective, the vividness of depiction unfailing, and the power to create "atmosphere" (not only different in each of the three main divisions of the theme, but subtly varied in almost every canto) comparable to that of such noted masters of this phase of artistry as Poe and Conrad. Though certain of Dante's figures of speech, mainly in the *Paradiso,* are grotesque or too homely in their application, his judgment of what is congruous and "convincing," at least in so far as concerns invention, was almost infallible. In his *Inferno* the tortures, the victims, the demons, and the mythological monsters seem appropriate and real in their detailed, appallingly physical presentation. But when he came to write of Paradise, he knew that the "things which eye hath not seen and ear hath not heard" could not be represented by terrestrial forms, and alone among poets has created a Heaven sufficiently unlike our earthly life to be other than hopelessly naïve and absurd to us.

Not only is Dante a supreme story-teller, but his narrative manner is essentially modern. It may even be maintained that our present-day technique of narration was born with Dante—was invented and for ever shaped by him. Homer's way of telling a story is not our way, nor is Virgil's; Dante's whole method of attacking a subject, his transitions, his handling of dialogue, his management of anticipation, suspense, surprise, and dramatic situation are almost precisely our own. The point may be in some measure illustrated by setting side by side prose translations of the openings of cantos in the *Iliad*, the *Odyssey*, the *Aeneid*, and the *Divine Comedy*. Typical of Homer are these:

> Thus kept the Trojans watch; but the Achaians were holden of heaven-sent panic, handmaid of palsying fear, and all their best were stricken to the heart with grief intolerable. Like as two winds stir up the main, the home of fishes, even the north wind and the west wind that blow from Thrace, coming suddenly; and the dark billow straightway lifteth up its crest and casteth much tangle out along the sea; even so was the Achaians' spirit troubled in their breast.
>
> But Atrides was stricken to the heart with sore grief, and went about bidding the clear-voiced heralds summon every man by name to the assembly, but not to shout aloud; and he himself toiled amid the foremost. So they sat sorrowfully in assembly, and Agamemnon stood up weeping. . . .
>
> —*Iliad* ix.

> Now when they had sped in flight across the palisade and trench, and many were overcome at the hands of the Danaans, the rest were stayed, and abode beside the chariots in confusion, and pale with terror, and Zeus awoke, on the peaks of Ida, beside Hera of the golden throne. Then he leaped up, and stood, and beheld the Trojans and Achaians, those in flight, and these driving them on from the rear, even the Argives, and among them the prince Poseidon.
>
> —*Iliad* xv.

> Then Odysseus of many counsels stripped him of his rags and leaped on to the great threshold with his bow and quiver full of arrows, and poured out all the swift

shafts there before his feet, and spake among the wooers:

"Lo, now is this terrible trial ended at last; and now will I know of another mark, which never yet man has smitten, if perchance I may hit it and Apollo grant me renown."

With that he pointed the bitter arrow at Antinous.
—*Odyssey* xxii.

Virgil is somewhat less antique of flavour, but is unlike us in the construction of his long sentences and in his use of the historical present:

Soon as Turnus raised up the flag of war from Laurentum's citadel, and the horns rang with their hoarse notes, soon as he roused his fiery steeds and clashed his arms, straightway men's hearts were troubled; all Latium at once is leagued in startled uprising, and her sons rage madly.
—*Aeneid* viii.

Meanwhile there is thrown open the palace of omnipotent Olympus, and the Sire of gods and King of men calls a council to his starry dwelling, whence, high-throned, he surveys all lands, the Dardan camp, and the Latin people. Within the double-doored hall they take their seats, and the king begins:
—*Aeneid* x.

Dante occasionally echoes the classical manner—thus the extended comparison with which he opens the twenty-fourth canto of the *Inferno*—but not often. The first lines of his cantos, turned into English prose, might almost be mistaken for the beginnings of chapters in some novel of to-day dealing with adventures in strange lands. Such passages may be dramatic, as:

"Through me is the way into the woeful city. Through me is the way to everlasting pain. Through me is the

> way unto the lost people. Justice moved my lofty Maker; the Divine Power fashioned me, the Highest Wisdom, and the Primal Love. Before me were no things created, save eternal; and eternal I endure. Leave every hope, ye who enter."
>
> These words in sombre hue I beheld written over the summit of a gate.
>
> —*Inferno* iii.

Or they may simply continue the flow of the narrative, as:

> Nessus had not yet reached the other side, when we plunged into a wood which was marked by no path. Not green were the leaves, but of a dusky hue; not smooth the branches, but gnarled and twisted; no fruits were there, but poisonous thorns. Those savage wild beasts that hold in hate the cultivated tracts between the Cecina and Corneto have no thickets so rough and so dense. Here the foul harpies make their nests. . . . Broad wings have they, and human necks and faces, feet with claws, and their huge bellies feathered; they utter mournful cries on the strange trees.
>
> —*Inferno* xiii.

In either case the turn of both thought and phrase is that of a Maupassant rather than of a medieval poet. The style of Chaucer is nothing like so modern, nor that of Cervantes, nor of the first novelists. Not until the nineteenth century, indeed, did the technique of story-telling, developed and refined through many generations, become at the same time so direct and so trenchant.

But the art of Dante is not the result of intuition; it is carefully wrought, conscious art. Among previous writers only Virgil, from the study of whom he says he learned his craftsmanship, and perhaps Sophocles approach him in the matter of painstaking, self-critical effort, nor have many gone beyond him in it since. Now, the miracle about this art is its isolation. Sophocles had Aeschylus to build upon, who was himself preceded by Phrynichus and other "lost" dramatists; Virgil had Ennius and Lucretius in his own tongue and the still living tradition of all Greek epic and elegy from Homer to the Alexandrians, for every educated Roman of his day was bilingual. But prior to Dante there was absolutely no vernacular Italian poetry save amoristic and metaphysical trifles—nothing ambitious in scope or considerable in length. Even the verse form of his masterpiece—the terza rima so fluid and close-knit for sustained narrative, yet so lyrical as to make the whole *Divine Comedy* "one prolonged song"—appears to have been his own invention. But though the work of literary pioneers is usually naïve, inspirational, and discursive; though a perfected and deliberate technique is usually evolved only in a period which is the artistic flowering of long-continued antecedent endeavour, no instance unless that of Flaubert can be found of more minutely detailed foreplanning more scrupulously executed than Dante's in the case of the *Divine Comedy*. In the words of Grandgent: "With all its huge bulk and bewilderingly multifarious detail, it is as sharply planned as a Gothic cathedral. Dante had the very uncommon power of fixing his attention upon the part without losing sight of the whole: every incident, every character receives its peculiar development, but at the same time is made to contribute its exact share to the total effect. The more one studies the poem, the clearer become its general lines, the more intricate its correspondences, the more elaborate its climaxes."

The three parts of the *Divine Comedy*—each of which ends with the words *le stelle* (the stars)—contain almost exactly the same number of lines: 4,720 in the *Inferno,* 4,755 in the *Purgatorio,* and 4,758 in the *Paradiso*. At the end of the *Purgatorio* the poet explains that he must draw

## INTRODUCTION

that division of his poem to a close, because all the pages allotted to it are full and the restrictions of his art suffer him to proceed no further! There are an even hundred cantos altogether—thirty-three in each part, if the first canto of the *Inferno* be reckoned as introductory to the whole. Hell is divided into nine circles; Purgatory into nine stages (counting the waiting place of the negligent at the foot of the mountain and the Terrestrial Paradise at its top, as well as its seven cornices); Heaven into nine spheres, besides the absolute Empyrean heaven. The circles of Hell are guarded in each instance by creatures of classical mythology appropriate to the sins punished in each. No wonder that Dante says the labour of his great work kept him lean for many years, when to this precision of design he added an indefatigable care for minutiae, so that every tercet was fashioned according to his will and crowded with other meanings than those which its words in themselves convey.

For scarcely less obvious than the narrative excellence of the *Divine Comedy* is the fact that this poem is not merely a narrative. It is an allegory as well—indeed, it seems to be several allegories at once, so that each detail may be taken to mean several different things, to fit into one or another scheme of interpretation. This pilgrim, Dante, who goes through the spirit realms is not only an explorer of the abodes of the damned, the penitential, and the blessed; he is the human soul encountering temptation, probing the depths of sin with the help of reason, and led to salvation by celestial aid; he is Dante's own soul turned from error to God—or the whole fabric of symbolism may be understood to apply to Mankind in the mass, or to contemporary politics rather than to moral or religious matters at all. Now one thread of allegory shows more prominently, now another; but it is rare that several threads cannot be discerned at once; and they are present even in the very smallest particulars of the story.[2] It is doubtful whether any other piece of allegorical writing in all literature is so well worked out as the *Divine Comedy,* so that the literal fiction never stultifies the figurative sense, nor vice versa.

Allegory was popular in the Middle Ages. The *Odyssey* was unknown to Dante; but the sixth book of the *Aeneid* furnished a familiar model for such a journey as he tells of, and he may have been acquainted with some of the numerous medieval legends dealing with visions of the other world. But his account of Hell, Purgatory, and Heaven was unique in its strong element of spiritual autobiography, whereby, as Dean Church points out, it anticipated *Pilgrim's Progress, Wilhelm Meister, Faust,* Rousseau, *The Excursion,* and so much else of subsequent literature; unique also in its orderly schematic division of each of the three realms of the dead into abodes appropriate for their respective inhabitants; and still more strikingly unique in Dante's peopling them with his own more or less famous contemporaries recently deceased. This procedure, involving moral judgments which were the poet's own, reveals his love of good and intense hatred of evil; but it is not true, as it has been charged, that he thus sought to give vent to his political animosities. Guelfs and

[2] Much of the scholarship expended on the *Divine Comedy,* especially at first, has been concerned with bringing to light the hidden meanings of the poem. The Notes in the present volume attempt only occasional elucidations, and these generally the most obvious, as specimens of its figurative method. An example of what the devoted ingenuity of a modern enthusiast can discover in, or read into, Dante, may be seen in the elaborate Interpretative Analysis prefixed to Mr. Courtney Langdon's text and translation; yet even if the poet did not mean everything that Mr. Langdon sets forth (and Mr. Langdon does not claim that he did), it impressively remains true that only the greatest and most self-consistent works of the human intellect will thus admit of being passed through the prism of a mind of another time and civilization; similarly Mr. Thomas Dwight Goodell has shown in his *Athenian Tragedy* how the *Ajax* of Sophocles can be interpreted equally well on three distinct planes of sophistication, representing respectively the viewpoint of the average Greek, of a Greek intellectual, and of a modern rationalist.

Ghibellines were ranged side by side alike amid the tortures of the abyss and the joys of Paradise. Dante knew none of our modern cant about hating the sin and loving the sinner; his feelings toward the individual were always fervent, and his opinions were doubtless often prejudiced (it could scarce have been otherwise with a man of such strong convictions), but in each case they represented a just appraisal according to his lights. Affectionate memories did not stay him from placing his old master, Brunetto Latini, among the damned.

But as the *Divine Comedy* is something more than a narrative, so also is it something more than an allegory. In its pages the whole of medieval Catholic civilization is summed up and becomes articulate. Dante was not one of the pioneers of human thought; his vision in no way outwent his own times. His universe was the narrow, static, compartmented universe of scholasticism; the great ideas of the Renaissance, just ahead, find no presage in him; the concept of "Progress," which has opened such vistas to the modern mind, never dawned upon his. But no other man—not even Dryden or Tennyson—has so completely spoken for the age in which he lived. "He entered on his great poem," says Dean Church, "to shadow forth, under the figure of his own conversion and purification, not merely how a single soul rises to its perfection, but how this visible world, in all its phases of nature, life, and society, is one with the invisible, which borders on it, actuates, accomplishes, and explains it." Consequently the theology, the philosophy, the cosmology, the geography, the physical science, the social and political theory, the ethics and the dialectic of the thirteenth century—all the mighty synthesis which Albertus Magnus, Thomas Aquinas, and the other great Schoolmen evolved out of Aristotle and Church doctrine—yes, and the mysticism of the thirteenth century, too—find place in the *Divine Comedy*. It is the full, perfect, eternal expression of the beliefs and ideals of the entire Middle Ages.

The stylistic qualities which went into the making of this colossal work, and the effect which they produce, are somewhat alien to our English poetic tradition. For us, sublimity is associated with vastness and vagueness. Our inevitable example of "the grand style" is Milton's *Paradise Lost* with its stupendous, dimly outlined landscapes and its deep, swelling harmonies. Now, for obvious reasons, Dante and Milton are grouped together in our minds: they both depicted Heaven and Hell in their poems; both were strong personalities, of great dignity, pride, resolution, and high moral sense; each wrote his masterpiece in the latter part of his life, when fallen upon evil days and forced out of the field of public affairs by the triumph of his political foes; Milton is the voice of the Protestant Reformation as Dante is of the Catholic Middle Ages. But in literary manner they were almost antithetical. Milton's imagination obscurely glimpses the gigantic; Dante's imagination sharply and precisely visualizes the definite, the concrete, the limited. Dante works, as it were, with the fine point of an engraver's tool, drawing minute details in clear outlines; he carefully depicts one torture chamber after another of a Hell geometrically designed and accurately charted. Milton with the broad brush of an impressionistic painter barely suggests the physical features of his Hell:

> A dungeon horrible, on all sides round,
> As one great furnace flamed; yet from those flames
> No light; but rather darkness visible
> Served only to discover sights of woe,
> Regions of sorrow, doleful shades, where peace
> And rest can never dwell, hope never comes
> That comes to all, but torture without end
> Still urges, and a fiery deluge, fed
> With ever-burning sulphur unconsumed.
>
> . . . . . . . . .
>
> Beyond this flood a frozen continent

> Lies dark and wild, beat with perpetual storms
> Of whirlwind and dire hail, which on firm land
> Thaws not, but gathers deep, and ruin seems
> Of ancient pile; all else deep snow and ice,
> A gulf profound as that Serbonian bog
> Betwixt Damiata and Mount Casius old,
> Where armies whole have sunk: the parching air
> Burns frore, and cold performs the effect of fire.

And when explorers traverse it, he says:

> Through many a dark and dreary vale
> They passed, and many a region dolorous,
> O'er many a frozen, many a fiery Alp,
> Rocks, caves, lakes, fens, bogs, dens, and shades
> of death.

It is this kind of writing that we most naturally think of as sublime. Dante was not incapable of magnificent effects of the same sort, and on rare occasions attempted and achieved them. The sounds of woe which assail his ears when he has first entered through the gate of Hell ("a tumult that goes whirling on for ever in that air dark without change, like the sand when the whirlwind breathes") or again when he stands "above the dolorous valley of the abyss," the myriad souls of the lustful borne on the blast of the infernal hurricane, the distant wailings heard and the fiery mosques of the city of Dis beheld far off across the murky water, and the approach of the Angel helper who shakes the shores of Styx with the tempest roar of his coming are sublime as Milton understood sublimity and as we most easily understand it. But in the main, Dante describes with the sober exactitude of the traveller who has seen and experienced the things of which he writes. Such his story represents him to be; hence the method is appropriate and the result "convincing." The burning tombs of the heretics are like the cemetery of Arles; the landslide guarded by the Minotaur is like that which fell into the Adige near Trent; the dikes bordering the brook carrying off the overflow of Phlegethon are like those on the coast of Flanders or along the Brenta river, *but not so thick or high*; the face of the giant Nimrod is of the same dimensions as the pine-tree cone of bronze standing before Saint Peter's in Rome, and a single arm of Lucifer larger in comparison with a giant's whole stature than a giant is larger than Dante. The plan and ordering of each division of his Hell are carefully set forth. In wealth of realistic detail the great Florentine vies with the authors of *Gulliver's Travels* and *Robinson Crusoe*.

Sustained elevation is the outstanding characteristic of Milton's poetry; that of Dante's is probably picturesqueness. For this quality, no other writer of verse, save perhaps Browning, has even approached him. His journey through Hell is one long sequence of vivid, unforgettable pictures. He seizes upon the striking incident, the dramatic pose or gesture. Paola and Francesca floating lightly through the darkling air of storm, Ciacco dropping back into the mire to rise no more, Farinata standing upright in his fiery tomb, Capaneus outstretched but tameless beneath the falling flames, Thaïs in all her loathsomeness, Vanni Fucci lifting hands of unspeakable insult to God, Mosca and Bertrand de Born in the valley of the dismembered schismatics, Ugolino wiping his mouth deliberately upon his victim's hair before beginning his story, and fastening with dog-like teeth upon the hated head when his words were ended—these are but a few of the many figures instantly evoked before our vision by the trenchant art of Dante,—figures singled out of the thronging hordes of lost humanity scarcely less graphically sketched than they. Whether dealing with the individual or with the mass or with natural scenery, this poet always finds the essential attribute and the right word to make the reader see clearly something that is worth being clearly seen.

## INTRODUCTION

And yet in his own unfamiliar way, Dante also is sublime. He, too, writes in "the grand style." His sublimity lies in part in his never-failing moral earnestness, and in the sheer force of character, the greatness of spirit which is revealed in his poem; this sort of sublimity he shares with Milton. But he is most of all sublime, not like Milton by virtue of his amplitude, but by virtue of his incomparable intensity. It is a quiet, a subdued intensity, for the most part. Only now and then, as in his outburst to the spirit of the simoniacal Pope Nicholas III and in *Purgatorio* v, does he somewhat let himself go; and even then one feels that more is held back than is expressed. And it is an intensity that is wedded to his pregnant brevity, and is inseparable from it. His simple, concise phrases are full of an infinitude of meaning and reach the heart like the "still, small voice" that shook Elijah far more than did earthquake or fire or tempest. So, in Francesca da Rimini's story of how love mastered her and Paola, she tells of their sitting and reading an old romance together: "We were alone and without any fear." All their piteous tragedy is foreshadowed in the magical collocation of those commonplace words. And she says that when the spell of the romance had done its work, "Upon that day we read no more therein." Such lines are sublime like the odes of Sappho in the absolute perfection of their utterance, at once the triumph of art and the quintessence of poignant human emotion. That is Dante at his tenderest. But set beside it the words of one of Hell's most thorough-going reprobates: "Bestial life, not human, pleased me, mule that I was; I am Vanni Fucci, a beast, and Pistoia was a fitting den for me." Nothing could be more different in tone, yet in either instance the art of maximum economy with maximum content is the same. Something of that terse, restrained, yet vibrant intensity of compact statement may be felt even in the simplest narrative passage recording Dante's own feelings and experiences:

"The day was departing, and the dusky air was taking from their labours the living things that are on earth; and I, all alone, was preparing to sustain the struggle, both of the journey and of the pity, which memory, that errs not, shall relate."

The contrast between Milton and Dante extends even to the verse forms which they respectively employed. The vehicle of each poet is characteristic of his own peculiar genius and is suited to give expression to that genius and to accentuate its difference from the genius of the other. The unrhymed pentameter of *Paradise Lost,* fashioned not line by line but in long verse periods of many lines (interminable, highly involved sentences couched in somewhat ponderous diction and with often inverted word order) that thunder on and on with almost overpowering resonance, is admirably in keeping with the majestic and shadowy creations of the English poet. The orderly, unbroken, quietly vigorous flow which marks the terza rima of the *Divine Comedy*—at once sinuous and sinewy—is no less natural to its author. John Addington Symonds has eloquently stated the distinctive effect produced by each form. "Milton's blank verse is like a fugue voluminously full upon an organ of many stops: Dante's *Rime,* terse, definite, restrained within precise limits, has no . . . surges and subsidences of Miltonic cadence, but, instead, a forceful onward march as of serried troops in burnished coats of glittering steel. His lines support each other, gathering weight by discipline, and by the strict precision of their movement. Or, to use another metaphor, they are closely welded and interlinked like chain armour, so that the texture of the whole is durable and supple, combining the utmost elasticity with adamantine hardness." Dante's verse is far more varied in tone than Milton's; now it is sweet and limpid, now austerely strong.

A poet who writes in so new and difficult a medium as

was the terza rima, who packs his lines with meaning, who insists on getting certain ideas into a certain space, and who indulges in manifold allegory and symbolism, must inevitably at times be uncouth or obscure. Hence it is not without justice that critics have pronounced the *Divine Comedy* "rough and abrupt; obscure in phrase and allusion, doubly obscure in purpose." Dante "does not scruple, on occasion, to sacrifice elegance or even clearness to brevity, vigour, or pictorial effect. He expected to be minutely studied, not cursorily read." His design to make of his poem a synthesis of the thought and knowledge of his age forced the inclusion of many things which are not easily put in rhyme, and which are as abstruse as they are frequently uninteresting to the average modern reader—though but few of them appear in the *Inferno*. His verses are also beclouded by occasional bits of sheer pedantry characteristic of the Middle Ages. Direct by nature, he yet chooses at times, for the sake of recondite statement or reference, to express himself in the most tortuous, roundabout way.

Perhaps a more strongly developed sense of humour would have saved Dante from these and other extravagances. But of this faculty he possessed little, though more indeed than did Milton, who exhibits almost none. Dante's humour in the *Inferno* is mainly of a grim, grotesque sort which alone would befit so terrible a theme. It is found chiefly in the cantos dealing with the barrators and the Malebranche; touches of it occur elsewhere. The only other kind that appears in his writings is a gentle, dignified banter, illustrated in the episode of the lazy Belacqua (*Purgatorio* iv) and in two letters written in Latin verses to his admirer, Giovanni del Virgilio, near the end of his life. But any large dash of the comic spirit in Dante's nature, with the ironical self-examination which it engenders, would probably have been fatal to some of those burning convictions, ideals, and loyalties which were the basis of his whole career and work.

Aside from pure lyrists who express only themselves, Theodore Watts-Dunton has distinguished two classes of poets according as their vision is "relative" or "absolute." "Between relative vision and absolute vision the difference seems to be this, that the former only enables the poet, even in its very highest exercise, to make his own individuality, or else humanity as represented by his own individuality, live in the imagined situation; the latter enables him in its highest exercise to make special individual characters other than the poet's own live in the imagined situation." A poet of relative vision can never entirely forget himself in portraying a character. The men and women who inhabit his pages are more or less coloured by his own personality; his nature is visible in their nature. The poet of absolute vision, on the other hand, creates characters objectively, and so loses himself in them that in recording their words and deeds he does not so much work his imagination as he is worked by his imagination. There is practically no limit to the number of different people he can draw, and each is both true to humanity in general and yet an unduplicated individual. Watts-Dunton also calls relative vision "egoistic imagination," and absolute vision "dramatic imagination." As poets possessing absolute vision, he names only "Shakespeare, Aeschylus, Sophocles, Homer, and (hardly) Chaucer."

Though conjectures as to the mental processes of genius are at best hazardous, it comes to the same thing, apparently, if we say that characterization with some writers is constructive or synthetic, with others creative. In constructive characterization, the author deliberately builds up his characters, detail by detail, into what he chooses to make them, devising speech or action to establish this or that trait. Such characterization can be very subtle, complex, and lifelike, as in the hands of Euripides or Browning or Ibsen. But it would seem that a few writers (the poets for whom Watts-

## INTRODUCTION

Dunton claims absolute vision, and perhaps some novelists) at once or shortly conceive their characters entire and, as it were, let them speak and act for themselves in the imagined situations. Characterization with one type of author is mainly a conscious, with the other type mainly a subconscious process. The constructive author may know little more about his characters than he actually tells. The creative author knows (subconsciously) everything about his, and as much of it is presented as the imagined situation or sometimes sheer chance calls forth; his characters are more than lifelike; they are alive. Those with even the fewest lines in Shakespeare and Aeschylus will yield the impression, on close scrutiny, of being not merely what they show, but complete individuals.

At first thought, one might suppose Dante a poet of absolute vision. The people met on his pilgrimage through the other world have a marvellous distinctness. But this distinctness proves on examination to be pictorial. If they exhibit a mood or trait, they do so as may the features of a person in a painting. Our essential impression of Farinata is established by the initial description:

> Erect he reared his breast and countenance,
> As though of Hell he entertained great scorn.

His own words which follow only confirm that picture of dignity, pride, and fortitude; beyond it we learn nothing more of him save his loyalty to faction and country. None of these traits is foreign to Dante's own nature. Again, the recital of Francesca is only that of any erring woman who has preserved her sense of delicacy. It is true, most of the dramatis personae of the *Divine Comedy* are too briefly encountered to afford a chance for detailed portrayal. The poet's own figure is no doubt purposely made colourless that it may better stand for mankind in general. (In the *Inferno,* for instance, he proves a craven throughout, as representing the human soul overawed by the terrors of infinite doom; the real Dante was nowise lacking in courage.) There was every opportunity, however, to delineate Virgil and Beatrice. The former is Dante's best-drawn character, Beatrice being a failure as the result of his too zealous and not well judged attempt to idealize her; yet Beatrice herself was no more difficult a presentation of the ideal than was Aeschylus' Athena in the *Eumenides,* and how indistinct appears even Dante's Virgil beside that bright embodiment of all that is gracious and wise and good, such as the people of Athens would fain believe their tutelary goddess to be!

Homer, Dante, Shakespeare—it is a commonplace of criticism that these three figures stand alone and apart, above all others in the history of the world's literature. And they are, indeed, of the same general degree of greatness; and certainly their number cannot be augmented by any poet who has ordinarily been suggested as a fourth beside them—not by Milton, whom the congenial admiration or literary chauvinism of some English critics would thus exalt, nor by Goethe, similarly preferred by Germans and by German-minded people of other nationalities. But if the actual manifestation of genius, and not merely the universal recognition of it, be the basis of our rating, one can hardly see how either Aeschylus or Sophocles or Euripides can be excluded from the company of the highest, both in view of the surviving tragedies by which we know them and in consideration of the fact that they wrote almost one hundred plays each, many of those lost having been esteemed by antiquity among their masterpieces; recent years have witnessed a steadily better appreciation of these men, and their eventual place seems fairly sure. Hence, the "peers" of the realm of letters are rightly not three, or even four, but six.

## INTRODUCTION

The position one assigns to Dante in such a group—if indeed it be not futile to attempt to distinguish superiority and inferiority among approximate equals—must inevitably depend on how much importance one attaches to the ability to draw character. To some of us, "absolute vision" appears the divinest of literary powers. Supremely important or not, Dante's lack of it is shared by only one of the other five, Euripides, with whom he should naturally be associated in our minds, rather than with any of the rest, alike for the similarity and the contrast between them and for the essential parity of their genius. For though Euripides was himself notable for very fine characterization of the constructive sort, he least of the six attained to "the grand style"—another matter of tremendous weight in appraisal; he was an artist of much greater range than Dante, but less sustained performance; both were sensitive, intensely individual spirits of decided convictions who found themselves at variance with their fellow citizens, so that both died in exile; both were dealers in ideas no less than in poetry—Euripides the more acute and original thinker, Dante the better balanced. Shakespeare, Sophocles, and Homer, on the other hand, submerged their probably genial personalities; they were not prophets or propagandists, but held the mirror up to nature. Aeschylus alone combined the office of a seer with objectivity.[3]

[3] The first great Athenian dramatist was the one poet of universal genius who has yet appeared: he seems to have had the gift for instinctive, creative characterization in more unmixed form than any other writer; and yet Dante's spiritual insight, on which so much stress has been laid of late, cannot really compare (considering that the Florentine had the advantage of having thirteen Christian centuries behind him) with that which is manifested in the *Eumenides,* for instance, as any English reader can see for himself by reference to Gilbert Murray's rendering and interpretation of that play. But all this does not necessarily mean that Aeschylus is the greatest figure in literature, or even as great as Homer or Shakespeare, or greater than Sophocles; for magnitude of achievement as well as many-sidedness must be taken into account.

To say that Dante's rank among the immortals is beside Euripides, wherever that may be, is not at all the startling assertion that it would have seemed a generation ago, before Professor Murray and other enlightened scholars rescued the author of the *Medea, Troades,* and *Bacchae* from age-long misunderstanding and depreciation. Members of the prevalent Dante cult would be satisfied with no rating save the highest for their idol, just as members of the Shakespeare cult have been prone to resent any imputation against the moral character or artistic inerrancy of theirs; but an author's worshippers are eventually his worst enemies, for they provoke reaction. It is a curious fact that Dante himself, in the fourth canto of the *Inferno,* reckons the master poets of the world to be six, among whom he claims a place. The passing of time, which brought forth Shakespeare, and our increased knowledge of classical literature enable us, while keeping their number the same, to better their personnel enormously, so that the great Italian would not feel chagrined even though he should be judged fifth or "sixth in that sage company."

#### BIBLIOGRAPHICAL SUGGESTIONS

To those readers who wish to have further knowledge of Dante are especially recommended Dean Church's *Dante and other Essays* (Macmillan), John Addington Symonds' *Introduction to the Study of Dante* (Macmillan), and Charles Hall Grandgent's *Dante* in the "Master Spirits of Literature" series (Duffield). The Introduction, the observations at the beginning of each canto, and the Notes in Grandgent's edition of the Italian text of the *Divine Comedy* (Heath) are also of the greatest value. For compact information as to the poet's times, life, and writings, E. M. Gardner's *Dante* (Dutton) is unsurpassed. Dante Gabriel Rossetti's exquisite

## INTRODUCTION

translations in his *Early Italian Poets* render accessible to English readers the entire *Vita Nuova* and also specimens of the work of numerous authors just prior to Dante or contemporary with him, thus affording examples of the sort of poetry current in Italy at the time of the *Divine Comedy*. An excellent history of Italian literature as a whole is that of Richard Garnett (Appleton).

# INFERNO

## PRELIMINARY NOTE

HELL, according to Dante, is a vast subterranean cavity, the shape of a funnel or inverted cone, narrowing into a point at the centre of the earth, where Lucifer stands fixed in eternal ice. The sides of this funnel-shaped cavity do not descend with unbroken slant, but are fashioned into terraces, like stairs, one below another. Each terrace extends entirely around the cone, so that each is an enormous circle, the one nearest the top the greatest in circumference and each of the others smaller than the one next above it. These circular terraces are of varying width, and the descent from one to another is a cliff of different height and steepness in every instance. Each circle is devoted to the punishment of a different sin, and the sins grow constantly more heinous and the punishments more terrible as the bottom of the abyss is neared, which is itself the last and worst circle; there are eight other circles above it—hence nine in all.

Dante conceived of the northern hemisphere of our globe as containing all the habitable lands—Europe, Asia, and Africa—of which the exact centre was Jerusalem, directly above the medial axis of Hell. The southern hemisphere he thought to be entirely covered with water except for the Mountain of Purgatory, which rose just at the antipodes to Jerusalem. Like his contemporaries, the poet accepted the Ptolemaic system of astronomy, according to which the earth is stationary and the centre of the universe, and has revolving about it nine spherical heavens, one within another. The innermost is the heaven of the Moon, beyond which are successively the heavens of Mercury, Venus, the Sun, Mars, Jupiter, Saturn, and the fixed stars. Outside this last is the Crystalline heaven, called the Primum Mobile because on it depends the motion of all the others as they all revolve about the earth. And finally, outside the Crystalline heaven, is the boundless, motionless Empyrean, the true abode of God and his saints and angels.

In the foot-notes a roughly approximate pronunciation of Italian proper names and a few others occurring in the text is given in phonetic spelling. No attempt is made to record such subtleties as the difference between the open and closed sounds of *e* and *o*. The syllabification is deliberately inconsistent; for just as the English word *Virginia*, for example, may be represented as three syllables (*Vir-gin-ya*) or as four syllables (*Vir-gin-i-a*), so Italian names permitting similar alternatives have been syllabified in each instance as fits the metre where they occur or as otherwise makes their pronunciation clearer.

Pronounce ä as in *arm*, ā as in *late*, â as in *bare*, ee as in *see*, ĕ as in *met*, ĭ as in *pin*, o as in *go*, ŏ as in *for*, oo as in *moon*, g as in *get*.

# INFERNO

## CANTO I

*The wood of error. The mount of righteousness.
The three beasts. The coming of Virgil. His
prophecy and counsel.*

In the mid-journey of our life astray
  I found myself within a dark wood, where
  The right way had been lost. And now, to say
How was that wood, is a hard task: so drear     4
  It was, and wild and savage, that full sore
  Even to think of it renews my fear.
So bitter is it, death were little more;     7
  Yet to declare the blessing which I found,
  Whate'er I saw within, I tell it o'er.
I know not how I entered there; so sound     10
  A slumber held me at the time I left
  The true path, that it weighed my senses down.
But when I came to where the valley's cleft,     13
  That with its dread had pierced my heart, was closed
  By a great hill, before this did I lift

---

1. The date assumed by Dante for the events of his poem is Eastertide, 1300, when he was thirty-five years old and hence half-way through man's allotted life-span of "three score and ten years."

2. The "dark wood" symbolizes the "worldly" life, with its manifold distractions and temptations, amid which man loses his way. It may also be interpreted politically, as the troubled state of Italy in Dante's time.

10-12. "The soul's sleep," says Saint Augustine, "is forgetfulness of God."

15. *a great hill.* This symbolizes the ideal life of virtue. In line 77 it is called "the delectable mount," which phrase Bunyan strikingly parallels in his *Pilgrim's Progress* with "the Delectable Mountains." Interpreted politically, the hill is civil order.

Mine eyes, and saw the shoulders of it robed 16
  With light already of that planet's rays
  Which guideth men aright on every road.
Then was my terror less that through the space 19
  Of a most piteous night had ever lain
  Deep in my heart's lake; and as in a daze
One who with spent breath wins to shore again, 22
  Turns him, when safe, the perilous sea unto
  And gazes,—so my spirit, which amain
Was still in flight, turned back and would review 25
  The passage that of souls had suffered none
  Alive to issue, having passed it through.
After my limbs a little rest had won, 28
  O'er the lone slope so went I as to keep
  The lower foot ever the firmer one.
Yet scarce had I addressed me to the steep,— 31
  Behold, a panther, swift and full of grace

---

17. According to the Ptolemaic system of astronomy, which the medieval world accepted, the sun moved about the earth and hence could be called a planet. It typifies the light of God's grace.

26-27. The life of sin leads inevitably to death.

30. In ascending a hill, one puts the greater weight on the lower foot.

32 *ff.* The three beasts symbolize three different kinds of sin, but their precise significance is in dispute. The traditional interpretation is that the panther represents sensuality, the lion pride or ambition, and the wolf avarice. These may be considered respectively as sins of incontinence, violence, and fraud—the three main divisions of evil punished in Hell. But certain commentators, among them Flamini and Grandgent, maintain that it is the wolf which represents incontinence, and the panther fraud. They argue that the beasts must have a personal significance to Dante as well as to mankind in general; and Dante hoped to prevail against the panther and might have done so against the lion as well, but was put to rout by the wolf; and it is inconceivable that avarice or any other sort of fraud must be regarded as the poet's especial weakness. But it may be submitted in rebuttal that Dante's actual encounter was with the panther; he fled aghast at the mere sight of the lion and wolf, which may therefore be taken to symbolize graver transgressions, the very aspect of which as eventual possibilities dismayed him. Moreover, the order of appearance is suggestive; sensuality may be regarded

## CANTO I

And clad with spotted coat! Nor did she leap
Away when I approached, but face to face 34
   Ever opposed me, so that many a time
   I needs must falter and my steps retrace.
The hour was the first of morning's prime, 37
   And with those stars the sun was mounting up
   That rose beside him when the Love Divine
Set them, so fair, in motion. A good hope, 40
   Therefore, alike the dawning of the day
   And the sweet season gave that I should cope
Well with that creature of a skin so gay. 43
   Yet this my panic in no measure stayed
   When I espied a lion in the way,
That as it were against me came, with head 46
   Upreared and so with ravenous hunger torn
   The very air did seem to be afraid.
A she-wolf too there was, by cravings worn 49
   Till laden full with leanness she appeared,
   Who many folk ere this hath made to mourn;—
Now heavy was my heart, for as she neared, 52
   All hope to scale the height relinquished I,—
   Such was the terror that her aspect stirred.
And even as one who wins right eagerly 55
   Is at a change of fortune overcome
   In spirit, with weeping and despondency,—
Thus I, by that relentless beast undone, 58
   Which, ever advancing, steadily back did force
   My steps to where all silent is the sun.

---

as especially the sin of youth, and the violence rooted in pride or ambition that of manhood, and cupidity with all its frauds that of old age.

   Interpreted politically, the panther is Florence, the lion France, the wolf the Papacy.

   38 *ff*. According to medieval tradition, the universe was created at the Vernal Equinox. Hence the constellation amid which the sun rises in the spring would be that in which it made its first journey across the sky.

While I was plunging on the downward course, 61
  Lo, one appeared before me in my need
  Who seemed from long disuse of utterance hoarse;
Beholding whom in that great waste, I cried 64
  To him: "Have thou on me compassiön,
  Whate'er thou art, spirit or man indeed!"
"Not man," he answered; "once I was a man. 67
  My parents were of the race of Lombardy
  And both of them by country Mantuan.
*Sub Julio* was I born, though latterly, 70
  And 'neath the good Augustus lived at Rome
  During the time of false gods and their lie.
A poet I was; and of Anchises' son, 73
  The just, I sang, who journeyed forth from Troy
  After the burning of proud Ilion.
But thou, why turnest thou back to such annoy? 76
  Why dost thou climb not the delectable mount
  Which is the source and cause of every joy?"
"And art thou, then, that Virgil and that fount 79

---

*67 ff.* It is the shade of the Roman poet Virgil, who was born near Mantua in the region which was afterwards Lombardy. Throughout the poem, he symbolizes human reason in its utmost attainment unaided by the light of divine grace. One of the great figures of classical antiquity, who might be regarded as summing up in his person the wisdom and the virtues of the pagan world, was a natural choice to embody this abstraction; and Virgil was selected because to the Middle Ages, which were unacquainted with Homer, he was the greatest of all poets, and also, by reason of legends which had grown up about him, was considered no less pre-eminent as a sage—at least till Aristotle was discovered in the twelfth century. He was supposed to have foretold unconsciously, in his fourth *Eclogue,* the coming of Christ. Moreover, as Dante declares in lines 82-87, Virgil was his own favourite author, his teacher of literary expression and his poetic model; and Virgil had himself told in the *Aeneid* of a descent to the lower world. Therefore he is especially fitted to be Dante's counsellor and guide.

70. During the lifetime of Julius Caesar, but so near its close as to be identified rather with his successor, Augustus.

73. *Anchises' son.* Aeneas, the hero of the *Aeneid,* Virgil's chief poem.

From whence a stream of speech so broad doth swell?"
Thus I replied to him, with bashful front.
"O glory and light of poets, the long zeal 82
And the great love—may these avail me now,
Because whereof I searched thy volume well.
Thou art my master and my author; thou 85
Alone art he from whom I learned the good
Fair style by which my fame and honour grow.
Behold the beast that turned me in my road! 88
Help me against her, famous sage, for she
Makes tremble all the pulses of my blood."
"To take another course behooveth thee," 91
He said, when he observed my tears, "if fain
Thou would from out this wilderness win free;
For she that causeth thee to weep, no men 94
Permits to pass her way, but evermore
Impedes their going until she slayeth them.
Her nature hath so virulent a store 97
Of evil that she cannot satiate
Her greed, and gorged is hungrier than before.
She mates with many creatures, and will yet 100
With many another, till the Hound shall come

---

101 *ff*. Here the political allegory temporarily overshadows the spiritual. The ideal purger and deliverer of Italy, whom Dante prophesies under the name of "the Hound" (*Veltro*), cannot be identified. Says Grandgent: "As the prediction was still unfulfilled at the time of writing, Dante naturally made it vague. . . . We know that the poet entertained great hopes of the youthful leader, Can Grande della Scala, in Dante's last years the chief representative of the Imperial power in Italy. It is possible that he so constructed his prognostication as to make its application to Can Grande evident in case those hopes should be realized, but not obtrusive in case they were not. 'Veltro' easily suggests Can Grande; 'Feltro e Feltro' may point to the towns of Feltre and Monte Feltro. Dante's conception of the just Emperor was perhaps influenced by current stories of the Grand Khan of Tartary, who was said to despise wealth and to live simply in a 'felt' tent, and whose title had a strange likeness to the name of the Imperial Vicar General."

And bring to mortal anguish her estate.
Not land nor treasure will he feed upon, 103
   But wisdom, love, and valour; and between
   Feltro and Feltro lieth his sovereign home.
That lowly Italy he shall redeem 106
   For which the maid Camilla died and wounds
   Cut off Euryalus, Turnus, Nisus. E'en
Back into Hell again, through all the towns, 109
   He shall hunt this one with unwearying chase.
   By envy first she issued from Hell's bounds.
Now I adjudge for thee the best of ways 112
   Is that thou follow, and I thy guide will be
   And lead thee hence through an eternal place
Where thou shalt hear the hopeless shrieks, shalt see 115
   The ancient spirits in pain, each so oppressed
   He cries to die once more and utterly.
Then shalt thou see those who contented rest 118
   In fire, because expecting in the end,
   When it may be, to come among the blest,—
To whom if thou desirest to ascend, 121
   A worthier spirit than I will guide; with her
   I leave thee, when our ways diversely wend.
For he that is on high the Emperor 124
   Me who was rebel to his law restrains,
   That none through me come to his Heaven there.
He governs everywhere, and there he reigns; 127
   There is his city and his exalted seat.

---

107 *ff.* Camilla was a Volscian warrior maid. She, Euryalus, Turnus, and Nisus are characters in the *Aeneid* who fell, fighting on one side or the other, in the war between the Trojans and the Latins.

114 *ff.* That is, through Hell and Purgatory. Beatrice will assume the office of Virgil when the time comes for him to go back to his place in Hell and for Dante to be conducted through Heaven, from which Virgil, who died a pagan, is excluded. Allegorically, the meaning of this change of guides is that human reason (Virgil) cannot investigate divine matters; here it must give place to theology (Beatrice).

O happy, whom a place he there assigns!"
And I to him: "Poet, I do entreat 130
  Thee by that God thou knewest not, to lead
  My steps, that from this ill and worse than it
I may escape, e'en whither thou hast said, 133
  Till I have seen Saint Peter's gate and those
  Thou tellest of, so darkly destinied."
Thereon he set forth, and I followed close. 136

## CANTO II

*Dante's misgivings. Virgil's reassuring story: the compassion of Beatrice; her charge to Virgil. A heart renewed.*

Day was departing, and the dusky air
   Was taking all things on the earth that are,
   Each from his labours. I alone prepare
That I may undergo the double war 4
   Of the long road and sights thereon so sad,
   Which memory shall relate, that doth not err.
O Muses, O high genius, now give aid! 7
   Mind which recordedst all that I did see,
   Here shall thy noble powers be displayed.
Thus I began: "Poet who guidest me, 10
   Ere thou commit me to that arduous pass,
   Consider if my worth sufficient be.
Thou sayest that the sire of Silvius, 13
   While yet corruptible, went down into
   The immortal world and there in body was.
If gracious then were the Almighty Foe 16
   Of evil, thinking on the high effect
   And who and what should spring from him, e'en so
It seemeth not unmeet to the intellect; 19

---

1. It is the evening of Good Friday.

7. Dante invokes the Muses in Canto i of both the *Purgatorio* and the *Paradiso,* but in Canto ii of the *Inferno* because here is really the beginning of that book, Canto i being introductory to the *Divine Comedy* as a whole.

13-14. *the sire of Silvius, While yet corruptible.* Aeneas (as told in *Aeneid* vi) while still in his mortal body, subject to corruption.

16-17. *the Almighty Foe Of evil.* The Deity. God, Christ, the Blessed Virgin, Beatrice, and apparently Virgil himself, are sacred names which are uttered as rarely as possible in Hell.

## CANTO II

For father of Rome and of her Empire's sway
He was already in high Heaven elect
(And both of these—the very truth to say— 22
Were 'stablished for the holy place where great
Peter's successor hath his seat to-day).
He in that journey thou didst celebrate 25
Learned things which of his triumph the causes were
And of the papal mantle and estate.
Afterwards went the Chosen Vessel there 28
To bring assurance of that faith which sets
The soul upon salvation's thoroughfare.
But I?—why should I go? and who permits? 31
Aeneas I am not; I am not Paul.
Nor I nor others deem it me befits.
Then if I yield me to this path, I fall 34
Mayhap but into folly;—wise art thou,
And better than I can speak, thou knowest all."
As he who unwills what he willed but now, 37
And with new thought changeth his whole design,
And from the thing begun doth quite withdraw,—
E'en such was I upon that dim incline; 40
And on reflection the resolve which ne'er
Gave pause in forming, I would fain resign.
"If rightly I interpret what I hear," 43
Replied that noble shade, " 'tis cowardice
That doth impede thy spirit, very fear,
Which oft so cumbers men, from enterprise 46
Most honourable it turneth them to flee,
As falsely seeing turns a beast that shies.
I will declare, from dread to set thee free, 49

---

26-27. Observe Dante's sense of the intimate relationship between the Empire and the Papacy.

28. *the Chosen Vessel.* Saint Paul (so called in Acts ix, 15). In Second Corinthians xii, 2-4, he visits Heaven, and in the medieval *Vision of Saint Paul* Hell also.

❦ 45 ❦

Wherefore I come, what sayings I did receive
  When first my pity was aroused for thee.
I was with those whose state is negative. 52
  A lady called to me, so blest and fair
  I prayed her to command what she would have.
Her eyes more brightly shone than any star, 55
  And with angelic utterance soft and pure
  She thus began to tell her mission there:
'O spirit courteous, of Mantua, 58
  Whose fame yet liveth in the world, and so
  Shall ever live, as long as time endure!
A friend of mine and not of fortune—lo, 61
  He hath such hindrance on his desert way
  That terror turned him; he doth backward go;
And much I fear, from what I have heard say 64
  Of him in Heaven, I sped for his defence
  Too late, he is already so astray.
Now hie thee forth, and with thy eloquence 67
  Help him, and in all other needful ways,
  And solace me by his deliverance.
'Tis Beatrice who sends thee; from a place 70
  I come to which I would return; and love,
  That speaketh now, brought me before thy face.
When I again am with my Lord above, 73
  I will commend thee often unto him.'
  Then she was silent; I to speech did move:
'Lady of virtue, through whom alone our stem 76
  Of human kind surpasses all contained
  Within that heaven of narrowest circling rim!

---

52. That is, in Limbo, where instead of positive pain the only punishment is exclusion from the presence of God. See Canto iv, 40-45.

70. Beatrice is throughout the poem at once the real Beatrice Portinari, fondly idealized, and the symbol of revealed truth or theology which supplements human reason, symbolized by Virgil.

78. The heaven of the Moon, which is the innermost and first encircles the earth.

## CANTO II

So pleasing unto me is thy command,     79
  Were it already done I seem too slow.
  Thy wish no further needs to be explained.
Yet tell me why thou dost not shrink to go,     82
  From mansions where thou longest to return,
  Down even to this centre here below.'
'Since thou art fain so deeply to discern,     85
  In few words I will tell thee why,' she said,
  'I do not fear to come unto this bourn.
Of those things only should we be afraid     88
  Which have the power to work us harm or bale;
  Of the rest, no—in them is nought to dread.
I am made such by God, so doth avail     91
  His grace, they touch me not—your miseries;
  Nor of this burning doth the flame assail.
A gentle Lady is in Heaven, who sees     94
  The hindrance dire for which I bid thee speed;
  Her pity breaketh judgment's stern decrees.
She called upon Saint Lucy in her need:     97
  "Now stands in want of thee thy votary's fate,
  And I commend him to thy care," she said.
Saint Lucy, foe of all things cruel, thereat     100
  Rose straightway up, and came the place towárd
  Where I beside the ancient Rachel sat.

---

92. *your*. The antecedent is the inhabitants of Hell in general. Similarly, "the flame" in the next line is inapplicable to Limbo, where there is none.

94. The Virgin Mary. Allegorically, divine mercy.

97. Saint Lucy is probably the Christian martyr of Syracuse, who to preserve her virginity from violence tore out her eyes. She was consequently the patron saint of all with diseased eyes. Dante here suggests that she is his own patroness, and elsewhere tells of suffering from weak sight. Allegorically, Saint Lucy represents divine light, illuminative grace.

102. *Rachel.* In Genesis, the daughter of Laban and wife of Jacob. Allegorically, divine contemplation.

"Beatrice," said she, "thou true praise of God, 103
  Why succourest thou not him who loved thee so
  That for thy sake he left the vulgar crowd?
Hearest thou not how sad he cries in woe? 106
  Seest thou not how death confronts him on
  That flood than which no sea can wilder show?"
Ever on earth to seek their good were none 109
  So prompt, to 'scape from evil none so fleet
  As I when she had spoken; and anon
I came down hither from my blissful seat, 112
  Trusting thy comely speech, which unto thee
  Does honour, and unto them that hearken it.'
After she had addressed these words to me, 115
  Weeping, she turned her lucent eyes away,
  Wherefore she made me haste more speedily;
And thus I came to thee, as she did say— 118
  Yea, rid thee of the monster which but now
  To the fair mountain barred thy shortest way.—
What is it, then, with thee? Why haltest thou? 121
  Why lodgest in thy heart such coward fear?
  Why art not bold and confident enow,
When three such blessed ladies for thee care 124
  Within the court of Heaven, and I plight
  My word to give thee good in so great share?"
As flowerets, by the chillness of the night 127
  Bent down and closed, are lifted and unfold
  Upon their stems, when sunshine bathes them white,—
Thus was it with my courage weak and cold; 130
  And I began as one delivered free,
  So much good daring did my spirit hold:

---

108. "The flood of human life, a flood more stormy with passion and darker with evil than the ocean with its tempests."—Norton.

124. The three blessed ladies who concern themselves in Dante's behalf are set over against the three beasts of Canto i.

## CANTO II

"O she compassionate, who succoured me! 133
   And courteous thou, who didst obey right swift
   The words of truth she uttered unto thee!
Thou hast with yearning for this path so chafed 136
   My heart by what thou sayest, that I have
   Resumed my earlier purpose, which I left.
Now lead; one will is in us twain, whereof 139
   Thou art the guide, the master thou, and lord."
   So spake I; and when he did forward move,
I entered on the deep and savage road. 142

## CANTO III

*The gate of Hell. The antechamber to the abyss: the neutrals between good and evil. The river Acheron. Charon. The ferriage of the damned.*

Through me ye go unto the dolent city;
 Through me ye go to everlasting pain;
 Through me ye go among the lost for ay.
Justice impelled my Maker; me Divine 4
 Omnipotence established, Wisdom sheer
 Above all wisdom, Primal Love most fain.
Before me none of things created were, 7
 Unless eternal; I eternal stand.
 All hope abandon, ye who enter here.

---

1-6. In the opening lines of this canto sublimity is so wedded to simplicity and to carven perfection of form that here, even more than elsewhere, the translator feels helpless in his inability to "sacrifice on the altars of all the gods at once." This being impossible, the version given above chooses to attempt to preserve something of the elevation and emotional tone of the original, at whatever cost to either rhyme or literalness. Those who would prefer a "closer" rendering, or any readers to whose ears the barely assonantal correspondence of the first and third lines may seem an unpleasant and quite too daring licence, are offered the following alternative translation:

> *Through me ye go unto the city of woe;*
>  *Through me ye go to endless pain thereof;*
>  *Through me to dwell among the lost ye go.*
> *Justice impelled my Maker, throned above.*
>  *The Power Divine was my establisher,*
>  *The Highest Wisdom, and the Primal Love.*

The second line might instead be rendered, *Through me to everlasting pain thereof,* with gain of dignity but further loss of syntactic parallelism; or, *Through me ye go, undying pains to prove,* which gives more of the "bell-tolling" effect of the original, but departs from its simple directness of phrasing. Each reader is invited to select, from the alternatives offered, those lines which would make a version most pleasing to his own taste.

## CANTO III

These words in sombre charactery I scanned,  10
  Set high above a gate; whereat: "Their sense,
  Master, is dire for me," said I, unmanned.
And he, as one who hath experience:  13
  "Here it is meet thou leave all fear behind,
  All cowardice be dead from this time hence.
We to the place have come where thou shalt find  16
  Those wretched people, as I told thee, who
  Have lost Right Knowledge, the highest good of mind."
He took me by the hand and onward drew,  19
  With cheerful mien whence I might comfort keep—
  Thus led me in, the secret things unto.
Here sighs and lamentations and deep  22
  Wailings resounded through the starless air,
  So that I, hearing them, began to weep.
Strange tongues, and outcries horrible of despair,  25
  Accents of anger, words of woe, a shriek
  Of voices high and hoarse, and, mingled there,
The sound of smitten hands—all this did make  28
  A tumult that still whirleth without cease
  For ever in that air for ever black,
Even as the sand doth when the whirlwind breathes.  31
  Then I, my head girt round with horror, said:
  "Master, what is it I hear? What folk are these
That in their misery seem so vanquishèd?"  34
  And he: " 'Tis thus the dreary souls suspire
  Who evil fame nor praises merited.
They are commingled with that caitiff choir  37
  Of angels who rebelled not, nor remained
  Faithful to God, but were for self entire.
Heaven cast them out,—would not by them be stained;  40
  Hell hath no place for them in its abysses,
  Lest for the damned some glory thus be gained."

---

18. *Right Knowledge.* That is, the knowledge of God.

And I to him: "What grievous thing oppresses 43
  Their spirits to such moaning?" He replied:
  "That will I tell thee briefly as suffices.
They have no hope of death, and they abide 46
  In life so blind and utterly debased,
  All other lots they envy, theirs beside.
The world will let no whisper of them last. 49
  Mercy disdaineth them, and justice too.
  Let us not talk of them; look and go past."
While I observed, a banner came into view, 52
  Which, swaying hither-thither, rushed amain;
  It seemed to scorn repose, so fast it flew:
And thronging after, followed such a train 55
  Of people that I ne'er in my surmise
  Would have conceived death had so many ta'en.
Some of their number I could recognize; 58
  I saw and knew the shade of that one who
  The great refusal made through cowardice.
This was of recreants that wretched crew— 61
  Forthwith I understood and deemed it sure—
  Hateful to God and to his enemies too.
These miserable ones, who never were 64
  Alive, went naked all, and felt the goad
  Full sharply of the wasps and gadflies there.

---

52-69. They who on earth wavered and trimmed, here follow an ever-shifting banner. Not having clothed themselves with righteousness, they now are naked. In life they shunned the stings of conflict, and in death they are stung eternally by wasps and gadflies.

59-60. The maker of "the great refusal" is usually thought to be Celestine V, who abdicated the Papacy five months after his election in 1294. Other identifications have been suggested—notably Esau and Pontius Pilate. This last, for which Mr. Courtney Langdon argues, seems much the most appropriate of all to a modern reader; but in view of the intensity of Dante's feelings toward his contemporaries, and the fact that Celestine's "refusal" placed the poet's enemy, Boniface VIII, in the papal chair, the customary interpretation appears to be the most probable.

## CANTO III

They made their faces to run down with blood,    67
  Which, mixed with tears and fallen at their feet,
  By loathsome worms was gathered up for food.
But looking on ahead, I saw a great    70
  River, with many folk upon its shore.
  "Master, now grant to me," said I thereat,
"That I may know who these are, and wherefore,    73
  As even by this feeble light is shown,
  They seem so ready for the passage o'er."
And he to me: "This will be clear anon,    76
  When for a space our footsteps shall be ended
  Upon the joyless strand of Acheron."
Then with my glance ashamed and downward bended,    79
  I kept me silent till we drew anear
  The stream, in dread my asking had offended.
And lo, an old man, white with ancient hair,    82
  Coming toward us in a bark; he cries:
  "Woe to you, wicked spirits! Hope not e'er
To look on Heaven with your sinful eyes.    85
  I come to lead you to the other side—
  Into eternal darkness, fire and ice.
And thou who standest, living, there—now wide    88
  Avoid thee, and depart from these, the dead!"
  But when he saw that still I would abide:
"Thou shalt obtain thy ferriage," he said,    91
  "Not here—by other ports, another way—
  And by a lighter vessel be conveyed."
To him my guide: "Vex thee not, Charon—nay!    94
  So is it willed where will and power concur.
  Inquire no further, thou, of what I say."

---

70-71. *a great River.* Acheron, river of woe, taken over from the classical Hades along with Charon, the ferryman of the dead.

91-93. That is, on the angel's bark, from the mouth of the Tiber to the mount of purification, as described in the second canto of the *Purgatorio*.

Then were the shaggy jaws grown quieter 97
  Of him, the steersman of the livid marsh,
  Who had about his eyes great wheels of fire.
But all those weary, naked souls did gnash 100
  Their chattering teeth, and pale became each face,
  Soon as they heard the bitter words and harsh.
They blasphemed God; their parents; the human race; 103
  And of their birth and of the seed that sowed,
  Alike the origin, the time, the place.
Then did they presently, sore weeping, crowd 106
  Together down to the accursed shore
  That waiteth every man who fears not God.
Charon, the demon, with his eyes aglower 109
  Like embers, beckons them, collects them all;
  He smites whoever lingers, with his oar.
As autumn leaves one after other fall 112
  Until the branch beholds its bravery gone
  To strew the earth, so, like a bird at call,
The evil brood of Adam, one by one, 115
  At signals cast themselves from off that shore
  Into the boat. Thus they depart anon
Over the dusky water—and before 118
  They can be set upon the farther strand,
  This one a fresh assemblage throngs once more.
"My son," the courteous master now explained, 121
  "All those who perish subject to the ire
  Of God are gathered here from every land.
To cross the stream they eagerly aspire, 124
  For Heaven's justice doth incite them so,
  Their fear is all converted to desire.
This way a righteous soul doth never go; 127
  And hence thou knowest, if Charon frets at thee,

---

114. *a bird.* That is, a trained falcon.

The import of his words, what thing they show."
Thereon the gloomy plain so violently
   Trembled that the remembrance left behind
   Of terror still with sweat doth cover me.
The tearful ground gave forth a blast of wind
   Out of which a vermilion flame did leap
   That conquered all my faculties of mind,
And prone I fell like one o'erwhelmed by sleep.

129. Charon's words prove that Dante is destined for salvation.

# CANTO IV

*The first circle: Limbo. The virtuous pagans and the unbaptized. The honoured ones of old. Poets and philosophers.*

A peal of thunder shattered in my brain
   The heavy trance, and even like to one
   Wakened by force, I started up. Again
I stood erect, nor sooner thus had done,     4
   Than searchingly I bent my freshened sight
   All round, to learn whither I now had come.
This is the truth: I found me on a height     7
   Above the valley of the abyss of woe
   Which gathers roar of wailings infinite.
Dark and profound and misty was it, so     10
   That though I peered within, I still could see
   Nothing whatever of the depths below.
"And now down into that blind world must we     13
   Descend," began the poet, all deathly pale;
   "I will go first, and thou shalt follow me."
Then I, who had observed his colour fail,     16
   Said: "How shall *I* speed, when it even dismays
   Thee, who alone to cheer me didst avail?"
But he replied: "The anguish of the race     19
   Who yonder dwell paints me with pity thus,
   Which thou dost take for terror on my face.
Let us go on; the long way urges us."     22
   So entered he, and caused my entering,
   The circle that first girdles the abyss.

---

1. During his swoon Dante has in some unexplained manner been conveyed across Acheron.

## CANTO IV

| | |
|---|---:|
| Here, as it seemed to me from listening, | 25 |
|   Was naught of lamentation beyond sighs | |
|   Which set the eternal air to quivering. | |
| From sorrows without torment these had rise, | 28 |
|   Of infants and of women and of men | |
|   That were in crowds both many and great of size. | |
| "Thou dost not ask," said the good master, then, | 31 |
|   "What spirits are these thou seest? I would have | |
|   Thee know, ere thou go on, they did not sin; | |
| And yet, if merit be theirs, it cannot save, | 34 |
|   Because they lack baptism, and thereby | |
|   The portal of that faith thou dost believe. | |
| And if they lived ere Christianity, | 37 |
|   They knew not how to worship God aright; | |
|   And numbered even among these am I. | |
| For this one reason we are lost, in plight | 40 |
|   Only so far afflicted that we live | |
|   Desiring, without hope of Heaven's sight." | |
| The words he uttered made my heart to grieve, | 43 |
|   Because I knew how goodly folk there were | |
|   Suspended in that Limbo negative. | |
| "Tell me, my master; tell me, noble sir!" | 46 |

---

25 *ff.* The souls of the virtuous heathen and of unbaptized infants, whom Dante, following the savage theology of his day, places in Hell (since all mankind, by the fall of Adam, are infected with sin, and can be saved from eternal punishment only by faith in Christ), suffer no physical torment, as they committed no heinous offence, but are exiled from the sight of God, and dwell sighing in darkness. "Such is the life of those devoid of true knowledge of God: their minds are enveloped in ignorance, and their hearts are full of a vague longing forever unsatisfied. But those among them who combine wisdom with virtue are illumined by mortal intelligence—a light dim compared with the vision of God, but bright beside the obscurity in which their less gifted fellows dwell."—Grandgent.

To prove that faith by which we overthrow
All error, I began, "did any e'er
Through his own merit or through Another's go  49
From hence, thereafter to a blessed fate?"
And he, divining that which I would know,
Answered: "When I was new in this estate,  52
I saw a Mighty One who hither bent
His steps, with sign of victory coronate.
The shade of our first parent forth he hent  55
And that of his son Abel, and of Noah,
Moses lawgiver and obedient,
King David, Abraham patriarch of yore,  58
And Israel with sire and children his
And Rachel for whose sake he laboured sore,
And many others, and brought them unto bliss,  61
Concerning whom let it be understood,
No human souls were ever saved ere this."
For all his words we paused not on our road,  64
But through that wood, the while, advancing were—
'Tis thus I name those crowded spirits: a wood—
And no great journey had we gone from where  67
I slept, when I espied a fire whose blaze
Prevailed against the night of half that sphere.
We still were distant from it a little space,  70
Yet not so far but I could see, in part,

---

47-48. That is, to verify the teaching of the Church by discovering whether Christ indeed descended into Hell and carried off the souls of the Patriarchs, who, having anticipatively believed in him, there awaited redemption by the shedding of his blood.

49-53. *Another's . . . a Mighty One.* The utterance of Christ's name in Hell is thus avoided.

52. Virgil had died in 19 B.C.

60. Jacob served Laban twice seven years before he won Rachel. See Genesis xxix.

67-68. *from where I slept.* That is, in swoon.

## CANTO IV

That people of distinction held that place.
"O thou that honourest both science and art, 73
Who may these be who stand in such esteem
That from the others' mode they are apart?"
And he to me: "The high exalted fame 76
Which echoes of them through that world of thine
Above, wins grace of Heaven, preferring them."
At this: "Give honour to the bard sublime!"— 79
The sudden words resounded in my ear—
"His shade returns that left us for a time";
And when the voice was still, I saw appear 82
Four stately spirits coming thitherward,
Whose faces neither sad nor joyful were.
"Mark him who beareth in his hand that sword"— 85
Thus unto me began the master kind—
"And walks before the other three, their lord.
Homer it is, the poet of sovereign mind; 88
Horace the satirist comes next to him;
Ovid is third, and Lucan last behind.
Because each shares with me, as he did win, 91
The name with which by one I was addressed,

---

72 ff. In this passage the recurrence of the word "honour" and its derivatives makes it echo as a *motif* throughout. A literal rendering would be: ". . . that honourable folk possessed that place. . . . 'O thou that honourest both science and art, who are these that have such honour that it separates them from the others' mode?' And he to me: 'The honoured renown of them which sounds in that life of thine, wins grace in Heaven which thus advances them.' At this a voice was heard by me: 'Honour the sublime poet,'" etc. Most translators reproduce this recurrence, but in our language such frequent and close repetition is unpleasant to the ear; I have preserved only so much of it as good English style will allow.

85 ff. Dante's roster of the supreme poets is conditioned by the fact that he knew little or no Greek. The reputation of Homer (in whose hand, as the poet of war, a sword is placed) was so great as to insure his inclusion; but the Greek dramatists and lyrists were only shadowy names to Dante.

They do me honour, and they do well therein."
United thus, I saw the goodliest 94
  School of those monarchs of high song, e'en that
  Which like an eagle soars above the rest.
After they spoke among themselves somewhat, 97
  They turned to me with sign that I should be
  Most welcome, and my master smiled thereat.
And greatly more besides they honoured me,— 100
  Yea, for they made me of their number, so
  That I was sixth in that sage company.
Thus we proceeded even into the glow, 103
  With talk of things that silence best would suit
  Now, but deserving then our speech; and lo—
We came unto a noble castle's foot, 106

---

106 *ff*. The castle probably symbolizes the abode of human accomplishment unaided by divine revelation, its seven walls the seven cardinal virtues (prudence, temperance, fortitude, justice, understanding, knowledge, wisdom), its seven gates the seven sciences (grammar, rhetoric, logic, arithmetic, geometry, astronomy, music), the streamlet eloquence. Its enumerated inhabitants are either (1) famous figures in the history of Rome or her parent Troy (with the single exception of the Moslem Saladin, whose noble qualities won admiration even from his crusader foes), or (2) men of learning. In the first group are: Electra (not the sister of Orestes celebrated by the Attic dramatists, but the mother of Dardanus the founder of Troy); Hector, Aeneas, and Julius Caesar; King Latinus and his daughter Lavinia, whom Aeneas won in Latium as told in the *Aeneid;* the maiden warriors, Penthesilea and Camilla, who fought respectively for the Trojans against the Greeks and for the Latins against the Trojans; the earlier Brutus, founder of the Roman Republic; and four virtuous Roman ladies—the Lucretia who was ravished by Sextus Tarquinius, Cornelia the mother of the Gracchi, Julia the daughter of Julius Caesar and wife of Pompey, and Martia the wife of Cato the Younger. The second group is presided over by Aristotle, "the master of those who know," venerated in Dante's time as a literally infallible oracle and through the great Schoolmen the basis of all medieval science and philosophy. It comprises the Greek philosophers Socrates, Plato, Zeno, Thales, Heraclitus, Diogenes, Democritus, Anaxagoras, and Empedocles; Dioscorides of Cilicia, who in the first century A.D. wrote a work on the medicinal qualities of plants; the Roman Seneca,

## CANTO IV

Girt seven times with lofty walls around,
And by a pleasant streamlet fenced about.
This we crossed over as it were solid ground;   109
Through seven gates did we together go—
Within, a meadow of fresh verdure found.
People were there with thoughtful eyes and slow,   112
Their aspect one of great authority;
They spoke but seldom and with voices low.
We then withdrew aside, and standing by,   115
Watched from a place where they could all be seen,
For it was open, luminous, and high;
And there before us on the enamel green   118
The mighty spirits were shown to me—ah, these
'Tis glory to have looked upon, I ween!
I saw Electra, 'mid great companies,   121
And in them Hector and Aeneas knew;
Caesar, all armèd, with his falcon eyes;
And King Latinus and his daughter, who   124
Beside him sat—Lavinia; paladin
Camilla and Penthesilea too.
I saw that Brutus who expelled the Tarquin;   127
Lucrece, Cornelia, Julia, Martia; and
Alone, apart, the noble Saladin.
When I a little raised my glance, beyond   130
I saw the master of all those who know
Seated amid a philosophic band.
They look toward him and greatest honour show;   133
And there I saw Plato and Socrates,

---

whose field was moral philosophy; Averrhoës, a Spanish Moor of the twelfth century, who wrote a commentary on Aristotle; three great physicians—Galen of Roman times, Hippocrates of Greek, and the Arabian Avicenna (Ispahan, 980-1037); Orpheus, Livy, Tully (i.e. Cicero), representing music, history, and oratory, respectively; Ptolemy, the great astronomer of ancient Alexandria; and Euclid, the Greek mathematician.

  Who next him stand, before the others; Zeno,
Thales and Heraclitus, Diogenes,     136
    Democritus, who based the world on Chance,
    And Anaxagoras, Empedocles,
And that collector of the lore of plants,     139
    E'en Dioscorides; moral Seneca,
    Averrhoës, who made the great comments,
And Galen and Hippocrates I saw,     142
    And Avicenna, Orpheus, Livy, Tully,
    Ptolemy, Euclid the geometer—
It is impossible that I should fully     145
    Recount them; me, my theme doth onward bear,
    And short of truth the tale is often wholly.
We that were six become but two. We fare     148
    Another way—so wise a guide is mine—
    Out of the quiet into the trembling air.
I enter where no light doth ever shine.     151

---

148. The other four poets let Dante and Virgil go on their way alone.

## CANTO V

*The second circle. Minos, the apportioner of dooms. The wanton in the whirlwind. Paolo and Francesca da Rimini.*

From the first circle we descended so
  Unto the second, which engirds less space
  And greater pain, that goads to cries of woe.
There dread and snarling Minos hath his place;     4
  He searches out their guilt who enter in,
  And sends them as he doth himself enlace.
For when the ill-starred soul has come to him,     7
  Then straightway it confesses utterly,
  Whereon that grand inquisitor of sin,
Perceiving its appointed place to lie     10
  In Hell, the circle number shows by mode
  Of times his tail wraps him to signify.
Ever before him stands a multitude;     13
  Each goeth up to that high chancery
  In turn, speaks, hears, is hurled to its abode.
"O thou that to the woeful hostelry     16
  Art come," said Minos, ceasing the discharge
  Of his great office on beholding me,
"Look how thou enterest, whom thou trustest; large     19
  Though the gate is, let it not thee betray."
  "Now wherefore criest?" spake my leader sage.

---

2-3. The circumference of the circular terraces grows smaller and smaller as the funnel-shaped pit of Hell is descended. In the preceding circle the punishment caused no more than sighs.

4. Minos is the mythological figure assigned to the second circle (Charon being reckoned in the first). In classical mythology he was the King of Crete, so just on earth that after his death he was made judge of the dead. Dante transforms him into a tailed and ferocious demon.

## THE INFERNO OF DANTE

"Hinder him not upon his destined way. 22
  So is it willed where will and power concur;
  Inquire no further, thou, of what I say."
And now at last the dolorous strains I hear 25
  Of anguish; now the lamentations smite,
  Mighty and manifold, upon my ear.
I came unto a place mute of all light, 28
  That bellows like the ocean in a storm,
  Fierce-beaten when the winds contending fight.
The infernal hurricane, that rest hath none, 31
  Hurtles the spirits on; its rage malign,
  Whirling and dashing them, fulfils their doom.
When they arrive at ruin's sheer incline, 34
  Then the sharp cries, the moaning, the complaint;
  Then they blaspheme against the Power Divine.
I understood that to this punishment 37
  The carnal sinners are condemned and cast,
  Whose reason subject to desire is bent.
As in the winter are the starlings fast 40
  Borne on their wings in wide and throngèd troop,
  So are the evil spirits on that blast.
Hither and thither it drives them, down and up; 43
  Never expectancy of peace have they;
  Not even of less pain is there any hope.
And as the cranes go chanting their sad lay, 46
  Making in air a long line of themselves,

---

28. *mute.* Void. Compare Canto i, line 60.

31-39. The second circle is given over to the punishment of those whose especial sin was lawless sexual passion. As on earth they were blindly swept onward by their uncontrolled desires, so here in darkness they are caught up, hurried headlong, tossed, and buffeted by tempest winds. Throughout the *Inferno* there is generally a symbolic correspondence between the offence punished and the mode of punishment.

40 *ff.* The similes from bird life are appropriate to the storm-borne spirits.

## CANTO V

Thus by that steep commotion on their way
I saw the shades borne, uttering their wails; 49
   Wherefore I said: "Master, who are these folk
   Whom this dark tempest so doth scourge with ills?"
"The foremost of them," he in answer spoke 52
   To me, "of whom thou fain wouldst learn, of yore
   Held many nations 'neath her Empress yoke.
To wantonness so was she given o'er, 55
   That licence, by decree, she lawful made,
   To blot the blame which she had won before.
She is Semiramis, of whom 'tis said 58
   That she succeeded Ninus, erst his wife.
   That land the Soldan rules, her sceptre swayed.
The next because of love took her own life, 61
   Nor to Sichaeus' ashes loyal clove;
   Then Cleopatra, she with lust arife;
And there is Helen, for whose sake did move 64
   The circle of so many sorrowing years;
   Yonder the great Achilles, who with love
Strove at the last; see, Paris with Tristram nears" . . . 67

---

58. Semiramis was the legendary Queen of Assyria—the wife of Ninus (equally legendary founder of Nineveh) and amazonian ruler after his death. Her amazing licentiousness culminated, according to one story, in a union with her own son, Ninyas; and some authorities, supposing that Dante confused the names Ninus and Ninyas, follow a MS. variant and read line 59: "She suckled Ninus [Ninyas], then became his wife."

61. Dido, Queen of Carthage, in her passion for Aeneas was false to the memory of her dead husband, Sichaeus. See *Aeneid* iv. She is placed here rather than among the suicides (Canto xiii) apparently because Dante seems not to regard self-destruction reprehensible in those without the enlightenment of Christianity. So Lucretia is in the first circle among the virtuous pagans, and Cato the Younger in Purgatory.

61 *ff.* Throughout the rest of this canto, the word "love" echoes with constant reiteration, as did "honour" in Canto iv.

66-67. One version of the death of Achilles is that he was slain by Paris while on a love-tryst with Polyxena, the daughter of Priam.

And he a thousand more did point and name,
  Whom Love from life divided with his shears.
But when I heard my teacher tell each dame 70
  And cavalier of olden time, my mind
  Was 'wildered; pity seized me and o'ercame;
And: "Poet," said I, "much am I inclined 73
  To speak with those twain who together go
  And seem to be so light before the wind."
And he: "Thou shalt observe until they blow 76
  Nearer; then pray to them by that love's force
  Which leads them, and they will obey." And so,
Soon as the wind had usward bent their course: 79
  "Ye weary souls," my voice uplifted I,
  "If One forbid not, come and talk with us."
As doves, when summoned by their longing, fly 82
  On open, steady wings to the sweet nest,
  Borne onward by desire across the sky,
These issued from the band 'round Dido massed, 85
  And floated toward us through the air malign,
  So strong to them was sympathy's behest.

---

Paris the lover of Helen and Tristram the lover of Iseult go side by side as the great adulterers of classical and medieval romance, respectively.

73. The pair of lovers who excite Dante's especial interest and compassion are Paolo and Francesca (frän-chĕs'-kä) da Rimini. Francesca, who is the one that answers Dante, was the daughter of Guido Vecchio da Polenta, lord of Ravenna; it was with her relatives that Dante spent the last and probably the happiest years of his exile, and it is not unlikely that he had earlier received courtesies at their hands that caused him in this passage to treat her story with such tenderness and beauty. She was married to Giovanni Malatesta, of Rimini, called "Giovanni the Lame" (Gianciotto). Deformed of body, he sent his handsome brother Paolo as his deputy to the wedding, so one account runs; and Francesca supposed Paolo the real bridegroom, and only later discovered the trick. An amour sprang up between these two, and eventually they were discovered together by Giovanni and forthwith slain.

## CANTO V

"O living creature, gracious and benign,     88
  Who this murk air dost thread to visit us
  Now, who have stained the world incarnadine,
Were but the Sovereign of the Universe     91
  Our friend, 'tis for thy peace would rise our prayer,
  Since thou compassionest our woe perverse.
Of what it pleases thee to speak and hear,     94
  That will we hear and speak, ere doth increase
  The wind again, that now is hushed, to stir.
The land where I was born sits by the seas     97
  Upon that shore to which descends the Po,
  With all his followers, in search of peace.
Love, that the gentle heart is quick to know,     100
  Enkindled this one for the fair form ta'en
  From me in manner that grieves me even now.
Love, that doth one beloved in turn constrain     103
  To love, so dear a fondness in me bred
  That, as thou seest, it doth yet remain.
Love to one death our steps together led;     106
  But Cain awaiteth him who quenched our life."—
  So wafted were to us the words they said;
And hearkening to those spirits and their grief,     109
  I bowed my head and stayed for such a space

---

92. Note the pathos of the word "peace" on Francesca's lips. Peace is what she herself, tossed for ever by the whirling blast, would most long for; it so haunts her mind that a little later she thinks of the Po's descent to the sea as a quest for peace.

102. "In manner that grieves me even now" is usually understood to depend on "ta'en" and to refer to the suddenness of her death, which gave her no opportunity to repent and so escape Hell. But it may possibly depend on "enkindled" and refer to the trick which made her suppose she was marrying Paolo instead of Giovanni.

107. Their murderer will be doomed to the place of Cain, the first ring of the ninth circle and the abode of those who violate the bond of kindred blood.

The poet asked: "What fancy dost thou weave?"

When I made answer, I began: "Alas! 112
  How many sweet thoughts and how much desire
  Led these two onward to the dolorous pass!"
Then turned to them, as who would fain inquire, 115
  And said: "Francesca, these thine agonies
  Wring tears for pity and grief that they inspire:—
But tell me,—in the season of sweet sighs, 118
  When and what way did Love instruct you so
  That he in your vague longings made you wise?"
Then she to me: "There is no greater woe 121
  Than the remembrance brings of happy days
  In misery; and this thy guide doth know.
But if the first beginnings to retrace 124
  Of our sad love can yield thee solace here,
  So will I be as one that weeps and says.
One day we read, for pastime and sweet cheer, 127
  Of Lancelot, how he found Love tyrannous:
  We were alone and without any fear.
Our eyes were drawn together, reading thus, 130
  Full oft, and still our cheeks would pale and glow;
  But one sole point it was that conquered us.
For when we read of that great lover, how 133
  He kissed the smile which he had longed to win,—
  Then he whom naught can sever from me now
For ever, kissed my mouth, all quivering. 136

---

112. From here to the end of the canto the lines are Dante Gabriel Rossetti's translation of this passage.

123. *thy guide*. Virgil, who now, exiled from God and "desiring without hope," remembers his earthly happiness and glory.

128. They were reading the French prose romance of Lancelot, telling of his love for Guinevere.

## CANTO V

    A Galahalt was the book, and he that writ:
      Upon that day we read no more therein."
    At the tale told, while one soul uttered it,     139
      The other wept: a pang so pitiable
      That I was seized, like death, in swooning-fit,
    And even as a dead body falls, I fell.     142

---

137. In the romance it was Prince Galahalt (not to be confused with Galahad) who acted as intermediary first to bring Lancelot and Guinevere together to the consummation of their desires. Francesca here says that in the case of herself and Paolo it was the book that was the intermediary.

## CANTO VI

*The third circle: the gluttonous beneath the rain.
Ciacco. His prophecy for Florence. Of the future
estate of the damned.*

When consciousness was mine again, that closed
  Before the sorrow of those kindred two
  By which my senses wholly were confused,
New torments and tormented souls anew     4
  On every side around me I behold
  Whithersoe'er I look or turn or go.
In the third circle am I—of the cold,     7
  Heavy, accursed, and eternal rain;
  Its law and quality for ever hold.
Large hail, dark water, and snow pour down amain     10
  Through the dun air; as though it were decayed
  Doth smell the soil of that bedrenchèd plain.
There Cerberus, a creature strange and dread,     13
  With triple dog-throat barks o'er them whose fate
  It is to be submerged. His eyes are red,
His beard is black with grease, his belly great,     16
  Sharp-nailed his paws; he mumbles with his jowl
  The spirits whom he doth rend and lacerate.
The pelting deluge maketh them to howl     19

---

1-21. Dante while still unconscious has been transported to the next circle. Here are punished those who were intemperate in eating and drinking. Says Longfellow: "Instead of the feasts of former days, the light, the warmth, the comfort, the luxury, and 'the frolic wine' of dinner tables, they have the murk and the mire, and the 'rain eternal, maledict, and cold, and heavy'; and are barked at and bitten by the dog in the yard." Cerberus, the mythological figure placed in this circle, is with his three gaping maws appropriately the symbol of voraciousness; and the swinish wallowing in the mud and the dog-like barking of the sufferers suggest the bestiality of their former mode of life.

## CANTO VI

Like dogs; with one they shield the other side;
   They often turn themselves, the wretches foul.
When Cerberus saw us, the huge worm, he wide      22
   Opened his mouth and showed his savage teeth;
   No limb he kept from quivering. My guide,
Spreading his palms upon the ground, took earth      25
   And threw it with full fists, a double load,
   Into those ravenous gullets; and therewith,
Even as a dog that bayeth at the goad      28
   Of hunger, falls to quiet and doth strain
   Only at eating, once he hath his food,—
Thus did those visages with filthy stain      31
   Of demon Cerberus, who thunders so
   Above the spirits, for deafness they are fain.
Over the shades we passed who undergo      34
   The grievous rain, and set our feet upon
   Their emptiness, which doth as bodies show.
They all were lying on the ground save one,      37
   Who raised himself out of his miry bed
   To sit, when he beheld us near him come.
"O thou conducted through this Hell," he said      40
   To me, "look, recognize me if thou mayst,
   For not till thou wast made was I unmade."
And I to him: "The anguish which thou hast      43
   Perchance withdraws thee from my memory,
   So that meseemeth I never on thee gazed.
But tell me who thou art, thus dismally      46
   Consigned and to such punishment that if
   Others are greater, none can loathlier be."
And he: "Thy city, which is now so rife      49

---

22. *worm.* A term used broadly for any disgusting creature.

24. *No limb*, etc. That is, he quivered all over in his eagerness to seize them.

42. That is, the speaker did not die till after Dante was born.

With envy that the sack doth overflow,
   Held me within her in the sunlit life.
'Ciacco' ye once were wont to call me; now       52
   For the pernicious sin of gluttony
   I languish in this rain, as seest thou.
But not alone am I in misery;       55
   All these the like for like offences pay";—
   And for a space no further word spake he.
I answered him: "So thy distress doth weigh       58
   Upon me, Ciacco, that it bids me weep;
   But if thou knowest, tell me: what shall they
Who live in that divided city reap?       61
   Is any righteous amid all their throng?
   And why did such great discord on her leap?"
" 'Twill come," he said, "after contention long       64
   To blood; the party of the forest groves
   Will drive out their opponents with much wrong.
Then in the course of three suns it behooves       67
   That they shall fall, the other faction mount,
   Through force of him who with the tide now moves.
A great while these shall wear a haughty front,       70
   Holding the others burdened down, howe'er
   They weep and are ashamed on this account.

---

51. *the sunlit life.* Coming from the wretch doomed to eternal darkness and storm, this phrase for earthly existence contains an infinitude of pathos. Throughout the *Inferno* similar expressions are found now and again on the lips of sinners, striking the same note of despairful yearning.

52. *Ciacco* (chäk'-ko) means "hog." It may have been a nickname won by the man's habits; or it may have been only a diminutive of Jacopo. Boccaccio, who has given some account of him as a *bon vivant*, calls him by no other name.

64-75. Here Dante (writing, of course, some time later) introduces a "prophecy" of what would happen immediately after Easter, 1300, the date at which he lays the story of the *Divine Comedy*. The long feud between the Bianchi or White Guelfs and the Neri or Black Guelfs

## CANTO VI

Two men are just, but none doth heed them there; 73
   Pride, avarice, and envy are the three
   Sparks that have set the hearts of all on fire."
The lamentable sound here ended he; 76
   And I to him: "Prithee, instruct me still!
   Bestow a little further speech on me.
Of Farinata and Tegghiaio tell, 79
   So worthy! Jacopo Rusticucci, Arrigo,
   And Mosca, and the rest intentioned well.
Where are they? Teach me! Make thou me to know! 82
   Fain would I learn if Heaven's joys enfold
   Or Hell empoisons them." And he thereto:
"The place of blacker spirits all these doth hold, 85
   Whom different sins deep toward the bottom weigh;
   Shouldst thou descend so far, thou mayest behold.
But when thou art in the sweet world, I pray 88
   Recall me to the memory of men.
   No more I answer thee; no more I say."
Therewith he rolled askance his forthright eyen 91
   And looked at me a little—then bent lower

---

culminated in bloodshed on May 1, 1300; and in June, 1301, the former (called "the party of the forest groves" because their leaders, the Cerchi, had come from the woodlands of Val di Sieve and were said to be rude and boorish) expelled their chief antagonists from Florence. The Neri returned in 1302, however, aided by the wiles of Pope Boniface VIII (who formerly had moved "with the tide") and banished six hundred Whites, among whom was Dante. Since it was ominous of his own misfortune as well as that of his party, the poet fitly calls Ciacco's prophecy "the lamentable sound."

73. Who are referred to is not known.

79-81. For Farinata (fä-ree-nä′-tä) see Canto x. For Tegghiaio (těg-gee-ä′-yo) and Jacopo Rusticucci (yä′-ko-po roos-tee-koo′-tchee) see Canto xvi. For Mosca (mo′-skä) see Canto xxviii. Arrigo (är-ree′-go) is not mentioned again and cannot be certainly identified.

89. Most of the damned crave to be remembered on earth. Only the traitors and a few others whose sins were especially shameful have no desire for fame.

His head, and fell back with the blind again.
And said my guide to me: "He nevermore 94
  Shall rouse, until the angel's trumpet sounds;
  But when in glory cometh the adverse Power,
Each shall revisit his sad grave, the bounds 97
  Of mortal flesh take on again, and hear
  That which to all eternity resounds."
So passed we through the mixture foul and drear 100
  Of spirits and of rain, with slackened pace,
  Touching upon the future life, though 'twere
But slightly; for: "Shall these torments increase, 103
  My master," said I, "after the great Sentence,
  Or shall they be as burning, or be less?"
And he to me: "Return unto thy science, 106
  Which says that as a thing is perfect, pain
  And pleasure too it findeth more intense.
Though these accursed folk can ne'er attain 109
  To true perfection, yet to the extent
  They will of coming closer to it then."
Along a route which circled round, we went, 112
  Speaking far more than I record, till we
  Came to the point at which is the descent.
Here we found Plutus, the great enemy. 115

---

96. *the adverse Power*. Another periphrasis for the name of Christ.
99. That is, the doom pronounced at the Last Judgment.
106. *thy science*. The teaching of Aristotle.
115. Plutus, in classical mythology the god of riches, is the guardian of the next circle, where misers and extravagant spenders are punished. He is called "the great enemy" because of Saint Paul's statement in First Timothy vi, 10: "The love of money is the root of all evil." In the next canto (line 25) Dante says: "No throng as large I marked in other states."

## CANTO VII

*The fourth circle. Plutus. The avaricious and the prodigal. Concerning Fortune. The descent to the fifth circle. The marsh of Styx. The wrathful and the sullen.*

"*Pape Satan,*" thus with his clucking voice,
  "*Pape Satan aleppe,*" Plutus began.
  Thereon, to comfort me against the noise
(For he knew all things): "Let not fear unman        4
  Thy heart; no power," said the benignant sage,
  "Hath he thy going down this rock to ban"—
Then turned himself unto that swollen visage:        7
  "Peace, thou accursed wolf," commanded he;
  "Consume thee inwardly with thine own rage.
Not without cause into the deep go we;              10
  So is it willed on high where Michaël
  Took vengeance of the proud adultery."
As sails, which by the wind are made to swell,      13
  Fall in a tangled heap when snaps the mast,
  Now to the ground that cruel monster fell.
To the fourth hollow we descending passed,          16
  Advancing on the dismal slope which thus
  Hath in its sack the sum of evil vast.
Justice of God, who can so numerous                 19

---

1-2. The words of Plutus, apparently a cry of warning or appeal to Satan on beholding the intruders, are obviously meant by the poet to be unintelligible, save to Virgil; hence the many ingenious attempts to interpret them are futile.

12. The word "adultery" is used in the ancient sense of any sort of act of violence or rebellion against God. Its reference here is to the revolt of Lucifer and his angels, in the overthrow of whom in battle the archangel Michael was especially prominent.

Pile up the penalties I saw and pains?
And why is guilt of ours so ruinous?
As yonder on Charybdis' wild expanse 22
  The surge doth break against the surge it meets,
  So have the people here to counter-dance.
No throng as large I marked in other states; 25
  Both on this side and that, loud howling, they
  Rolled forward with their chests enormous weights.
They clashed together; then backward from that fray, 28
  Wheeling, recoiled and shouted severally:
  "Why hoardest thou?" "Why flingest thou away?"
Thence round that gloomy circle did they ply 31
  On either hand, till opposite thereto
  Again they met with their opprobrious cry,
And turned once more and traversed each anew 34
  His half ring to the former tilting ground.
  Then I, with heart as it were piercèd through,
Said: "Master, who these people are, expound; 37
  And tell me if they all were clerics, here
  Upon the left of us, these tonsure-crowned."
He answered: "Each and every one, they were 40
  Of mind so squinting in their former place
  That with no measure used they money there.
And such most plainly now their utterance bays 43
  Whene'er they come to the two points of this
  Circle where diverse guilt divides their ways.
They on whose heads no hairy covering is, 46
  Were priests and popes and cardinals, wherein
  Doth culminate the utmost avarice."
"Master," said I, "among these folk I ween 49

---

22. *Charybdis.* The famous whirlpool in the Straits of Messina, celebrated in classical literature.

26-35. The opposing bands are formed respectively of the wasters and the amassers of wealth, which is symbolized by the great weights they roll before them.

## CANTO VII

There surely must be some that I should know
  Who were polluted by this kind of sin."
But he to me: "Vain thoughts combinest thou. 52
  The undiscerning life they followed cloaks
  Their sordid souls against discernment now.
For ever will they come to these two shocks,— 55
  Some from the sepulchre rise up again
  With the fist closed, and some with shaven locks.
Ill giving and ill keeping—these have ta'en 58
  The heavenly world from them and to this strife
  Set them; to speak less bluntly, I disdain.
Now mayest thou see the mockery, how brief, 61
  Of gifts that Fortune can bestow for boon,
  O'er which men buffet in their mortal life;
For all the gold that is beneath the moon, 64
  Or ever was, could not give rest unto—
  Of all those weary souls—a single one."
"Master," said I to him, "declare and show: 67
  This Fortune which thou namest—what is she
  That holds earth's blessings in her clutches so?"
"O foolish creatures," then responded he, 70
  "How great an ignorance doth on you fall!
  My judgment of her now receive from me.
That One whose wisdom far transcendeth all 73
  So made the heavens and gave each a guide
  That every part doth shine reciprocal
To every other and equal light provide. 76
  Thus too for worldly splendours he ordained
  A general minister who should preside
And make at times her bounties, falsely named, 79

73-96. Virgil tells Dante that just as God set Intelligences (angels) to control the movements of the various heavenly spheres, so too he ordained a power, Fortune, who should administer the destinies of men on earth. Being one of the primal creations, without free will and wholly God's instrument, she is undeserving of human blame and indifferent to it.

From folk to folk, kindred to kindred, pass
  Beyond prohibiting by human mind.
Therefore one people rules, another race  82
  Doth languish, in accord with her decrees,
  Hidden, as lies the serpent in the grass.
Your knowledge cannot thwart her; she foresees,  85
  Judges, and so her governance pursues
  As o'er their realms the other deities.
Her permutations know not any truce;  88
  Necessity compels her to be swift;
  Another soon his turn obtaineth thus.
That Power is she against whom all men lift  91
  Their curses; ill repute and blame amiss
  Even those who ought to praise her bring for gift.
But she is blessed and hears naught of this;  94
  Among the other primal creatures, lo,
  She turns her wheel and joyeth in her bliss.
Let us descend, now, unto greater woe.  97
  Each star that on our setting-out arose
  Is sinking; 'tis forbid to linger so."
Straight to the bound across the circle's close,  100
  Under whose bank wells forth a spring, we fared;
  Thence boiling down a cleft the water flows.
Darker than purple-black its stream appeared,  103
  And where that dusky wave falls to the abyss,
  We followed by a rugged path and weird.
A marsh that hath the name of *Styx* there is,  106
  Where spreadeth out this dismal little brook
  Beneath the grey, malign declivities.

---

100-105. Up to this point Dante and Virgil have been walking along the exterior rim of the fourth circle. Now they cross that circle to its inner boundary bank, on the other side of which, looking inward upon the fifth circle and just below the crest of the steep slope descending thither, a little spring bubbles up and pours its water down a considerable declivity into this next division of Hell.

## CANTO VII

| | |
|---|---:|
| Then, as I stood intently gazing, folk | 109 |
|   Besmeared with mud I saw in that lagoon, | |
|   All naked, and most wrathful in their look. | |
| They smote each other not with hands alone, | 112 |
|   But with their heads and chests and feet; also | |
|   They tore each other with their teeth. "My son," | |
| Said the good master, "thou beholdest now | 115 |
|   The souls of those whom anger overcame; | |
|   And further, I would have thee surely know | |
| That other people are beneath this same | 118 |
|   Water, whose sighs, as plainly thou mayest see, | |
|   The bubbles on it everywhere proclaim. | |
| Fixed in the slime, they say: 'Sullen were we | 121 |
|   Aforetime in the sweet, sun-gladdened air, | |
|   And filled with smoke of rage continually. | |
| Now lie we sullen here in the black mire.' | 124 |
|   This hymn they gurgle in their throats, for they | |
|   Have not the utterance of words entire." | |
| Wide round the filthy fen upon our way, | 127 |
|   Between the dry bank and the slough, we passed, | |
|   With eyes regarding those that guzzling lay | |
| Therein, until we reached a tower at last. | 130 |

109-126. The fifth circle is devoted to the punishment of anger. Those whose rage was violent buffet and rend each other upon the surface of the muddy pool; the sulky or sullen lie hidden in the mire of its bottom.

## CANTO VIII

*Fifth circle. The signal fires. The boatman Phlegyas. The crossing of Styx. Filippo Argenti. The city of Dis. The demons deny entrance.*

I say, continuing, that long before
  Unto the foot thereof we ever came,
  Our gaze had sought the summit of that tower,
For there we saw two beacons burn, whose flame    4
  Another answered back, so far away
  That hardly could the eye perceive its beam.
Then turning to all wisdom's fountain sea:    7
  "What means this fire? What answereth that?" said I.
  "And tell me: those that lit them, who are they?"
"Across the turbid wave thou mayst espy    10
  What is expected, if 'tis not concealed
  By reek of the morass," he gave reply.
Never hath cord an arrow yet impelled    13
  That sped through air so swiftly from the bow

---

1. According to Boccaccio, the first seven cantos of the *Inferno* were written before Dante's banishment; were left in Florence when he went into exile; and were only restored to him some years later, whereupon he resumed the work which he had in the meantime abandoned—hence the word "continuing" in the opening line of Canto viii. This story is not generally believed; and certain of the passages in the earlier cantos must have been written after his banishment. But there is some evidence at least that Dante's original scheme of the *Inferno* was different from that which he actually followed, and that the change of plan was made not far from this point. Hitherto, one of the Seven Deadly Sins has been punished in each circle, and a single canto has been devoted to each, whereas Canto xii-xxxiv deal only with the passage through the seventh, eighth, and ninth circles. This looks as though Dante had begun with the intention of completing the *Inferno,* the *Purgatorio,* and the *Paradiso* in ten or twelve cantos each, and the work grew under his hand.

## CANTO VIII

  As sped a little vessel I beheld
Approach us through the water even now,     16
  A single boatman steering it, who cried:
"So art thou come, fell cursed spirit, thou!"
"Phlegyas, Phlegyas," answered him my guide,     19
  "This time thou callest in vain; but till we pass
The marsh, no longer, shalt thou have us bide."
As one who learns some great deception has     22
  Been practised on him, and resents the fraud,—
So in his gathered wrath grew Phlegyas.
Into the skiff descended my dear lord,     25
  Bidding me enter after him; and lo,
It seemed not laden till I was aboard.
Soon as we both were in, the ancient prow     28
  Set forth upon its way, dividing more
Than was its wont the waters of the slough.
Then, while we traversed the dead channel o'er,     31
  One full of mud rose up in front of me
And said: "Who art thou, come before thine hour?"
I answered: "Though I come, I do not stay.     34
  But who art thou, that art so foul?" Thereto:
"Thou seest I am one who weeps," said he.
And I to him: "With weeping and with woe,     37
  Thou spirit maledict, do thou remain,
For thee, all filthy as thou art, I know."
Both hands unto the boat he stretched out then,     40
  Whereat my wary master thrust him back,

---

19. Phlegyas, the boatman of Styx and mythological guardian of the fifth circle, was a son of Mars and King of the Lapithae. In his vengeful wrath he burned the temple of Apollo at Delphi, and therefore is placed in Tartarus by Virgil in *Aeneid* vi. His boat seems to be Dante's own invention.

32. This is Filippo Argenti (fee-leep'-po är-jĕn'-tee), of Florence. His family, the Adimari, were political opponents of Dante.

Saying: "Off! Down with the other dogs again!"
And after threw his arms about my neck, 43
   Kissed me, and cried: "O soul indignant thus,
   Blessed be she who bore thee, for thy sake!
That was on earth one proud and tyrannous; 46
   No goodness doth adorn his memory;
   And hence his shade is likewise furious.
How many who are deemed great kings shall lie 49
   Hereafter in this place like swine in mud,
   Leaving behind them only infamy!"
Then said I: "Leader mine, in truth I should 52
   Rejoice to see him soused beneath this swill
   Before we ever leave its squalid flood."
And he to me: "Thou shalt obtain thy will 55
   Or e'er the shore reveal itself. 'Tis meet
   To gratify a wish thus suitable."
Nor was it long until I saw those wet 58
   And muddy folk so fiercely on him fall
   That still I praise and thank my God for it.
"Have at Filippo Argenti!" cried they all; 61
   And the Florentine, in passion raging sore,
   Turned his own teeth against himself, withal.
We left him there, of whom I tell no more; 64
   But on mine ears smote wailings unsubdued,
   So that I peered intently on before.
"My son," now said to me the master good, 67
   "The city that is named of Dis draws near,
   With heavy people, vast in multitude."

---

44. It is Dante's indignation against evil that Virgil commends.

68. "Dis" was another name used by the Romans for Pluto, the god of Hades. Dante applies it both to Lucifer and to the region within the city walls which gird the lower and more terrible depths of Hell.

## CANTO VIII

And I: "Its minarets already, sir,     70
  I see distinctly yonder in the vale,
  Vermilion, as though issuing from fire."
He answered: "The eternal fire of bale,     73
  There kindled, maketh them with ruddy flame
  Glow as thou seest in this nether Hell."
At length into the fosses deep we came     76
  Which all that joyless city gird and moat,
  Whose walls did unto me of iron seem.
Yet not before wide circuit round about,     79
  We reached a place where loud the boatman saith
  To us: "Here is the entrance! Get ye out!"
Of those once rained from Heaven, I saw beneath     82
  The gates more than a thousand; angrily
  They shouted: "Who is it—who—that without death
Goes through the kingdom of the dead?" And he,     85
  My leader sage, a sign unto them made
  That he would speak with them in secrecy.
Then their great scorn they somewhat checked, and said:     88
  "Come only thou, and that one let begone
  Who in this realm so boldly dared to tread.
Let him return on his mad way alone,—     91
  Try if he can; for thou shalt here remain,
  Who unto him so dark a land hast shown."
Judge, Reader, if at that accurst refrain     94
  I did not grow discomfited full sore.
  Methought I ne'er should win to earth again.

---

70. *minarets.* Literally, "mosques." The word, with its Mohammedan associations, suggests a city of those alienated from God. What Dante sees are the burning tombs of the sixth circle, the space just inside the walls. This circle would seem to be almost on a level with the marsh of Styx, which forms the fifth, but the phrase "in the vale" shows there is at least a slight depression, either inside or outside the ramparts.

82. *those once rained from Heaven.* The erstwhile rebel angels, now demons.

"O my loved guide, who seven times and more 97
  Hast rendered unto me security
  And rescued from deep peril that stood before,—
Leave me not thus undone," entreated I, 100
  "And if our farther progress be denied,
  Let us go back together speedily."
He that had brought me hither then replied: 103
  "Fear not; our passage none can from us take,
  By Such a One 'twas given us. Do thou bide,
Waiting me, here; comfort and feed thy weak, 106
  Dejected spirit with good hope; for thee
  I will not, in the world below, forsake."
Thus the sweet father goeth a space from me, 109
  And I remain in doubt, while "no" and "yes"
  Contend within my head for mastery.
What he proposed to them, I could not guess; 112
  Yet stood he there not long before that rout
  Poured in again, vying in eagerness.
Right in my master's face, who stayed without, 115
  They shut the gates, these foes of ours; and now
  To me, with lingering steps, he turned about.
His eye was fixed upon the ground, his brow 118
  Shorn of all boldness, and with sighs he said:
  "Who hath forbidden me the abodes of woe?"
Then unto me: "But thou, be not dismayed, 121
  Though I am wroth. This trial will I subdue,
  Whate'er to thwart us be within essayed.

---

105. *By Such a One.* By God himself.

110. *"no" and "yes."* That is, that Virgil will not or will return to him.

112-117. Virgil, typifying human reason, is powerless against the demons, quintessential evil. Here only the heavenly aid of special grace will avail.

## CANTO VIII

| | |
|---|---:|
| In sooth their insolence is nothing new. | 124 |
|   At a less secret gate it once was shown, | |
|   Which stands unbolted still. 'Twas o'er it thou | |
| The dread inscription sawest; and thence adown, | 127 |
|   E'en now descends the slope precipitous, | |
|   Passing the circles unaccompanied, one | |
| Who shall set wide the city unto us." | 130 |

---

124-127. The demons had similarly resisted Christ on his descent into Limbo, to rescue the Patriarchs, after his crucifixion. In consequence the outer gate of Hell was broken open and so remained. Compare Canto iii.

## CANTO IX

*Before the gate of Dis. The Furies. The coming of the angel. Entrance to the city. The sixth circle: heretics. The fiery tombs.*

That hue which cowardice had painted me
  When I beheld my guide turn back, repressed
  His own new colour the more speedily.
He stopped like one who doth attentive list,      4
  Because the eye not far could lead his sight
  Through the black air and through the heavy mist.
"Yet it must be that we shall win this fight,"      7
  He said, "unless . . . One promised us such aid.
  But till it come, how long doth seem the wait!"
I noted well that he had overlaid      10
  His opening words with others different
  In purport from those former ones he stayed;
Yet still he gave me fear, because I lent      13
  To his unfinished phrase perchance more fell
  A meaning than was really his intent.
"Into this bottom of the gloomy shell      16
  Doth any ever come from that first grade
  Where they who are but reft of hoping dwell?"
So questioned I, and he in answer said:      19
  "This journey which I wend, on very rare
  Occasion is by any of us made.
'Tis true I once before descended here,      22

---

1. *That hue.* The pallor of fear.
8. *One.* Beatrice.
16. *shell.* The Italian word is *conca;* perhaps the meaning is not "shell" but, rather, "a large conical receptacle," in which case "well" would be a better translation.
17-18. That is, from Limbo, where Virgil resides.

## CANTO IX

By cruel Erichtho's arts, who would compel
   The shades their bodies to resume and wear.
My flesh was naked of me no great while 25
   When she required me there within to go
   And fetch a spirit out of Judas' hell.
That is the darkest place and the most low, 28
   And farthest from the heaven encircling all.
   Be reassured, for well the way I know.
This marsh that doth the mighty stench exhale 31
   Engirds the woeful city round about,
   Where, save with wrath, we enter not the pale."
And more he spake, but I recall it not, 34
   Because mine eyes were wholly fixed; I viewed,
   O'er a high tower's summit, where the hot
Flame burned, three hellish Furies, stained with blood, 37
   Who of a sudden had uprisen there—
   Women, to judge by limbs and attitude.
With greenest hydras were they girt; for hair 40
   They had small serpents and cerastes e'en,
   Which round their savage temples did they wear.
And knowing well the handmaids of the queen 43
   Of everlasting dole, he said to me:
   "These are the fierce Erinnyes that are seen.
Lo there, Megaera on the left hand; she 46
   On the right, Alecto, weeping; in the midst
   Tisiphone"; and silent then was he.
Each with her nails made rending of her breast, 49

---

23. *Erichtho.* A Thessalian sorceress in Lucan's *Pharsalia*.
27. *Judas' hell.* The lowest circle, where Judas and other traitors are confined.
37-63. The Furies, or Erinnyes (Alecto, Megaera, and Tisiphone), in classical mythology avengers of the murder of kinsmen and the violation of other peculiarly sacred ties, seem used by Dante to symbolize man's remorseful memories of former sins. He calls them "handmaids" of the mythical Proserpina, Pluto's queen, whom Theseus and his friend

Smote with her palms, and shrieked so loud a moan
That I, for dread, close to the poet pressed.
"Let come Medusa! Change him into stone! 52
'Twas wrong we did not the assault requite
Of Theseus," they all shouted, looking down.
"Turn thee about, and keep thine eyes shut tight; 55
For if the Gorgon showeth, and thou see,
No reascending is there to the light!"
Thus cried the master, and himself turned me, 58
And trusted not my hands unto that work,
But screened me also with his own.—O ye
Who have unclouded understanding, mark 61
The lesson which doth its concealment make
Beneath the veil of verses strange and dark!
And now drew nigh over the turbid lake 64
The crash and uproar of a fearful sound,
Whereat did both the shores begin to shake, —
A noise to which no likeness could be found 67
But of a wind, by adverse heat set free,
That strikes a forest in its might unbound,
Shatters the boughs, lays low, and bears away: 70
Rolling up dust, it goeth on superb,
And makes the wild beasts and the shepherds flee.

---

Pirithoüs tried to carry off. Pirithoüs was slain in the attempt; and Theseus was fastened to a great rock, but was later set free by Hercules in defiance of the infernal powers. Therefore the Erinnyes now call for the Gorgon Medusa to come and turn Dante to stone, that for him there may be no deliverance. The hidden meaning to which attention is directed in this passage appears to be that remorse may bring despair, symbolized by Medusa (that is, despair of receiving the mercy of God), which hardens the heart; reason (Virgil) exhorts man to turn his eyes upon his evil conscience, but no longer permits him to look when there is prospect that this petrifying despair will come to him.

68. *a wind, by adverse heat set free.* Heat in the adverse or opposite quarter of the heavens causes a vacuum, which the air rushes to fill; thus a great wind may be generated.

## CANTO IX

He loosed mine eyes and said: "Direct thy nerve 73
  Of vision now across that ancient scum,
  There, where the marish smoke is most acerb."
As frogs, when doth the hostile serpent come, 76
  All vanish through the water as they ply
  Till huddled in the mire is every one,
More than a thousand ruined souls saw I 79
  Thus flying before him who did o'erpass
  The ferriage of the Styx with footsteps dry.
Ever he swept the dense air from his face 82
  With left hand moved before him as he went,
  Nor otherwise it seemed he weary was.
Clearly I saw he from above was sent, 85
  And looked unto my guide, who silently
  Signed me to stand in quiet and lowly bent.
Ah, how disdainful he appeared to me! 88
  He reached the gate, and with a little rod
  He opened it; resistance none had he.
"Outcasts of Heaven, O despicable brood," 91
  Upon the horrid threshold he began,
  "Why hath such insolence in you abode?
Why spurn ye at that Will which never can 94
  Be of its purpose balked or made to fail,
  And which hath oftentimes increased your pain?
To butt against the Fates doth what avail? 97
  Your Cerberus, if call to mind ye would,
  Goes therefore with raw chin and gullet still."
Then he returned along his miry road, 100
  And spake no word to us, but wore the guise
  Of one whom other cares constrain and goad
Than touch the folk that are before his eyes; 103
  And toward the city we, with hearts composed

---

98-99. Cerberus was chained by Hercules and dragged to the upper world.

After his holy utterance, bent our ways.
We entered there, for none our steps opposed;
And I, most fain of their estate to know
Who by so vast a fortress were enclosed,
No more was in, than round I gazed, and lo,
I saw a spacious plain on every hand,
Filled full with torment and with cruel woe.
Just as at Arles, where Rhône doth stagnant stand,
Or Pola, the Quarnaro gulf anear
Which bounds Italia and bathes her land,
The sepulchres make all the ground appear
Uneven, 'twas on every side the same
Here; but the manner was far bitterer here.
For in among the tombs was scattered flame,
Whereby they glowed with hotness as intense
As any craft requireth, iron to tame.
Their lids were lifted and thrown back, and thence
A wailing rose; no sufferers could be stirred,
Save the most wretched, unto such laments.
"Master, what people are the souls interred
Within these coffers," said I, "who with drear
Outcry of anguish make themselves thus heard?"
"The arch-heretics and their followers are here,

---

112-116. At Arles (ärl), where the delta of the Rhône begins, there was a great cemetery, dating from Roman times down through the Middle Ages, with many imposing tombs. Another was formerly at Pola (po'-lä), but this has disappeared. The gulf of Quarnaro (quärnä'-ro) is situated at the northern end of the Adriatic and marks the northeastern confines of Italy.

127. By "heretics" Dante apparently means materialistic free-thinkers —"atheists"—or else they would have been in the ninth bolgia of the eighth circle, with the schismatics. In life denying immortality, in death they inhabit tombs of undying pain. It should be noted that just as Upper Hell begins with the circle of the virtuous pagans and unbaptized infants, souls stained by no grievous sin of commission but unpossessed of saving faith, even so does Lower Hell begin in this sixth circle, which

## CANTO IX

Of every sect," he answered, "nor dost thou deem
  How greatly laden is each sepulchre.
Here like with like is buried; yet their teen           130
  Differs as do in heat these monuments."
  Then, turning to the right, we passed between
The tortures and the lofty battlements.               133

---

also contains souls whose sin is unbelief, but this time of a graver sort, —for instead of merely not knowing "how to worship God aright," they denied his existence. Similarly, too, around Hell as a whole, outside of all its circles, is the zone of the passive neutrals between good and evil; these did not even lack understanding of righteousness, but only the zeal to perform it.

132. The course of the poets through Hell is regularly toward the left —that is, the sinister way, as they probe deeper and deeper into evil. (Later, in ascending the Mount of Purgatory they invariably move to the right.) Here in the sixth circle and again when approaching Geryon (xvii, 31) they turn to the right in Hell. The reason for these exceptions is obscure, though many explanations have been attempted.

## CANTO X

*Sixth circle. Farinata the undismayed. Cavalcante Cavalcanti. Of the extent of knowledge among those in Hell. Exile foretold for Dante.*

Along a narrow path my master goes
  Between the tortures and the city wall,
  And I behind his shoulders follow close.
"O power supreme, that through the circles foul     4
  Thus leadest," I began, "as pleases thee,—
  Speak, and my longings satisfy, withal.
Those in the tombs—could they be seen by me?     7
  The coverings even now are open thrown,
  And no one keepeth guard." Then answered he:
"All shall be closed when they return anon     10
  Here from Jehoshaphat, clad in former wise
  With bodies they have in the world laid down.
The burial place of Epicurus lies—     13
  His and his followers'—upon this side,
  Who held the soul but with the body dies.
So shalt thou presently be satisfied     16
  Touching the question which thou didst reveal
  To me, and in the wish thou still dost hide."
And I: "Dear leader, I do not conceal     19
  My heart from thee excepting through desire
  Of brevity; this did thy teaching seal."—
"O Tuscan, thou that midst the city of fire     22
  Walkest alive, with speech so courteous,

---

11. It was believed that the Last Judgment would take place in the Valley of Jehoshaphat, near Jerusalem. See Joel iii, 2, 12.

18. *the wish.* That is, probably, to see some Florentine heretics, who were numerous in those days.

## CANTO X

May it please thee now to stop a little here!
Thy language plainly showeth thee, like us,     25
   A native of that noble land whereto
   Perchance o'er much was I injurious."
This was the sound that suddenly had issue     28
   From one of those ark-tombs, whereat in fear
   A little nearer to my guide I drew.
He said: "Nay, turn! What doest thou? Lo, there     31
   Is Farinata, who has risen. From
   The waist thou shalt behold him, standing sheer."
Mine eyes were fixed already on that form;     34
   Erect he reared his breast and countenance,
   As though of Hell he entertained great scorn.
And now my lord with bold and ready hands     37
   Pushed me to him, the sepulchres between,
   Saying: "Make few thy words and clear of sense."
When I before him came, somewhat his eyen     40
   Regarded me, and almost in disdain
   He made inquire: "What ancestors were thine?"
And I, who to obey him was most fain,     43
   Hid not the truth, but all my lineage showed,

---

32. Farinata (fä-ree-nä'-tä) degli Uberti was leader of the Ghibellines in Tuscany in the middle of the thirteenth century. He expelled the Guelfs from his native city of Florence in 1248, but they returned in 1251 and drove out him and the other Ghibellines in 1258, whereupon he retired to Siena with his fellow exiles and organized a movement which resulted in the terrible defeat of the Florentine Guelfs at the battle of Montaperti in 1260—"the havoc and great slaughter which dyed the Arbia (är'-byä) red." This left him master of Florence, and he again expelled his adversaries. Two years after his death in 1264, the battle of Benevento crushed the Ghibellines; the Guelfs again returned, and so bitter were their memories of Montaperti that the Uberti were excluded from all subsequent decrees of amnesty. Farinata was a brave and able man, as Dante (himself now of Ghibelline tendency) fully appreciated; but as a materialist he is placed among the heretics, one of whom the inquisitor had declared him (nearly twenty years after his death) together with his sons and grandsons.

Whereat he raised his brows a little. Then
He said: "Fiercely adverse to me they stood, 46
  And to my fathers and my party yond
  On earth, so twice I scattered them abroad."
"If they were driven out, yet they returned 49
  Both times from every quarter," I answered him;
  "Thy kindred not so well that art have learned."
Now alongside of this one, to the chin 52
  Uncovered, there appeared another shade,
  Upraised, I think, upon his knees within.
He looked around, as though desire he had 55
  To find if some one else were there with me,
  And when he saw his expectation fade,—
Weeping: "If through this prison blind," said he, 58
  "Thou goest by loftiness of genius,
  Where is my son? why is he not with thee?"
I answered: "Of myself I come not thus, 61
  But by his aid who waiteth there,—toward whom
  Mayhap thy Guido was contemptuous."
The words he spake and manner of his doom 64
  Already had revealed him past surmise;
  To be explicit I could thence presume.

---

51. In addressing Farinata, Dante uses the plural (*voi*, etc.) to indicate especial respect—so too with Cavalcante and in Canto xv with Brunetto Latini, but the singular with all others of the damned. Nearly every translator accordingly changes the English pronoun from "thou" and "thy" and "thee" to "you" and "your"—and thus secures precisely the opposite effect from what is desired and what Dante achieves; for in English "you" is not more formal and reverential than "thou" but less so!

61-66. Dante recognized Cavalcante Cavalcanti, the father of Guido (gwee'-do) Cavalcanti. Guido had been Dante's best friend, and was next to him the greatest poet of the age; therefore Cavalcante naturally felt they should be together. It is not known why Dante says Guido was perhaps contemptuous toward Virgil—whether in literary judgment or, as a sceptic, toward Reason. The most plausible interpretation of the whole reply to Cavalcante would be that Dante means that he was able to take his (poetic) journey through Hell because he followed the

## CANTO X

Then springing suddenly to his feet, he cries: 67
   "Saidst thou? He *was?* Lives he not anywhere?
   Strikes not the blessed light upon his eyes?"
And when of some delay he was aware 70
   In my response, he fell back in that chest
   Again, nor evermore did he appear.
But that heroic soul at whose request 73
   My footsteps I had stayed, bowed not his head,
   Changed not his aspect, flinched not in the least.
"If badly they have learned that art," the thread 76
   Of former speech he now resumed, "I trow
   It more tormenteth me than doth this bed.
But of that queen who reigneth here below, 79
   Not fifty times rekindled shall be the face
   Ere thou the hardness of that art shalt know.
And as thou wouldst to the sweet earth retrace 82
   Thy steps, inform me why in all their laws
   The people are so fierce against my race."
Whence I to him: "The havoc that once was 85
   And the great slaughter that dyed the Arbia red

---

example of Virgil (see Canto i, 85-87) in extended literary composition, whereas Guido, cultivating only the current Provençal type of poetry with its "short swallow-flights of song" to the entire neglect of the ancient model, could never, despite his undeniable genius, hope to achieve any such great work as the *Divine Comedy*. Guido was still alive at the date assumed for Dante's mystic journey, but was dead when the poem was actually written. He was a notable White Guelf, and hence one of those whom in Dante's priorate it had been necessary to banish from Florence, along with the leaders of the other party, for the sake of peace. The climate of Sarzana, Guido's place of exile, proved fatal to him, and he died in August, 1300.

79. *that queen who reigneth here below.* The moon, whose goddess, Diana, in her other aspect of Hecate was mistress of the black arts, and hence is here identified with Proserpina. Fifty lunar months from the date of the vision would be April, 1304. Dante was banished in 1302, and the first unsuccessful attempt for his return began in March, 1304.

Doth such devotions in our temple cause."
And thereupon he sighed and shook his head. 88
   "In that I was not single, nor had e'er
   Moved with the others, be assured," he said,
"Save for due reason. But I was single there 91
   When all consented to blot Florence out;
   Alone I openly defended her."
"So may thy seed have peace at last, the knot," 94
   I begged of him, "unloose for me, I pray,
   Wherein my understanding hath been caught.
It seems, if rightly hear I what ye say, 97
   That ye beforehand know what time shall bring,
   But in the present 'tis another way."
"Like one with faulty sight, we see a thing 100
   Clearly," he said, "which lieth far remote;
   So much of light still grants the Almighty King.
But when the event draws near, or now is wrought, 103
   Our minds are wholly void; of human state,
   Except as others tell us, know we naught.
And therefore thou mayst comprehend our fate: 106
   That all our knowledge will be dead and done
   When of the Future closed shall be the gate."
"Prithee, declare unto that fallen one," 109
   Said I, for my neglect compunctïous,
   "That with the living still is joined his son;
And if before I did not answer thus, 112
   Explain that 'twas because perplexity

---

87. The edicts against the Uberti were pronounced in the cathedral of San Giovanni. Dante perhaps uses the word "devotions" in irony because such vindictive enactments profaned the holy edifice.

91-93. When Florence was helpless after Montaperti, all the chiefs of the allied Ghibellines favoured her utter destruction, save only Farinata, who heroically rose in their midst and, declaring that this should never be while he lived to wield a sword in her defence, forced the rejection of the plan.

## CANTO X

(The same thou solvedst) already wrapped me close."
But now my master was recalling me, 115
   Whence I besought that spirit with eager haste
   To tell me who were in his company.
"More than a thousand are we, here encased," 118
   He said. "The second Frederick is below,
   And the Cardinal. I speak not of the rest."
Thereon he hid himself; and I unto 121
   The ancient poet returned, with thoughts applied
   To those dark words which seemed to bode me woe.
Forward he moved, and going by my side, 124
   Asked me: "What is it that doth so disturb?"
   And to his question I in full replied.
"Let memory," that sage enjoined, "preserve 127
   What thou hast heard against thyself. 'Tis meet
   Here to attend." His finger bade observe.
"When thou shalt come in presence of the sweet 130
   Radiance of her whose lovely eyes see all,
   She of thy life will tell the way complete."
To leftward then he turned his steps. The wall 133
   We quitted, and on toward the middle went
   Along a path that strikes into a vale
Which even thus high its noisome stench upsent. 136

---

119-120. *The second Frederick* is of course Frederick of Hohenstaufen, Emperor of Germany. He was generally considered an Epicurean infidel; certainly in his tolerance and in his independence of thought and action he was unique among the sovereigns of his age, of whom he was by far the greatest and the most enlightened. *The Cardinal* is Ottaviano degli Ubaldini, an ardent Ghibelline though attached to the papal court.

123. *those dark words*. The implied prophecy of Dante's banishment, line 81.

130-132. Beatrice, of course, is meant.

134. *on toward the middle*. That is, across the circle and toward the central abyss, which is the "vale" of line 135.

## CANTO XI

*On the brink above the seventh circle. Exposition of the lower depths: the violent, then last the fraudulent. The incontinent, above, less guilty. Of usury.*

Upon the verge of a high bank, composed
   Of mighty broken rocks, we now discover,
   Beneath, a yet more cruel throng enclosed.
And here so horrible a fume doth hover             4
   Of stench exhaled out of the deep abyss,
   For shelter we withdrew behind the cover
Of a great monument, whereon was this              7
   Written: "I hold Pope Anastasius, whom
   Photinus from the right way led amiss."
"It needs we to the dismal blast become             10
   Accustomed, ere beginning the descent,
   And then we shall not find it burdensome."
The master thus; and: "That the time be spent      13
   Not idly," said I, "compensation find."
   And he: "I have precisely that intent."
"My son," he now began to say, "confined          16
   Within these stones are circles three, more small
   From grade to grade, like those we left behind.
Full of accursed spirits are they all,               19
   But hearken how and why they bear such load,
   That sight hereafter may for thee avail.
Every malignant act, by Heaven abhorred,        22

---

4-5. The stench arises from the foulness of the sins punished in the lower depths of Hell.

8-9. Anastasius II was Pope from 496 to 498. There was a story that he was persuaded into heresy by Photinus, a deacon of Thessalonica.

22. *malignant act*. That is, deliberate sin, in contrast to the sins of impulse or incontinence punished in the circles already traversed.

## CANTO XI

Aimeth at injury, and such an aim
Makes others grieve, either by force or fraud.
But fraud, which only man commits, hath blame 25
The more with God, and hence the fraudulent
Are placed beneath and suffer greater pain.
All the first circle is of the violent; 28
But since to three may violence be done,
Three rings divide and form its whole extent.
To God, to self, and to one's neighbour, one 31
May offer violence;—with plain discourse,
I say, to them and theirs shall this be shown.
Lo, on one's neighbour death and wounds by force 34
May be inflicted, flame and pillage blight
His property, extortion drain his purse.
Wherefore all homicides, and all who smite 37
Maliciously, the outer ring torments—
Robbers and plunderers, too—in different plight.
To self and goods may one do violence; 40
So in the second ring must he deplore
His deed with unavailing penitence
Who of your world deprives himself, his store 43
Squanders and games away, and there, where he
Should dwell in joy, goes sorrowing evermore.
Violence may be done the Deity 46
By one's denying and blaspheming him
And scorning Nature and her bounty free;
And hence the smallest round doth seal the sin 49
Of Sodom and Cahors and all of those
Who speak despising God, their hearts within.
Fraud, that on every human conscience gnaws, 52

---

42-43. Wastrels and gamblers, who dissipate their wealth bodily, are distinguished from the merely prodigal, who are in the fourth circle.

50. Sodom stands for unnatural sexual vices; see Genesis xix. Cahors, in southern France, was notorious for its usurers.

A man toward them may practise who confide
  In him, or them that no such faith repose.
This latter mode seems only to divide 55
  The general bond of Nature's amities;
  And therefore in the second circle bide
Magicians, flatteries, hypocrisies, 58
  Falsification, theft, and simony,
  Panders and barrators—such filth as these.
In the other mode forgot are both the tie 61
  That Nature makes and what in after days
  Is added, causing special trust thereby.
Hence in the smallest circle, the mid-place 64
  Of all the universe and seat of Dis,
  For ever is consumed whoe'er betrays."
"Master," said I, "clearly proceedeth this 67
  Thine argument, and doth full well distinguish
  The fashion and the folk of the abyss.
But prithee tell me: those of the fat marsh, 70
  Those the wind driveth, those the rain beats down,
  And those encountering with reproaches harsh—

---

58-60. The translation follows the original in jumbling sins and sinners together in the same list. Barrators are traffickers in public offices, corrupt officials; barratry in the political sphere is analogous to simony in the ecclesiastical.

65. *Dis.* The name is here used, not for the city, but for Lucifer.

68. For the sake of more effective phrasing below, a hendecasyllabic line has here been used with even less suggestion of rhyme than in the other cases where one occurs. Any reader to whose ear it may be unsatisfactory can substitute in the text the following alternative version of lines 67-72:

> *"Master," said I, "clearly proceedeth this*
>   *Thine argument, distinguishing full well*
>   *The fashion and the folk of the abyss.*
> *But those of the fat marsh—I prithee tell—*
>   *Those the wind driveth, those the rain beats down,*
>   *And those encountering with reproaches fell—*

## CANTO XI

Why are they not within the fiery town 73
   Punished, if God is wroth with them? If he
   Is not, then wherefore are they so fordone?"
"What makes thine intellect," said he to me, 76
   "Thus err beyond its wont? Or is thy thought
   Bent otherwhere? The dispositions three—
Rememberest thou the words, or hast forgot, 79
   With which thy Ethics thoroughly doth explain
   Concerning them, that Heaven abideth not:
Incontinence, and malice, and insane 82
   Bestiality? and how incontinence
   Offends God least and hath the smallest blame?
If thou consider with intelligence 85
   This doctrine, and bethink thee who are those
   That have above, without, their punishments,—
Plain will it be why from these felons' woes 88
   They are divided, and Avenging Might
   Hammers upon them with less wrathful blows."
"O sun that healest all imperfect sight, 91
   So thine expounding gladdens me, that doubt,"
   Said I, "no less than knowledge gives delight.
Yet turn thee back a little, to the spot 94
   Where sayest thou an offence is usury
   To Heavenly Goodness, and unloose that knot."
"Philosophy points out," he answered me, 97

---

73. *within the fiery town.* Within the walls of Dis.

80. *thy Ethics.* The *Nichomachean Ethics* of Aristotle. Dante's scheme does not coincide with Aristotle's; his own division of injurious acts into those of violence and those of fraud is from Cicero (*De Officiis*) but he roughly equates sins of violence with the "bestiality" of the *Ethics*.

97 *ff.* The argument here given against usury, or interest (the taking of which the Middle Ages, so strangely to our own notions, condemned), is that the operations of nature are directly established by God and follow his art or processes of working, and according to the *Physics* of Aristotle human art is an imitation of nature; and that from nature and art man is commanded in Genesis (ii, 15: "And the Lord God took

"To him who heeds, nor only in one part,
   How Nature shapes her course most faithfully
By Intellect Divine and by its art;                                   100
   And if thou con thy Physics, thou wilt see,
   After not many pages, that your art
Doth follow her, so far as this may be,                             103
   As pupil follows master; so of a' kind
   Your art is grandchild to the Deity.
Now from these two, if thou recall to mind                 106
   The first of Genesis, to earn their bread
   And to advance, it doth behoove mankind;
And since the usurer pursues instead                               109
   Another course, Nature he doth disdain,
   Herself and follower; his hope is laid
Elsewhere. Now come; for journeying I am fain.       112
   The Fishes quiver on the horizon now,
   And wholly over Caurus lies the Wain,
And yonder far is found our way below."                         115

---

the man, and put him into the Garden of Eden to dress it and keep it";
and iii, 19: "In the sweat of thy face shalt thou eat bread") to
earn his bread and to advance; but the money-lender's gain is derived
neither from the operations of nature nor from his own toil—he flouts
both nature herself and her follower, art (industry).

113-114. That the constellation Pisces, or the Fishes, is on the horizon
and the Wain (Charles' Wain, the Great Dipper, Ursa Major) is over
Caurus (that is, in the northwest, Caurus being the name for the northwest wind), is the poet's characteristic circumlocution for saying that
the time is about 4 a.m. It is Saturday, the day before Easter.

## CANTO XII

*The Minotaur in the pass. Descent to the seventh circle. The first ring: Phlegethon. Doers of violence in the boiling blood. The warder centaurs. Nessus and Chiron. Tyrants, conquerors, and bandits. Across the stream.*

The place we reached for going down was one
  Of Alpine ruggedness, and from what lay
  There also, such as every eye would shun.
Like to that fallen ruin which one day             4
  Smote the Adige's flank this side of Trent
  Because of earthquake or defective stay
(For from the summit to the plain was rent        7
  The mountain's face, so that the shattered heap
  Of stones affords, though barely, a descent)—
Such was the pathway down that rocky steep;     10
  And on the broken verge of the ravine
  Sprawled at full length the infamy of Crete,
Which was conceived in the false cow. And when   13

---

1 *ff.* The descent into the seventh circle is steeper and farther than any previously encountered, thus separating the violent from the incontinent by a considerable space. A still greater chasm will presently be found between the violent and the fraudulent.

4-6. A tremendous slide of rocks which occurred on the road between Trent and Verona; it fell into the Adige (ä'-dee-jā), overwhelming villages along a stretch of three or four miles. Albertus Magnus, who describes it, imputes such landslides to earthquakes, or to water undermining the base of a mountain.

12-13. *the infamy of Crete,* etc. The Minotaur, monstrous compound of man and bull, is fitly the mythological guardian of the circle of the violent. He was born of the insane passion of Pasiphaë, the wife of King Minos of Crete, for a bull, to gratify which she concealed herself in the wooden figure of a cow; he is thus an emblem of sins against nature. To him in the Labyrinth were thrown the Athenian youths

## THE INFERNO OF DANTE

He saw us there, on his own flesh he bit,
   Like one whom anger overbears within.
My sage cried out to him: "Thou thinkest it         16
   Perchance to be that same Athenian Duke
   Who in the world achieved thy death. Now get
Thee gone, thou beast, for this one never took       19
   Instruction from thy sister, but is here
   That he upon your punishments may look."
Just as a bull doth from his halter tear             22
   The instant he receives the fatal blow,
   And cannot walk, but plunges here and there,—
I saw the Minotaur do even so;                 25
   And Virgil, wary, cried: "To the passage—run!
   While he is frenzied is the time to go!"
Thus we pursued our downward way, upon      28
   The dumpage of those stones, which from the weight
   Unwonted, often moved beneath my shoon.
Pondering I went; and: "Of this fallen freight,      31
   Haply," said he, "thou thinkest, guarded by
   That bestial rage whose power did I abate.
Now I would have thee know that formerly,       34
   When I went down into the nether Hell,
   This cliff had not yet fallen. But verily,

---

and maidens given yearly as satisfaction for the murder of Minos' son, and he devoured them; he is thus an emblem of murder and tyranny. He was finally slain by Theseus, here called the "Athenian Duke" (cf. the "Theseus, Duke of Athens" of Shakespeare's *Midsummer Night's Dream*), with the aid of Ariadne, the daughter of Minos and Pasiphaë.

29. *The dumpage of those stones.* The figure, as that of a discharged wagon-load, is graphic; so too is the touch that the stones moved beneath the weight of Dante's mortal body.

34 *ff.* Virgil explains that the rock slide resulted from the convulsion of nature attending the death of Christ on the cross, which occurred not long after Virgil's enforced expedition into the lower depths of Hell by command of the witch Erichtho (see Canto ix, 22-27).

## CANTO XII.

Not long it was (if I remember well) 37
  Before His coming who bore off from Dis,
  Out of the highest circle, the great spoil,
In every part the loathsome, deep abyss 40
  So trembled that the universe, methought,
  Was thrilled with love, whereby (some credit this)
The world has often been to chaos brought; 43
  And at that moment, here and otherwhere,
  The downfall of this ancient rock was wrought.
But fix thine eyes below, for now draws near 46
  The river of blood, and every one who by
  Violence injured others, boileth there.
O wicked, foolish, blind cupidity, 49
  That in the transient life doth urge us so,
  And in the eternal steeps us bitterly!
I saw a broad moat bended like a bow,— 52
  Such, in accordance with my guide's account,
  That it encompassed all the plain below.
And between it and where the bank 'gan mount 55
  Were archer centaurs, running in a file
  As on the earth it was their wont to hunt.
Perceiving us descend, they all stood still, 58
  And from the troop, with weapons ready got
  Beforehand, issued three as for our ill.

---

42-43. The doctrine referred to is that of Empedocles, which Dante probably learned from Aristotle.

47-48. The river of boiling blood is later called Phlegethon (Canto xiv, 130-135). The appropriateness of the punishment of tyrants, slaughtering conquerors, murderers, highwaymen—shedders of blood in general—is obvious. They stand in gore of depth varying proportionately as each may be said to have waded in it on earth.

49. Cupidity is held to be the mainspring of man's violence to his fellow man.

60 ff. The three centaurs, monsters half man and half horse, are Chiron, Nessus, and Pholus. Chiron, the good centaur, was the teacher of Achilles and other heroes. Nessus, who for hire carried people on

One of them cried out from afar: "To what  61
   Torments, O journeyers down the slope, come ye?
   Tell us from there. I draw the bow, if not."
My master said to him: "Our answer we  64
   Shall unto Chiron, there beside thee, make.
   Thy will was ever rash, unhappily."
Then unto me: " 'Tis Nessus, who for sake  67
   Of the fair Deianira met his death,
   And for himself himself did vengeance take.
He in the middle, at his breast beneath  70
   Gazing, is mighty Chiron, who upbrought
   Achilles; the third, Pholus, prone to wrath.
They range by thousands round the fosse, and shoot  73
   Whatever spirit from the blood hath dared
   To emerge farther than its crimes allot."
And now those monsters swift of pace we neared,  76
   And Chiron took an arrow; with its notch,
   Backward upon his jaws he put his beard.
When his great mouth he had uncovered: "Watch  79
   The one behind," he told his mates. "Have you
   Noted he moves whatever he doth touch?
Not so it is the feet of dead men do."  82
   And my good guide, close to his breast now drawn
   Where are together joined the natures two,
Answered: "He lives indeed, and thus alone  85
   To show him the dark vale behooveth me.
   Necessity, not pleasure, leads him on.

---

his back across the river Evenus, tried to abduct Deianira, the wife of Hercules. Hercules slew him with a poisoned arrow, but while dying he avenged himself by telling Deianira that a shirt stained with his poisoned blood would restore her husband's love for her, if this ever wavered. Deianira subsequently sent Hercules the shirt when he became enamoured of Iole, and the hero perished in torment. Pholus is mentioned by classical poets, but is undistinguished.

   84. Where the human trunk rose from the equine foreshoulders.

## CANTO XII

Leaving the Alleluia-song came she 88
  Who gave me this new office; I am no
  Fraudulent soul, and robber none is he.
But by that Power through which my footsteps go 91
  Along so wild a road, I pray thee spare
  One of thy band to be with us and show
Where is the ford, and on his back to bear 94
  This man across it, seeing that he may
  Not traverse like a spirit through the air."
On his right breast wheeled Chiron then to say 97
  To Nessus: "Turn and guide them. If ye chance
  To meet another troop, make it give way."
Now with our trusty escort moved we thence 100
  Along the edge of the red boiling flood
  Wherein the boiled were shrieking loud laments.
People I saw that e'en to the eyebrows stood 103
  Immersed, and the great centaur said: "Lo, there
  Are tyrants, dealers in rapine and in blood.
Here they bewail their pitiless mischiefs; here 106
  Is Alexander, with Dionysius fell
  Who gave to Sicily many a woeful year.
That head with hair for blackness notable 109

---

88. *she*. Beatrice.

89-90. *I am no*, etc. That is, we are not criminals destined for punishment in either this or the next circle.

91. *that Power*. God.

107-111. *Alexander*. Probably Alexander the Great, as a bloody conqueror; but possibly Alexander of Pherae, a Thessalian tyrant famous for his cruelties. In his *Monarchia,* Dante speaks approvingly of Alexander the Great. Dionysius is the famous ruler of Syracuse (*c.* 432-367 B.C.). As an example of Italian tyrants, Azzolino III (äts-so-lee'-no), or Ezzelino, son-in-law of the Emperor Frederick II and the most monstrous of Ghibellines (1194-1259), is coupled with Obizzo II (o-beets'-so) of Este (ĕs'-tä), a cruel and rapacious Guelf of the latter half of the thirteenth century, who was said to have been murdered by his own son (called his stepson by Dante, perhaps as a hint of bastardy).

Is Assolino; the other, blond one—he
Obizzo is, of Este; him did quell
His stepson in the world, in verity."  112
   Then to the poet I turned, who said: "Chief guide
   Let him be now, and me but second be."
After a little, the centaur paused beside  115
   A folk which, upward from their throats displayed,
   Were seen to issue forth that burning tide.
He showed to us apart a lonely shade.  118
   "In God's own bosom this one piercèd through
   The heart still honoured on the Thames," he said.
Then in the stream beheld I others who  121
   Lifted therefrom the head and shoulders clear,
   And recognized among them not a few.
And so the blood grew ever shallower  124
   And shallower, until it did but seethe
   The feet; our passage of the moat was there.
"Even as on this side thou dost perceive  127
   Diminish steadily the boiling gore,
   I wish thee," said the centaur, "to believe
That on the other ever doth it lower  130
   Its bottom, till it comes again to where
   Tyranny must with groans be suffered for.
Justice Divine requites with torment there  133

---

118-120. This is Guy de Montfort, who in church at Viterbo, during the celebration of the mass, stabbed Prince Henry, nephew of Henry III of England. The victim's heart was said to have been preserved in a casket (or cup) placed on a pillar on London Bridge.

133-138. Where the stream, completing its circuit, comes again to the place where the bloodiest of criminals are punished, may be found Attila ("the scourge of God," King of the Huns), Pyrrhus and Sextus, and Rinier (reen'-yâr) of Corneto (kor-nā'-to) and Rinier Pazzo (päts'-so), two noted Italian highwaymen of the thirteenth century. Pyrrhus may be either the son of Achilles, who committed such atrocities

## CANTO XII

Attila—he that was on earth a scourge—
Pyrrhus, and Sextus; and milks tear by tear
For ever, whom thereof the heat doth purge, 136
Rinier of Corneto and Rinier Pazzo too,
That on the highways did such warfare wage."
Then he turned back, and crossed the ford anew. 139

---

when Troy was taken, or Pyrrhus the King of Epirus, the great enemy of the Romans. Similarly, Sextus may be either of two men: Sextus Tarquinius, the ravisher of Lucrece, or Pompey the Great's younger son, who turned pirate.

139. Having deposited his double burden on the other bank of the stream, Nessus returned to his comrades.

## CANTO XIII

*Seventh circle. The second ring: the violent against themselves or property. The forest of the suicides. The harpies. Trees once men. Pier delle Vigne. The hunted wastrels. The broken, nameless tree.*

Ere Nessus yet had reached the other side,
  We forward bent our steps into a wood
  Wherein no path whatever was supplied.
Not green the foliage was, but dusky-hued;     4
  Not smooth, but gnarled and twisted, were the boughs,
  With poison-thorns instead of fruitage good.
In thickets not so cruel and dense do those     7
  Wild beasts that hate the farming lands, and roam
  Between the Cecina and Corneto, house.
Here the foul harpies, nesting, make their home,     10
  That chased the Trojans from the Strophades

---

2. The wood is the second of the three concentric rings into which the seventh circle is divided. The river of blood, together with its enveloping plain ranged over by the centaurs, was the first ring; the third will be a belt of sand on which fall flakes of fire. The forest, occupying all the space between the inner bank of the circular stream of boiling blood and the outer edge of the circular sand belt, is composed altogether of trees which are the souls of suicides, thus transformed. Having voluntarily quitted their mortal bodies on earth, such sinners are not allowed after death to wear the semblance of those bodies; they are further punished by being broken and lacerated by the harpies (symbolizing the gloomy, fearful thoughts that impelled them to self-destruction) and by the other inhabitants of this ring, the souls of spendthrifts, who are hunted by black, devouring hell-hounds, symbolic of their creditors.

9. The little river Cecina (chā'-chee-nä) and the town Corneto (kornā'-to) are here used to designate the northern and southern boundaries of the swampy, wooded country known as the Maremma between the mountains of Tuscany and the sea.

## CANTO XIII

With dire announcement of impending doom.
Broad wings have they, and human visages 13
   And necks, clawed feet, large bellies feathered o'er;
   They sit and wail upon the uncouth trees.
And the good master said to me: "Before 16
   We enter farther, thou must understand
   'Tis now the second round thy feet explore,
And shall be, till thou reach the horrible sand; 19
   Hence look about thee well, and thou shalt see
   What in my speech would ne'er belief command."
Plainings I heard breathed forth on every 22
   Side, but beheld none to make outcry thus;
   And so I stopped, bewildered utterly.
He must have thought those multitudinous 25
   Voices I deemed a people there to make,
   Hidden behind the trunks because of us.
Therefore my leader said: "If thou wilt break 28
   From any of these plants a tiny spray,
   'Twill prove thy supposition a mistake."
Then forth I stretched my hand a little way, 31
   And plucked a branchlet off from a great thorn;
   And the trunk cried: "Why dost thou mangle me?"
And when with blood it redly dark had grown: 34
   "Why dost thou tear me?" it began again
   Its protest. "Breath of pity hast thou none?
We that are now but stocks,—we once were men. 37
   Truly, more merciful should be thy hand
   Even had we the souls of serpents been."
As from a fresh, green log, which at one end 40
   Is burning, and at the other drips and loud
   Hisses with noise of the escaping wind,—
So from that broken twig came words and blood 43

---

11-12. See *Aeneid* iii.

Together forth; the sprig of foliäge
I dropped, and like to one in terror stood.
"If he, O injured soul," replied the sage, 46
"Had without this been able to believe
What he had seen but on my verses' page,
His hand would ne'er have grasped thee to bereave; 49
Yet was the thing incredible, and so
I prompted that which now myself doth grieve.
But tell him who thou art, that thus, to do 52
Thee some amends, thy fame on earth may he
Quicken. Return is granted him thereto."
"With thy sweet words thou so allurest me," 55
The trunk said, "that I cannot hold my peace.
Count it not grievous, should I tempted be
To talk at length. The keeper of both keys 58
Of Frederick's heart am I. So dextrously,
Locking it and unlocking, turned I these
That almost all men from his secrets I 61
Excluded—yea, and gave such faith to grace
That charge that sleep and health I lost thereby.
The harlot who from Caesar's dwelling place 64
Hath never turned away her strumpet eyes,
The common bane and vice of courts, to blaze
Kindled all minds against me; so likewise 67
Did these, inflamed, inflame the King august
That my glad honours turned to dismal sighs.

---

48. In the third book of the *Aeneid* Virgil tells how Aeneas found the soul of Polydorus imprisoned in a tree.

58 *ff*. The speaker reveals himself to be Pier delle Vigne, minister and confidant of Frederick II. He at length fell into disgrace, was imprisoned and according to some accounts blinded, and slew himself. Dante evidently believed him innocent of the charges preferred against him.

64. The "harlot" is Envy, and "Caesar's dwelling place" is the Imperial court.

## CANTO XIII

My mood disdainful and my soul's disgust,    70
  Thinking by death to bid disdain adieu,
  Made me unjust against myself, the just.
Oh, by this tree's new roots I swear, unto    73
  My lord I never broke my faith, but clave
  With most fit reverence; and I beg of you,
If either to the world indeed should have    76
  Return, uplift my memory, which still
  Lies prostrate from the blow that envy gave."
He paused; then said to me the poet: "While    79
  He now is silent, let not thy chance depart.
  Speak and inquire of him whate'er thou will."
But I: "Nay, ask thou yet, of what thou art    82
  Persuaded best would give content to me;
  For I cannot, such pity fills my heart."
"So may this man do freely that for thee,    85
  O prisoned spirit, which thy words entreat,
  I pray thee tell us," therefore began he,
"How in these knotted trunks the soul doth get    88
  Bound up; and if thou canst, inform us too
  If ever from such limbs escapeth it."
Then the trunk puffed amain, and the wind blew,    91
  Changing anon into a voice, e'en this:
  "Briefly shall it be answered unto you.
When from the body out of which amiss    94
  It rent itself, the passionate spirit goes,
  Minos consigns it to the seventh abyss.
It falls into the wood, nor is there chose    97
  A place for it, but whereso chance doth grant
  That flings it, like a grain of spelt it grows—
A sapling first, and then a savage plant.    100
  The harpies, feeding on its leaves off-torn,

---

84. It should be noted that pity is reckoned an entirely proper sentiment toward certain sinners, but not toward others.

At once give pain and to the pain a vent.
We for our spoils like others shall return, 103
  But not to be again in flesh arrayed,
  For 'tis not right to have what one doth spurn.
Here we shall drag them, and throughout the glade 106
  Of woe our bodies shall suspended be—
  Each on the thorn-bush of its wretched shade."
We were attentive still unto the tree, 109
  Thinking that it might wish to tell us more,
  When startled us a tumult suddenly,
As one is startled who perceives the boar 112
  And chase approach his post, and heareth loud
  The beasts and crashing branches, these before;—
And on the left hand, lo, two spirits, nude 115
  And briar-scratched, fleeing with rush so mad
  They broke through every barrier of the wood.
"Now haste thee, death; oh, haste thee to mine aid!" 118
  The foremost cried; and thinking his own pace
  Too slow, the other: "Lano, never sped
Thy legs so swift at Toppo's jousting-place"; 121
  And since of breath, perchance, he was in lack,
  Made of himself and of a bush one mass.
Behind them was the forest full of black 124
  Braches, all fleet and eager for their prey
  As, when the leash is slipped, a greyhound pack.
In that one who was crouching fastened they 127
  Their teeth, and him e'en piece by piece they rent;
  Anon they bore those piteous limbs away.

---

103. That is, they will go for their bodies at the Last Day, like other spirits. Compare Canto x, 10-12.

115 *ff*. One of the two spirits is Lano (lä'-no) of Siena, a member of the notorious "spendthrift brigade" (see Canto xxix, 125-132, and Note). He squandered a large patrimony and later was slain in the rout of the Sienese by the Aretines at the ford of Pieve del Toppo (top'-po) in 1280. The other is Jacomo da Sant' Andrea (yä'-ko-mo dä sänt än-drä'-ä) of Padua, another notorious wastrel.

## CANTO XIII

And now my escort took my hand and went 130
  Leading me to the thicket, which in vain
  Through its red fractures lifted up lament:
"O Jacomo da Sant' Andrea, what gain 133
  Hadst thou by making me thy screen?—what good?
  How for thy sinful life am I to blame?"
The master said when he beside it stood: 136
  "Who wast thou, that, through wounds so numerous,
  Art blowing forth thy dolorous speech with blood?"
"Ye spirits who are come," he answered us, 139
  "To view the shameful havoc that from me
  My limbs with violence hath severed thus,
Oh, at the foot of their unhappy tree 142
  Collect them! Of that town was I which for
  The Baptist her first patron changed; whence he
Will grieve her with his art for evermore; 145
  And did some glimpse of him not still remain
  Where of the Arno is the passage o'er,
Those citizens who afterwards again 148
  Upbuilt her on the ashes left thereof
  By Attila would but have toiled in vain.
I swung the gibbet-noose from my own roof." 151

---

132. In tearing Jacomo to pieces, the dogs also shattered the bush where he had tried to conceal himself.

143 *ff*. The identity of the shade inhabiting the bush is uncertain. He declares only that he is a Florentine, and that he hanged himself in his own house. Mars was the first patron of Florence, later exchanged for John the Baptist; and a fragment of his statue still stood till 1333 at the head of the Ponte Vecchio, the old bridge over the Arno (är'-no). The passage means, says Benvenuto da Imola, "that after Florence gave up Mars, that is, fortitude and valour in arms, and began to worship the Baptist alone, that is, the Florin, on which is the figure of the Baptist, they met with misfortune in their wars." By the fragment of Mars' statue yet remaining is symbolized the surviving remnant of valour which alone preserved Florence. Dante confounds Attila the Hun with Totila the Ostrogoth, who was commonly supposed to have destroyed Florence.

## CANTO XIV

*Seventh circle. The third ring: the violent against God and against nature. The fiery snow. Capaneus the blasphemer. The crimson rill. Of the Cretan Image and the origin of the rivers of Hell.*

Since love of native land now laid constraint
  On me, I gathered up the scattered leaves
  And gave them back to him whose voice grew faint.
Thence to the boundary line we came that cleaves     4
  Apart the second ring and third, and there
  A fearful mode of justice one perceives.
To make these new things manifest and clear,     7
  I say that we had reached a plain whose ground
  Refuseth any growing plant to bear.
The dolorous wood engarlands it around,     10
  As round the wood the dismal fosse doth spread.
  We stayed our steps upon its very bound.
Arid and thick the sand which formed its bed,     13
  Nor otherwise than that which once was stirred
  Under the feet of Cato was it made.
Vengeance of God, oh, how shouldst thou be feared     16
  By every one of those who read with awe
  Concerning that which to mine eyes appeared!
Full many a flock of naked souls I saw,     19
  Who all were weeping very miserably,

---

*3. grew faint.* Because the wounds of the torn branches, which permitted utterance, were ceasing to bleed.

15. The reference is to Cato of Utica—Cato the Younger—who marched an army across the Libyan desert in 47 B.C.

19-27. Three classes of offenders against God and nature are here punished in ways appropriate to each. The blasphemers lie impotent beneath the wrath of that Heaven which they once defied; the usurers

## CANTO XIV

And subject seemed they to a diverse law.
Some of them prostrate on the ground did lie, 22
 And some were sitting crouched together close,
 While others moved about continually.
They who went round were far most numerous, 25
 And fewest they who 'neath the torment pined
 Outstretched, but loudest in their cries were those.
Over the whole great waste of sand there rained 28
 With a slow fall dilated flakes of fire
 Like snow amid the Alps without a wind.
Even as the flames which in those regions dire 31
 Of torrid India Alexander on
 His host beheld fall to the ground entire—
Wherefore to trampling zealously upon 34
 The soil he set his troops, because each flame
 Was easier extinguished when alone—
So fell the eternal heat by which, the same 37
 As tinder by the flint and steel, the sands
 Were kindled for redoubling of the pain.
Unceasing was the dance of wretched hands 40
 That shook off, now on this side, now on that,
 The burning which for ever fresh descends.
"Master, who conquerest all," said I thereat, 43
 "Except the stubborn demons who forth-came
 Against us at the entrance of the gate,—

---

sit still, even as in the world when they should have been engaged in honest toil; the sexually perverted, somewhat like the unchaste of the second circle, are driven onward incessantly, as by their desires on earth. The members of this third class are the most numerous; the blasphemers least so.

31-36. Dante here seems to confuse two fictitious stories of Alexander: the one of a tremendous snowfall which his men trampled down as it descended; the other of flames which fell upon them. This confusion occurs also in Albertus Magnus, who therefore was probably Dante's immediate source.

## THE INFERNO OF DANTE

Who is that mighty one who for the flame 46
   Seems not to care, but scowling lies outspread
   As nowise by the fiery shower made tame?"
And he himself, aware of what I had 49
   Inquired concerning him, now loudly saith:
   "The same I living was, that am I dead.
Even though Jove should weary out his smith, 52
   From whom, incensed, he snatched the bolt that on
   My final day I was transfixèd with;
Though he should tire the others one by one 55
   In Mongibello's sooty forge with cry
   Of 'Help, good Vulcan, help!' as he upon
The field of Phlegra did, and should he ply, 58
   Hurling at me with all his might, e'en thus
   No joyful vengeance could he have thereby."
Then with a force I ne'er had heard him use 61
   The like till now, my leader spake: "In that
   Thine arrogance remains, O Capaneus,
Unquenchèd still, the harder is thy state. 64
   No torture save thy madness would be pain
   Unto thy rage justly proportionate."
Then turned he back to me with gentler mien, 67
   And said: "One of the seven kings who went
   Forth against Thebes is this. God in disdain
He held and seems to hold, unreverent; 70

---

46 *ff*. It is Capaneus, one of the seven mythical heroes who assailed Thebes. Capaneus declared that not even Jove himself should withhold him from taking the city, and for this impiety was smitten by a thunderbolt as he mounted the ramparts. Jove is here, as elsewhere, identified with Jehovah, and his war with the giants is alluded to by Capaneus—how he overthrew them on the battlefield of Phlegra with thunderbolts forged by Vulcan and his fellow smiths, the Cyclops. Mongibello (mon-jee-bĕl'-lo) is Mount Etna, whose crater was the reputed smithy of Vulcan.

61 *ff*. The impious words of Capaneus arouse even the equable Virgil to indignation.

## CANTO XIV

But as I told him, his own scornful mood
Is for his breast a fitting ornament.
Now follow me, with all solicitude 73
To set not on the burning sand thy feet
But ever keep them close beside the wood."
To where there poureth a swift rivulet 76
Out of the forest, we in silence came—
A brook whose redness makes me shudder yet.
As from the Bulicame flows a stream 79
Which afterwards the sinful women share,
So down across the sand flowed this, the same.
Its bed, both banks, and eke the margins near 82
On either side of it were formed of stone;
Whence I perceived our passageway was there.
"Among all other things which I have shown 85
To thee since first we entered by that gate
Whereof the threshold is denied to none,
Upon no object have thine eyes been set 88
So notable as this stream is, that o'er
Its channel doth all flames annihilate."
These were the words my master spake; wherefore 91
I begged him to vouchsafe the food and end
The hunger which he had bestowed therefor.
"In the mid-sea lieth a wasted land," 94

---

79-80. *The Bulicame* (boo-lee-kä'-mā) was a hot sulphurous spring near Viterbo. A portion of its stream was conveyed to the houses of the prostitutes of that town, who were not allowed to use the public baths. Its reddish colour and its emission of fumes make it apt for comparison with the brook (the overflow of the moat of boiling blood), which issues from the forest of the suicides, crosses the ring of sand, and plunges into the next circle.

86-87. *that gate,* etc. The outer gate of Hell, entered in Canto iii.

94 *ff.* The figure of the Old Man was doubtless suggested to Dante by the image of Nebuchadnezzar's dream (Daniel ii), but is used to symbolize the history of the human race as it passed successively through the traditional golden, silver, brazen, and iron ages with steady moral deteri-

He said, "that men call Crete, beneath whose king
The world of old was pure. And there doth stand,
Glad once with leaves and waters murmuring, 97
  A mountain which the name of Ida bore,—
Now desolate, like some forgotten thing.
Rhea for her son's hid cradle chose of yore 100
  This spot, and better to conceal him when
He wept, had clamorous outcry raised thereo'er.
Within the mountain is a great Old Man, 103
  Who doth his back toward Damietta hold
And looks at Rome, as 'twere a glass to scan.
His head is fashioned of the finest gold, 106
  And of pure silver are his arms and breast;
Then brazen even to the fork his mould;
And lower all is choicest iron and best, 109
  Save that the right foot is of bakèd clay,
Whereon he stands with weight the heavier pressed.
All parts, except the golden head, display 112
  A cleft, whence ever-dripping tears distil,
Which, gathering, through that cavern pierce their way.
From rock to rock they course into this vale; 115
  Acheron form they, Styx, and Phlegethon;
Then by yon narrow sluice descend until

---

oration. The left foot is the Empire; the right one of baked clay the Church, more fragile but the greater support of mankind. The Old Man is located on the island of Crete, as situated midway between the three continents of Europe, Asia, and Africa; his back is turned to Damietta (in Egypt, and famous for its association with the crusades), which here typifies the East where the great ancient monarchies were; his gaze is fixed on Rome, the present seat of authority. His tears represent the woes of humanity, arising from sin. None flow from the golden head, for the golden age was innocent of sin.

100. Mythology tells that Rhea took refuge in a cavern on the Cretan Mount Ida to give birth to the infant Jove, and caused her servants to clash spears and shields (whence in later times corybantic dances were celebrated) that his father might not find and devour him.

## CANTO XIV

They come to where is no more going down, 118
    And there they make Cocytus; I discuss
    Its nature not; thyself shalt see anon."
And I to him: "If from our world flows thus 121
    The present runnel, why doth it appear
    But on the border of this ring to us?"
"Thou knowest that the place is circular," 124
    He answered, "and though thou hast gone, always
    Descending leftward, toward the bottom far,
Part of the circle thou hast yet to trace; 127
    Then if new things to look on still remain,
    It should not bring amazement to thy face."
"But where is Phlegethon"—thus I again— 130
    "And Lethe, master? Thou dost not disclose
    Of one, and sayest the other is from this rain."
"In every question which thou dost propose 133
    Thou pleasest me," he said, "but the red wave
    That boileth should resolve thee one of those.
Lethe thou shalt behold,—not in this cave, 136
    But where the souls that, being penitent,
    Have had their sins remitted, go to lave."
And then he said: "It now is time we went 139
    Forth from the wood. See thou behind me tread.
    The banks, that burn not, a safe path present,
And every flamelet over them falls dead." 142

---

127. In their descent, Dante and Virgil had not yet made a complete circuit of the funnel-shaped cavity of Hell.
136-138. *not in this cave,* etc. That is, not in Hell, but in Purgatory.

## CANTO XV

*Seventh circle: third ring. The violent against nature. Brunetto Latini.*

One of the solid margins bears us now,
   And overhead mist of the brook doth shade
   From fire the borders and the stream below.
As bulwarks by the Flemish folk are made            4
   Between Wissant and Bruges to oppose
   The sea, whose billowy surge they hold in dread,
Or as the Paduans by the Brenta those                 7
   To save their villages and castles rear
   Before the heat melts Chiarentana's snows,—
Likewise are fashioned the embankments here,       10
   Although less thick and to a lower height
   The master builded these, whoe'er he were.
Already we had gone so far I might                  13
   No longer tell at all the place where grew
   The wood, though backward I should strain my sight,

---

1. *solid margins.* The stone banks which border the brook carrying off the overflow of Phlegethon. Along one of these the poets could safely walk (as the vapours thrown off by the little stream destroyed the fiery flakes that fell thereover) and so cross the sand belt to the next circle beyond.

4-12. The embankments are compared to the dikes along the coast of Flanders (Belgium) from Bruges to Wissant (once an important port between Boulogne and Calais) and to similar defences reared by the Paduans against the spring floods of the Brenta (brĕn'-tä) due to the melting snows in the mountainous district of Chiarentana (kyä-rĕn-tä'-nä); but, says Dante (note the realistic sobriety of his imagination as compared, for instance, with the swelling vagueness of Milton's), these in Hell are not so large, whoever built them. Dante elsewhere states that God made Hell, but he leaves open the question of whether certain of its details were created by the divine *fiat* or were the work of angels or devils.

## CANTO XV

When with a band of spirits met we, who 16
  Came now beside the dike; and passing by,
  They looked (as in the evening people do
At one another when the darkling sky 19
  Hath a new moon) with puckered brows at us,
  Like an old tailor at his needle's eye.
When by that company examined thus, 22
  Lo, I was recognized by one, who caught
  My mantle's hem and cried: "How marvellous!"
And while his arm was unto me stretched out, 25
  So on his roasted visage did I peer
  That the scorched countenance prevented not
My mind from knowing him, whereat more near 28
  Leaning, with face bent downward toward his own,
  I answered: "Ser Brunetto, art thou here?"
And he: "Be not offended, O my son, 31
  If back Brunetto Latini turn and go
  With thee a space, letting his troop pass on."
And I now: "From my heart I beg thee, do; 34
  And wouldst thou rather we should sit, withal,
  I will, if but my guide permitteth so."
"My son, whoe'er of this herd stops at all," 37
  He said, "must for a hundred years therefrom
  Lie prone, nor fan away the flames that fall.
Move onward, then; I at thy skirts will come, 40
  And later will rejoin my brotherhood
  Who go lamenting their eternal doom."

---

24. *My mantle's hem.* The embankment rose about the height of a man above the sandy plain.

30. Brunetto Latini (broo-nĕt′-to lä-tee′-nee), entitled "Ser" as a notary, was a prominent figure in the generation preceding Dante's. He was a man of great ability and learning, the author of an encyclopedic work in French, the *Tresor* (here referred to by its Italian title, *Tesoro*), and a shorter didactic allegory in Italian verse, the *Tesoretto*. If not actually Dante's teacher, he seems to have exercised a great influence upon him.

I durst not to his level from the road 43
  Descend, but kept my head bent down as one
  Is wont to do who walks in reverent mood.
"What chance or fortune ere thy days are done 46
  Hath brought thee hither," he began, "and who
  May this one be that guides thy footsteps on?"
"Yonder above in the fair life," thereto 49
  I answered, "in a vale I went astray,
  Before my years to fullness ever grew.
I left it but the morn of yesterday. 52
  That one appeared when I was there returning,
  And homeward leadeth me along this way."
"If thou wilt follow where thy star is burning, 55
  Thou needs must gain a glorious port anon,
  If true in the glad world was my discerning,"
He said; "and if I had not died too soon, 58
  Beholding Heaven thus kindly on thee look,
  I in thy labour would have cheered thee on.
But that ungrateful and malignant stock, 61
  Who came of old down from Fiesole
  And savoureth still of mountain and of rock,
For thy good deeds will be thine enemy, 64
  And rightly, for with crabbed sorbs confined,

---

51. The meaning is probably not "before I completed my days," but "before I reach my prime," Dante being thirty-five, the midway point of life, at the supposed date of the journey.

55. "Star" had better be understood in the metaphorical sense—the beacon star of Dante's mission—than astrologically in reference to his horoscope.

58. *too soon.* The meaning is merely "ere then"; Brunetto lived to a ripe old age.

61 *ff.* Fiesole (fĭ-ĕ′-zo-lā) is at the summit of a steep hill some three miles from Florence. Cataline and his followers took refuge there when driven from Rome, and tradition declared that Roman colonists combined with people of that town to found Florence. Dante, who claimed descent from the ancient Romans, regarded the rude Fiesolan admixture as the source of his city's woes.

## CANTO XV

To bear beseemeth not the sweet fig tree.
Ancient report on earth proclaims them blind—  67
  A greedy, envious, avaricious race;
  Then cleanse thee of the customs of their kind.
Thy fortune so great honour shall amass  70
  That both the factions are to crave for thee;
  But distant from the goat shall be the grass.
For litter let the beasts of Fiesole  73
  Each other rend, nor touch the plant, indeed,
  If on their dunghill one should rise to be,
In which may live again the holy seed  76
  Of those old Romans who remained there when
  The nest of so great wickedness 'twas made."
"If my desires were all fulfilled," I then  79
  Replied to him, "thou hadst not yet, I trow,
  Been banished from the natural life of men;
For in my mind is fixed, and stirs e'en now  82
  My heart, thy dear kind image fatherly
  As in the world those hours thou taughtest me how
One may attain to immortality;  85
  And while I live, should by this tongue be told
  The gratitude I cherish unto thee.
What of my course thou sayest, I note and hold  88
  With other text, till by a lady heard
  Who, if I win to her, can truth unfold.
Only this much be now to thee declared:  91
  If but my conscience chide me not thereo'er,
  For whatso Fate may will, I stand prepared.
Such news is to mine ears not strange; wherefore  94
  Let Fortune, as she pleaseth, make her wheel
  Revolve; his mattock ply the country boor."

---

85. That is, by fame.
89. *a lady*. Beatrice.

| At this my master turned on his right heel | 97 |

Backward, and looked at me, and then did say:
"Who layeth those words to heart, doth listen well."
But none the less I go upon my way 100
Talking with Ser Brunetto, and ask who
Are of most fame and chief in his array.
"Of some 'tis good to learn," said he thereto; 103
"Touching the others we had best be still;
For longer talk the moments are too few.
In brief, know all of them were clerks erewhile, 106
Men of great learning and of great renown,
And, one same crime on earth did all defile.
Priscian is of them, and Accorso's son 109
Francesco; and among that wretched kind,
If such vile scurf thou carest to look upon,
Is he the servants' Servant once assigned 112
From Arno's unto Bacchiglione's strand,
Where a sin-wasted frame he left behind.
More I would tell of; but my going and 115
My speech must not be lengthened, for I see
Yonder a new smoke rising from the sand.
People approach with whom I may not be. 118

---

97. Virgil's turn was toward the right to signify approbation, and in courtesy to avoid showing his back to Brunetto, who was on that side behind him.

109 ff. Priscian, the great Latin grammarian of the sixth century, is nowhere else accused of the vice for which Dante condemns him. Francesco d'Accorso (frän-chĕs'-ko däk-kor'-so) was a jurist like his still more famous father, Accorso da Bagnolo of Florence. He lived in Bologna and England in the thirteenth century. The third sinner, indicated but not named, is Andrea de' Mozzi, Bishop of Florence (on the Arno). Because of his scandalous life he was transferred by the Pope ("the Servant of servants"—Boniface VIII) to Vicenza, on the Bacchiglione (bäk-keel-yo'-nä).

118. The sinners in this ring were divided into groups, which were not allowed to intermingle.

Let my *Tesoro,* in which I still live on,
  Thy favour win;—I ask no more of thee."
Then he turned back; and he appeared like one    121
  Who on the plain before Verona tries
  For the green mantle; and of those that run,
No loser seemed, but he who gains the prize.    124

---

119. For the *Tesoro* (tĕ-so'-ro), or *Treasure,* see Note on line 30.
121-124. Brunetto ran as fast as the winner of the annual foot-race outside Verona. This contest was held on the first Sunday in Lent; the prize was a piece of green cloth.

## CANTO XVI

*Seventh circle: third ring. The violent against nature: Guido Guerra, Tegghiaio Aldobrandi, Jacopo Rusticucci. The roar of Phlegethon, plunging downward. The cord thrown into the abyss.*

I now was where I heard the booming sound,
  Like to the hum which bee-hives make, of falling
  Water that plunged through space to the next round,
When lo, three shades together, loudly calling, 4
  Issued upon the run from out a band
  That passed, beneath the rain of torment galling.
They came toward us, and each cried: "Stop and stand, 7
  O thou that by thy garb to us would seem
  A citizen of our corrupted land."
Ah me, what wounds, recent and old, by flame 10
  Burnt in upon the limbs of these saw I!
  It pains me still, even to think of them.
My teacher paused, attentive to their cry. 13
  "Now wait," he said, turning to me his face;
  "Persons are these deserving courtesy.
And were it not for the nature of the place 16
  Which darteth fiery arrows, I should feel
  Such speed in thee more than in them were grace."
They recommenced, as soon as we stood still, 19
  Their wonted wail, and when they came to us,
  Made of themselves, the three of them, a wheel.
As champions, naked and anointed, use, 22

---

1-3. The poets now hear the thunder of the waterfall, made by the brook along which they proceed, plunging over the tremendous precipice which separates the seventh circle from the eighth.

21. *Made . . . a wheel.* They ran round in a circle before Dante and Virgil so as not to incur the penalty for standing still (xv, 37-39).

## CANTO XVI

Watching for hold and vantage, ere essayed
Are blows and thrusts at one another,—thus
Circling around did each of them his head  25
Turn unto me, so that in opposite wise
His neck and feet continuous journey made.
"If of this yielding ground the miseries  28
Render ourselves and prayers contemptible,"
Said one, "and scorched and blackened visages,
Let our renown incline thy soul to tell  31
Us who thou art that dost securely so
Press with thy living feet the soil of Hell.
He in whose steps thou seest me to go,  34
Naked and hairless though he move, was greater
In rank and station than imaginest thou.
He was the grandson of the good Gualdrada,  37
And in his life did he with counsel and
With sword do much. His name is Guido Guerra.
The other, who behind me treads the sand,  40
Is Tegghiaio Aldobrandi, whose fame
Should in the world above most honoured stand.
And I who on the cross am stretched with them  43
Jacopo Rusticucci am; the dire
Moods of my wife for this deserve chief blame."
Could I have been protected from the fire,  46
Among them I had cast me down, nor earned
My teacher's blame, I think, for this desire;
But since I should have baked myself and burned,  49

---

34-45. All three were illustrious Florentines of the thirteenth century. Guido Guerra (gwee'-do gwĕr'-rä) was a distinguished Guelf soldier. His grandmother, Gualdrada (gwäl-drä'-dä), was noted for her beauty and modesty. Tegghiaio Aldobrandi (tĕg-gee-ä'-yo äl-do-brän'-dee) deserved honourable memory among his countrymen; for his advice, if followed, would have saved them from the defeat of Montaperti. Little or nothing is known of Jacopo Rusticucci (yä'-ko-po roos-tee-koo'-tchee).

Fear overmastered the good will whereby
To clasp them I thus eagerly had yearned.
" 'Twas not contempt but sorrow," began I, 52
"That your condition fixed within me so
Deeply that it will leave me tardily,
As soon as this my lord spake words unto 55
Me on account of which my heart inferred
That people were approaching such as you.
Yea, of your land am I—was ever stirred 58
With fondness when your deeds I did recall
And honoured names, or when thereof I heard.
For the sweet fruits I go, and leave the gall, 61
E'en as my truthful guardian promised me,
But to the centre first I needs must fall."
"So may thy soul a long while," answered he 64
In turn, "thy members animate and guide,
And so may thy renown shine after thee,
Tell us if courtesy and valour bide 67
Within our city as they were wont to do,
Or if therefrom they have departed wide;
For now Guglielmo Borsieri, who 70
Goes yonder with our fellows, gives us great
Grief by his words, and here he is but new."
"The upstart folk and sudden gains of late 73
Have bred in thee such pride and such excess,
O Florence, thou already weepest thereat!"
Thus I exclaimed aloud with lifted face. 76

---

63. *the centre.* The centre of the earth; the bottom of the cavity of Hell.

70. Guglielmo Borsieri (gool-yĕl'-mo bor-sĭ-â'-ree) appears in a story of Boccaccio's *Decameron* (1, 8).

73. Florence had grown greatly in population and in wealth at the end of the thirteenth century. Instead of "upstart" the translation should perhaps be "new-come" in reference to the immigration of inferior stock from the country; but I have judged it to apply, rather, to parvenus.

## CANTO XVI

The three, who found their answer in my cry,
Glances exchanged, as hearing truth express.
"If otherwhile others to satisfy 79
Cost thee so little, happy thou shalt be,
Speaking without constraint," they made reply.
"And therefore, if from these dim regions free 82
Thou stand beneath the radiant stars again,
When saying 'Thus it was' shall pleasure thee,
Ah, do not fail to tell of us to men." 85
At this they broke their wheel, and as they fled
Their nimble legs seemed to be wings. "Amen"
Could by no possibility be said 88
So quickly as they disappeared; wherefore
My master deemed it good to push ahead.
I followed him, and when we little more 91
Had gone, so near us was the water's din
We scarce could hear each other for the roar.
Just as that stream which first e'en to the brine 94
Flows east from Monte Viso separately
Upon the left-hand slope of Apennine
(Ere it descends, in lowly bed to be, 97
The name is Acquacheta called thereof,
And this it hath no longer at Forli)

---

94 *ff*. The first stream beyond Monte Viso (mon'-tā vee'-so) which flows eastwardly down the left slope of the Apennines in an independent course to the sea instead of into the Po is the Montone, which in one of its upper branches is called the Acquacheta (äk-kwä-kā'-tä), or Stillwater; at Forli (for-lee') it gives up that name and the Montone begins. The Montone falls (probably with a greater volume of water in Dante's day than now) at San Benedetto (bĕ-nĕ-dĕt'-to) over a ledge which, says the poet, is high enough to afford room for a thousand small cascades instead of the one great plunge that actually occurs—or which, according to another interpretation of line 102, is in the vicinity of a structure (the Benedictine monastery of San Benedetto) large enough to house a thousand people. The former sense seems preferable, but the translation in some measure preserves the ambiguity of the original.

Reverberates from the mountain, high above  100
  San Benedetto, falling in one bound
  Where for a thousand would be room enough,—
Thus o'er a brink precipitous we found  103
  That ruddy water thundering so that in
  A little time our ears would have been stunned.
I wore a cord girt round me; it had been  106
  Therewith that I had earlier thought to bind
  The panther with the gaily spotted skin.
This from about me I did all unwind,  109
  For so my leader now commanded me,
  And gave it to him, in a coil twined;
Then, turning to the right hand, cast it he  112
  Forth at some distance, nor the edge anigh,
  Into the chasm's black profundity.
"In sooth, some strange, new thing must needs reply,"  115
  Said I within me, "to this signal new
  Which thus my master follows with his eye."
Ah, how great carefulness befits one who  118
  Is near to those that see not deeds alone
  But with their wisdom even thoughts can view!
He said to me: "What I await will soon  121
  Arise, and that whereof thy fancies dream
  Must be discovered to thy sight anon."
Always to truth that doth a falsehood seem  124
  A man should close his lips, or thus should try—
  Else, although innocent, he incurreth shame;

---

106 *ff.* The cord has been the subject of much speculation by commentators, and has been allegorically interpreted in various ways—for instance, that it is the sign of the Franciscan order, and that Dante once thought to bind his fleshly lusts (symbolized by the panther) by joining that brotherhood, but that reason (Virgil) showed him that asceticism was no longer needed when once he had beheld the fate of incontinence, and might even lead to hypocrisy or fraud (Geryon).

112. *turning to the right hand.* Before making a long throw a right-handed man swings far around to his right.

## CANTO XVI

But here I cannot; therefore, Reader, by 127
   The verses of this Comedy I swear—
   So may the fame of them not swiftly die—
We saw come swimming up, through that dark air 130
   And gross, a shape that would right awesome be
   To every heart, though valiant howsoe'er,—
Like one returning who went down to free 133
   An anchor which hath grappled on a reef
   Or other object hidden in the sea;
Who upward stretches and draws in beneath. 136

## CANTO XVII

*Seventh circle: third ring. The monster Geryon, type of all fraud. The violent against God's and nature's law of livelihood: usurers. On the back of Geryon. The flight downward to the eighth circle.*

"Behold the savage beast with pointed tail,
  Who scaleth mountains, walls and weapons breaketh—
  Behold him who infects the world with bale."
Beginning thus, to me the master speaketh,     4
  And beckons him to come from out the void
  To where our rocky path its ending maketh.
And that uncleanly image of vile Fraud     7
  His head and shoulders landed on the shore
  But drew not to the ledge his tail abhorred.
His face the semblance of a just man's wore,     10
  Its aspect was of such benignity,
  But like a snake's was all his body lower.
Two taloned arms, covered with hair, had he;     13
  His breast and back and both his sides displayed

---

1 *ff.* The cord thrown from the brink of the cataract has summoned up the monster Geryon, symbol of fraud and therefore mythological guardian of the eighth circle, where the fraudulent are punished. In classical story Geryon is no such fantastic creature as here is pictured, but a giant, three-headed or three-bodied, who was a king in Spain. As one of the Twelve Labours, Hercules slew him and carried off his cattle. Dante, apparently following a medieval tradition that Geryon enticed strangers to his home and then killed them, makes him the type of fraud and gives him a single body compounded of three different creatures: the head of a just man (so that his frontal aspect is deceptively benignant), the arms of a rapacious beast, and all the rest the figure of a subtle serpent with venomous, stinging tail. The corrugations of his skin into the shapes of nooses and shields signify the snares and concealments of the fraudulent.

8. *the shore.* The stony edge of the precipice.

## CANTO XVII

Nooses and shields, as painted plain to see.
Cloth was by Turks or Tartars never made, 16
   Groundwork and broidery, with colours more,
   Nor by Arachne on her loom were laid
Such webs. As wherries sometimes on the shore 19
   Are part in water, part upon the land,
   Or, 'mongst the guzzling Germans, for his war
The beaver seats himself upon the strand, 22
   So lay that worst of monsters on the brim
   That shutteth in with stone the waste of sand.
All his tail quivered in the chasm dim, 25
   And twisted upward its envenomed end,
   Which like a scorpion's armed the point of him.
My guide said: "Now must we a little bend 28
   Our way aside, that beast malevolent
   To reach, who yonder doth his length extend."
So, turning to the right, we made descent, 31
   And ten steps closer to the sheer abyss
   To shun the flames and burning marl we went.
And when we came to him, I saw, from this 34
   Upon the sand a little farther on,
   Folk who were sitting near the precipice.
"That thou a full experience of this zone 37
   Mayst bear away, hie thee and witness how
   It is with these," my lord said hereupon.
"Brief be thy speech with them; and until thou 40

---

18. *Arachne.* She presumed to compete with Minerva in weaving, and was turned into a spider by the offended goddess.

21-22. The beaver was believed to catch fish by dangling its tail in the water.

31. In descending from the top of the embankment along which they had been walking, the poets could not have turned leftward as usual, the scalding brook being on that side of them.

36. These are usurers, offenders against both God and nature in their violation of the law of industry. See Canto xi, 94 *ff*.

Returnest, I will talk with this one, that
His mighty shoulders he may lend us now."
Thus on the utmost boundary desolate 43
Of that seventh circle, all alone I go
To where those people sit disconsolate.
Between their eyelids gushes forth their woe. 46
This side and that, his hands each sufferer plies
Against the flames, against the soil aglow.
The dogs in summer do not otherwise 49
With muzzle now and now with paw, when they
By fleas are bitten or by gnats or flies.
Scanning the visages of some who lay 52
Beneath that dolorous rain of fire, not one
I recognized of those I did survey;
But I perceived that from each neck hung down 55
A pouch of different colour and device,
And this, 'twould seem, their gaze doth feed upon.
Now when among them round I cast mine eyes, 58
Azure I saw upon a yellow purse
The semblance of a lion and eke the guise.
Then, as my glance pursued its onward course, 61
Another I observed, blood red, to show
The form, more white than butter, of a goose.
And one who had an azure, pregnant sow 64

---

*52 ff.* The fire-flakes had scorched their faces past recognition, but some could be identified by the armorial bearings on their purses, the sole object of their regard. (Allegorically, this may signify that the usurer forfeits his humanity and becomes but a money bag. So, too, were the avaricious and the prodigal of the fourth circle unrecognizable.) The azure lion was the escutcheon of the Gianfigliazzi family, the goose of the Ubriachi—both of Florence; the speaker, with the device of a sow, is one of the Scrovigni of Padua. Of Vitaliano (vee-täl-yä'-no) nothing is known. The yet-living usurer who is impatiently awaited is Giovanni Buiamonte of Florence, the "sovereign knight" (or as we should say to-day, the "prince") of usurers; the arms of his family were three eagles' beaks.

## CANTO XVII

Depicted on his argent sacklet cried
To me: "In this our ditch what doest thou?
Begone! but know, since thou hast not yet died, 67
That Vitaliano, once my neighbour, here
Shall have his seat upon my left-hand side.
A Paduan I with Florentines; mine ear 70
Full many a time they deafen, shouting thus:
'Soon may he come, the sovereign cavalier,
With pouch that triple-beakèd blazon shows!'" 73
And then he writhed his mouth, and thrust far out
His tongue, as doth an ox that licks his nose.
Now that my tarrying might vex him not 76
Who had admonished me to stay not long,
From those forwearied souls I turned about.
I found my leader by this time had swung 79
Upon that dreadful creature's back. To me
He said: "Now be thou bold. Now be thou strong.
By such stairs henceforth our descent must be. 82
Mount thou in front, and I midway will sit,
That thus the tail may do no hurt to thee."
As one so near the quartan's shivering fit 85
Already that his nails are pallid blue
And shade brings trembling, even the sight of it,
Such on the utterance of these words I grew; 88
But as beneath a worthy master's gaze
Servants are brave, in me his urgings drew
Forth shame. On those huge shoulders did I place 91
Myself. I tried to say, and found that I
Lacked voice for speech: "Hold me in thy embrace."
But he that oft in trials formerly 94

---

82. They will leave the seventh circle by aid of Geryon, the eighth by aid of the giant Antaeus, and the ninth by climbing down the side of Lucifer.

85. *the quartan's shivering fit.* An attack of quartan fever.

Had been my help, soon as I mounted, fast
Caught and sustained me in his arms on high.
And then he said: "Now, Geryon, move thee! Vast 97
Thy circles, gradual thy descending be.
Think of the novel burden which thou hast."
As from its station goeth backwardly 100
A little bark, so thence did that one fare,
And when he felt himself entirely free,
To where his breast had been, his tail he there 103
Turned round, and stretching, moved it like an eel,
And with his paws gathered to him the air.
No greater fear, I think, did Phaëthon feel 106
When he the reins abandoned, and the sky
Was scorched, as even yet is visible;
Nor wretched Icarus when he found that by 109
Melting of wax the feathers had begun
To leave his loins, while rang his father's cry,
"Astray thou goest!" than mine was when upon 112
All sides I saw the air, and vanished so
Was everything except the beast alone.
He swims unceasingly, but slow, most slow; 115
He wheels and settles, though this I but surmise
By wind against my face and from below.

---

106. *Phaëthon.* The son of Apollo, who tried to drive the chariot of the sun across the sky. He lost control of the horses, and Jove killed him with a thunderbolt to prevent a universal conflagration. The Milky Way was supposed to be the place where the heavens were scorched when the car veered from its course.

109. Icarus, in classical mythology, was the son of Daedalus, the wonder-artificer of Crete. Daedalus contrived wings for the escape of himself and his son from that island; Icarus flew too high, the heat of the sun melted the wax with which his pinions were fastened, and he fell into the sea and was drowned.

117. The wind blowing against Dante's face from the side indicated Geryon's wheeling flight; from below, the settling.

## CANTO XVII

Already on the right I heard arise 118
  The cataract's hideous roar from the abyss,
  And craned my neck, with downward peering eyes.
Then all the more that plunge of the precipice 121
  I feared, beholding fires and hearing lament;
  So, trembling, I the closer cling for this.
Now, for till then it was not evident, 124
  By the great evils that on every side
  Drew near, I saw our circling and descent.
Even as a falcon that hath never spied 127
  Or bird or lure though long upon the wing,
  Doth while his lord cries, "Woe, thou stoopest!" glide,
Down whence he darted first, through many a ring 130
  Weary to earth, and far from the falconer
  Lighteth, a sullen and disdainful thing,—
Thus at the bottom Geryon set us, near 133
  The base of the deep-furrowed rock; and lo,
  Being of our persons disencumbered there,
He sped away like arrow from the bow. 136

---

118. *on the right.* Their circling has brought them to the other side of the fall of Phlegethon from that on which they started.
128. *lure.* In falconry, the artificial figure of a bird, by which the falcon was recalled.

## CANTO XVIII

*The eighth circle—Malebolge. The first chasm: betrayers of women. The hurrying throng, lashed on by demons. The second chasm: flatterers, wallowing in filth.*

A place called Malebolge, all of stone
   And of an iron colour, lies in Hell,
   Like to the towering barrier round it thrown.
There yawns, exceeding wide and deep, a well     4
   Right in the middle of that field malign,
   And of its structure I in time will tell.
Hence the enclosure that remains between     7
   The well and foot of the high cliff is round,
   And valleys ten divide the space therein.
Even as the form presented by the ground     10
   Whereon, the ramparts better to defend,

---

1 ff. *Malebolge* (mä-lĕ-bol'-jä) means literally "Evil-pouches," hence "Evil-pits." The place by that name consists of ten narrow, concentric chasms which, together with the ridge walls or embankments that divide them from each other, occupy all the ground between the foot of the great cordon of cliffs which the poets have just descended with the aid of Geryon and the rim of the central pit of Hell. Each chasm describes a complete circle, one inside another, about the central pit; and the floor of each and the ridge wall that divides it from the valley lying next inside its circle are always lower respectively than the floor and corresponding ridge wall of the next outer valley, so that from the foot of the surrounding cliffs to the central pit or well there is a gradual descent. Across this area, from the outer precipice foot to the brink of the inner well, run several long ridges of rock, like the spokes of a wheel from outer rim to hub. Each ridge thus crosses every valley, but is pierced by an arch, bridge-like, where it spans each, so that the circuit of no valley floor is blocked. The poets reach one of these causeways at line 69 of this canto, and proceed along it over one valley or bolgia after another. In each chasm they see a different kind of fraud punished.

## CANTO XVIII

Many concentric moats a castle bound,—
Just such an aspect here those trenches lend; 13
  And as unto the outer bank small bridges
  From thresholds of such fortresses extend,—
So from the cliff's low base proceed rock ridges, 16
  Across the embankments and the chasms, down
  To where the well doth end them round its edges.
In this place, from the back of Geryon 19
  Cast off, we found ourselves; and to the left
  The poet held, and I behind moved on.
Upon the right we saw new miseries quaffed, 22
  New torments, scourgers new the lash who plied,
  With which was filled completely the first cleft.
Within were naked sinners; on our side 25
  They toward us moved, and on the farthermost
  As we did, but with longer, swifter stride.
The Romans thus, because of the great host 28
  In the year of Jubilee, upon the bridge
  Took measures that it might be easier crossed,—
Whence toward the Castle they that walk that edge 31
  Their faces turn and toward Saint Peter's go,
  But toward the Hill those on the other ledge.
Along the gloomy stone at all points, lo, 34

---

22 *ff*. Skirting the foot of the outer cliffs in a leftward direction, the poets have the first bolgia on their right. It contains pandars and seducers, who are lashed on by horned demons, even as in the world they were goaded by their evil desires. (The horns are symbols of adultery.) The file of pandars occupies the outer half of the chasm, and moves toward the right; that of the seducers the inner half and moves toward the left. The pandars are hence nearer to the poets and, advancing in the opposite direction to them, meet and pass them face to face. This division of the sinners into two bands going in opposite directions, each on its own side of the bolgia and keeping to the right, is compared to the movement of the crowds in Rome upon the bridge of Sant' Angelo during the Jubilee of 1300, in accordance with the traffic regulations then inaugurated. By the "Hill" is meant the Capitoline Hill.

I saw with great whips hornèd fiends abhorred,
   Who smote the backs of those that here have woe.
Ah, how at the first blows they made that herd 37
   Lift up their legs; truly, thereafter none
   Ever awaits the second or the third.
As I was passing on, mine eyes by one 40
   Of them were met; and instantly I said:
   "Him hath my sight already fed upon."
To scan his form my steps I therefore stayed, 43
   And with me also stopped my gracious guide
   Nor that I go a little back forbade.
To hide himself that driven spirit tried, 46
   Holding his head down, but all fruitlessly,
   For: "Thou that lookest on the ground," I cried,
"If true the features which thou wearest be, 49
   Art Venedico Caccianimico. What
   To such a bitter portion sendeth thee?"
He answered: "Willingly I tell it not; 52
   But thou compellest me with thine utterance clear,
   Which bringeth back the old world unforgot.
'Twas I persuaded Ghisola the Fair 55
   To do the Marquis' will, whatever way
   The shameful tale be told. Nor am I here
The only Bolognese who weepeth. Nay, 58
   This bolgia is so filled with us, I vow,
   That tongues less numerous are taught to say
*Sipa* from Reno to Savena now; 61

---

50. Venedico Caccianimico (vĕ-nĕ-dee'-ko kä'tchä-nee-mee'-ko) was of a notable Bolognese family. He procured his own sister, Ghisola (gee'-so-lä), as a mistress for the Marquis Obizzo of Este.

59-61. That is, the people now employing the Bolognese (bo'-lon-yeez) dialect on earth are fewer in numbers than the Bolognese who already occupy this bolgia. Bologna lies between the Reno (rä'-no) and Savena (sä-vä'-nä) rivers. *Sipa* was the Bolognese form of *si* ("yes")—or else, according to other authorities, of *sia*.

## CANTO XVIII

And if thereof thou pledge and proof wouldst join,
   Our avaricious hearts remember thou."
While thus he spake, a demon on his loin 64
   Smote with the lash, and cried: "Pandar, begone!
   There are no women here for thee to coin."
I sought again mine escort, and thereon 67
   Ere many steps were taken did we see
   From the embankment jut a ridge of stone.
This we ascended very easily, 70
   And left by it, on turning to the right,
   Those circling walls that stand eternally.
When we had come to where beneath the height, 73
   An arch, through which the scourged ones pass, doth yawn,
   My leader bade: "Stay now, and let the sight
Strike on thee of those others evil-born, 76
   Of whom the faces thou hast not yet seen,
   Since in the same direction they have gone."
So from that ancient bridge we viewed the train 79
   Come toward us on the other side, who fled
   Likewise before the cruel lash. Again
The master kind, without my asking, said: 82
   "Behold yon stately one, who for his pains,
   As he approacheth, seems no tear to shed.
What look of majesty he yet retains! 85
   Lo, Jason, who by courage and by guile
   Despoilèd of their ram the Colchians.

---

69. *a ridge of stone.* The beginning of one of the lines of bridges that run across the bolgias down to the central pit.
73-78. Standing upon the bridge span above the first bolgia and looking to his right, Dante for the first time sees the faces of the other file of inmates of that chasm, the seducers; for hitherto these have been moving in the same direction as himself, only faster.
80. *the other side.* The inner half of the bolgia's circuit.
87. *Despoilèd of their ram.* That is, carried off the Golden Fleece.

| Upon his way he passed the Lemnian isle, | 88 |
| After the bold and ruthless women there | |
| Had given all their males to death erewhile. | |

Among them with his words and tokens fair 91
  The maid Hypsipyle he deceived and won,—
  Her that deceived the others earlier.
To bear his child he left her there alone; 94
  Such guilt condemns him to such punishment,
  And also for Medea is vengeance done.
With him go all who use like blandishment; 97
  Enough is this of the first vale to know,
  And of the souls that in its jaws are pent."
We had already come to where unto 100
  The next bank joins the bridgeway's narrow spike
  And for a new arch makes a buttress so.
Here we heard people whining in the dike 103
  Beyond, who puff and snort amid the gloom,
  While on their bodies with their palms they strike.
The banks are crusted o'er with a green scum 106
  By vapours from beneath, which there condense
  And to the eyes and nose are burdensome.
So deep the place that nowhere might our glance 109
  Unto its bottom pierce, till we should go
  Right o'er the arch, where highest the eminence.

---

88-96. According to Greek legend, the women of Lemnos conspired to murder all males on the island. Their plan was carried through, save that Hypsipyle secretly spared her father. Later, she was seduced and abandoned by Jason; therefore he is punished in this bolgia, and also for his abandonment of Medea, by whose aid he had won the Fleece.

100 *ff*. The poets have now crossed the first bolgia and have come to the dividing embankment wall between it and the second chasm, over which their causeway-ridge will pass with another arching span. On this new bridge they proceed.

## CANTO XVIII

We mounted there, whence in the ditch below 112
   Discerned I folk immersed in excrement
   That seemed from the latrines of man to flow;
And while I searched the depths with gaze down bent, 115
   I saw one's head so smeared with ordure foul
   That clerk's or layman's 'twas not evident.
"Why starest thou at me"—thus did he bawl— 118
   "More than the others in their filth?" And I
   To him: "Because, if rightly I recall,
I have beheld thee when thy hair was dry. 121
   Alessio Interminei of Lucca 'tis;
   Hence most of all on thee is fixed mine eye."
And beating then his pate: "The flatteries 124
   Wherewith my tongue was never weary once,"
   He cried aloud, "have plunged me down to this."
Thereon my guide said unto me: "Advance 127
   Thy face a little farther, that thou so
   Mayst let thy vision reach the countenance
Of that unclean, dishevelled strumpet who 130
   With nasty nails doth scratch herself all o'er,
   Now standing on her feet, now crouching low.

---

112 *ff*. Gaining the summit of the bridge arching above the second bolgia, Dante beholds, in the narrow, noisome depths below, the next group of the fraudulent—flatterers—wallowing in human excrement. The revolting realism of the passage which follows is due to no lack of refinement on the part of the poet, but to his feeling that flattery is so loathsome that its fate must be no less so. As evidence that Dante's sensibilities were in nowise blunted, may be instanced the delicacy of his treatment of the difficult subject of unnatural sexual vice in Cantos xv and xvi—a delicacy so great that the casual or unsophisticated reader might not realize what was the sin there dealt with.

122. Of Alessio Interminei (ä-lĕs'-syo ĭn-tĕr-mee'-nä-ee) of Lucca (look'-kä), little is known. He lived in the thirteenth century.

| | |
|---|---:|
| Thaïs it is, the harlot, who of yore | 133 |
|    Asked by her lover, 'Thankest me much?' replied, | |
|    'Nay, past all measure!' to that paramour;— | |
| And let our sight herewith be satisfied." | 136 |

133. Thaïs is doubtless named to afford an ancient example of a flatterer, Alessio being a recent one. She is a courtesan in Terence's comedy *Eunuchus,* and the incident referred to is mentioned by Cicero (Dante's source) as an instance of flattery, in that she replied extravagantly as in line 135 to her lover's question instead of saying simply, "Yes, much."

## CANTO XIX

*Eighth circle: Malebolge. The third chasm: simonists. The protruding, burning feet. Pope Nicholas III. Of his expected fellows. Dante's indignant outburst.*

O Simon Magus, O his followers vile,
  Ye who the things of God, which ought to be
  The spotless brides of righteousness, defile
For silver and for gold rapaciously!     4
  Now it is meet for you the trumpet blow,
  Because in the third chasm suffer ye.
Already o'er the following tomb we go     7
  Upon the bridge of rock unto that part
  Which hath the middle of the fosse below.
Wisdom supreme, thou showest what wondrous art     10
  In Heaven, on earth, and in the abyss profound!
  How justly doth thy power give desert!
I saw the livid stone which formed the ground     13
  Was full of holes—the bottom and each side—
  All of like breadth, and every one was round.
No larger did they seem and not less wide     16
  Than those which in my beautiful Saint John
  The places for baptizing priests provide,

---

1. Simon Magus offered the Apostles money if they would give him the gift of the Holy Ghost (Acts viii). Hence the buying of ecclesiastical offices or other trafficking in spiritual things is called "simony" after him. This sin is punished in the third bolgia.

7. *tomb*. Receptacle for the dead, hence bolgia.

17. *my beautiful Saint John*. The Baptistery of Florence. It contained stalls or pits for the baptizers, one of which was formerly broken by Dante for the reason that he gives, hoping by this statement to silence slanderous accounts of his act.

| And one of which, not many years agone, | 19 |
|     I broke to save one drowning there—now let | |
|     These words of mine the truth to all make known. | |
| Out of the mouth of each a sinner's feet | 22 |
|     Protruded, and his legs unto the calf; | |
|     The rest of him concealed within was set. | |
| All had both soles afire, because whereof | 25 |
|     Their joints were twitching with such violent throes | |
|     That withes and ropes they would have snapped in half. | |
| Even as the blaze on oily objects flows | 28 |
|     Only along the surface wontedly, | |
|     It likewise did with these, from heels to toes. | |
| "Who is that one who showeth his agony, | 31 |
|     Master, more than his fellows quivering there, | |
|     And whom a ruddier flame doth lap?" said I. | |
| And he to me: "If thou wilt let me bear | 34 |
|     Thee down that bank which is the lower, so | |
|     Thou from himself his name and sins wilt hear." | |
| "My wish with thine," said I, "doth ever go. | 37 |
|     Thou art my lord and knowest thy will I keep; | |
|     And what I speak not, thou dost also know." | |
| Hence, coming to the fourth embankment steep, | 40 |
|     We turned and on the left hand made descent | |
|     Into the perforated, narrow deep. | |
| Ne'er from his haunch my guide benevolent | 43 |

---

*22 ff.* The simonist perverts spiritual things, so must stand inverted. Fire plays upon the soles of his feet, as an aureole stands about the head of a saint.

*35. that bank which is the lower.* The inner wall of the bolgia, which in each instance is of less height than the outer, since Malebolge as a whole slopes toward the central well.

*40-42.* That is, having crossed the bridge over the third bolgia and reached the embankment wall that separates it from the fourth, they descend the outer side of this bank, which is the inner side of the third bolgia, thus gaining the floor of that chasm.

## CANTO XIX

Would set me down until he reached the brack
Of him who with his legs did so lament.
"Whoe'er thou be that, planted like a stake, 46
Hast," I began, "thy upper half beneath,—
O wretched soul, if thou are able, speak."
I seemed a friar to whom confession saith 49
A treacherous murderer that to his side,
When fixed, recalls him, thus delaying death.
"Art thou already standing there?" he cried,— 52
"O Boniface, already standing there?
By several years the writ of doom hath lied.
Hast thou no longer for that wealth a care 55
For which thou didst not dread by trickery
To seize, and ravage then, the lady fair?"
Like those who feel themselves bemocked, grew I, 58
When naught they comprehend of what is said
To them and are unable to reply.
"Tell him immediately," thus Virgil bade, 61
" 'I am not he, not he whom thinkest thou' ";
And I, as he commanded, answer made.
With both feet fiercely wrenched the spirit now; 64
And later, sighing and with voice of woe,
He said to me: "Then I can serve thee how?

---

49-51. Assassins were sometimes buried alive upside down, and the comparison pictures one who, already fixed in his hole, recalls to his side the confessor that he may thus put off a little longer the moment when the earth will be thrown in upon him.

52 ff. The speaker is Pope Nicholas III, who died in 1280. Hearing Dante's voice, he thinks it is Boniface VIII come to take his place, and is surprised, knowing that Boniface's death was written in the Book of Fate to occur in 1303, whereas it is now only 1300. Boniface, Dante's great enemy, attained the Papacy by fraud, and was equally unscrupulous in the exercise of his prerogatives.

57. *the lady fair*. The Church, the bride of Christ.

58-60. Dante stands dumbfounded with astonishment at the words with which Nicholas mistakenly addresses him.

| If to learn who I am, thou carest so | 67 |
|---|---|

That down the embankment thou didst hither fare,
That I was clothed with the great mantle, know.
Truly was I a son of the She-bear,     70
  So eager to advance the cubs that yon
  Above engulfed I wealth, my own self here.
Beneath my head are thrust the others down     73
  Who had preceded me in simony,—
  Flattened between the fissures of the stone.
There, in like manner falling, I shall lie     76
  When cometh he whom I supposed thou wast
  When I with sudden question gave reply.
But now already longer do I toast     79
  My soles, thus planted upside down, than he
  Shall stand with glowing feet set uppermost;
For after him, out of the West, shall be     82
  A shepherd without law, of fouler deed—
  Yea, one most fit to cover him and me.
Like unto Jason he, of whom we read     85
  In Maccabees; as him his king of old,
  So this one he who governs France shall speed."
I know not if I here were overbold,     88
  But answer made I even in this strain:

---

69. *the great mantle.* The papal mantle with which the Pope was invested.

70. *the She-bear.* Nicholas belonged to the Orsini family, in whose coat-of-arms was a she-bear (*orsa*); hence he speaks of other members of that family, whose interests he furthered, as "cubs."

79-87. Nicholas declares that he has already stood thus inverted for a longer time than Boniface will stand before being relieved in turn by yet another simoniac Pope, worse even than they. The prophecy is of Clement V, of Gascony (the West)—as much a creature of the King of France as the high priest Jason is portrayed in the Second Book of Maccabees to have been of King Antiochus Epiphanes of Syria. It was during the pontificate of Clement that the seat of the Papacy was transferred to Avignon and the "Babylonish captivity" of the Church thus begun.

## CANTO XIX

"Ah, tell me now, what treasure manifold
Our Lord exacted of Saint Peter when 91
  He put the keys into his hands in trust?
  Surely he said but 'Follow me.' Again,
The grace of Peter and the others cost 94
  Matthias naught, when to that office he
  Was chosen which the guilty soul had lost.
Therefore abide; for thou art righteously 97
  Punished; and keep the money got so ill
  Which gave thee against Charles such valiancy.
And were it not for this, that I am still 100
  With reverence for the keys supreme imbued
  Which thou didst hold in the glad life erewhile,
Words I should use yet heavier and more rude, 103
  For sorrows to the world your avarice brings,
  Raising the wicked, trampling on the good.
Such shepherds meant the Apostle's visionings 106
  Of her that on the waters hath her seat
  Committing fornication with the kings—
Her that was born with seven heads of might 109
  And in her ten horns had authority
  While yet her spouse in virtue took delight.
Your god of gold and silver fashion ye,— 112
  Differing from the idolater wherein,

---

94-96. The reference is to the selection of Matthias as Apostle in place of Judas Iscariot. See Acts i.

98-99. Nicholas was charged with having been bribed to oppose Charles of Anjou, brother of Louis IX of France, in Sicily, where the conspiracy to expel the French culminated in the massacre of the Sicilian Vespers.

104. *your*. The reference is to Nicholas and others like him.

106 *ff*. See Revelation xvii, 1-3, for this vision of Saint John. Dante would seem to interpret the woman to stand for the Church, her heads for the Seven Sacraments, and her horns for the Ten Commandments; her spouse is the Pope. It will be observed that he deals freely with his source.

Save that his one and yours a hundred be?
To how much ill gave birth, O Constantine, 115
 Not thy conversion but that dower unmeet
 The first rich Father from thy hands did win!"
Now while I sang to him this burden sweet, 118
 Whether 'twere rage or conscience on him fed,
 He violently kicked with both his feet.
Truly I think my guide was pleased indeed, 121
 He listened with a look of such content
 Unto the sound of those true words I said.
Then in his arms he lifted me, close pent, 124
 And when he had me gathered to his breast,
 Upward retraced the way of his descent.
Nor did he weary thus to hold me fast, 127
 But to the peak of that arch carried me
 Which from the fourth wall to the fifth is cast.
Gently his burden then relinquished he— 130
 Gently, for rugged was the crag and steep,
 Nor even a goat might cross it easily.
Thence I beheld another valley deep. 133

---

116. *that dower unmeet.* The temporal power of the Pope, bestowed, according to legend, by Constantine the Great upon the Roman Bishop Sylvester. The document of this donation was not proved a forgery until the fifteenth century.

128. Virgil carried Dante not only out of the depths of the third chasm, but thereafter along the causeway till they reached the summit of the arch above the fourth bolgia, where they could best look down into it.

## CANTO XX

*Eighth circle: Malebolge. The fourth chasm: diviners and magicians, with reverted faces. Ancient prophets. Of the origin of Mantua. Other necromancers.*

Of a new punishment my verses tell,
  Theme for the twentieth canto to supply
  Of the first song, of those submerged in Hell.
Already was I minded thoroughly 4
  To look into the abyss revealed below,
  Which bathes itself with tears of agony.
And folk I saw, silent and weeping, slow 7
  Along the curve of the great valley pace,
  As in the world with litanies men go.
And as upon them lower fell my gaze, 10
  Between the chin and where the chest begins
  Each seemed contorted wondrously; the face
Was backward twisted even to the loins, 13
  And backward it behooved them to advance,
  For these from looking forward, fate restrains.
Perhaps indeed by palsy's violence 16
  Some one hath been thus wholly bent awry,
  But I ne'er saw nor credit such mischance.
So, Reader, may God let thee profit by 19
  This thy perusal, now thy thought bestow

---

3. *the first song.* The *Inferno,* the first of the three parts of the *Divine Comedy.*

7 *ff.* The inmates of the fourth bolgia are diviners, sorcerers, and other dealers in the forbidden "black arts" of magic. They are punished by having their heads twisted round on their shoulders, so that they, who had in life unlawfully looked into the future, can now look only behind them and hence must walk backward.

How I could ever keep my own face dry
When close at hand I viewed our image so                22
  Wrenched that the weeping of the eyes made wet
  Along the cleft the hinder parts below.
Truly, as on a rock I leaned of that                    25
  Hard crag, I wept until mine escort said:
  "Art thou but as the other fools, e'en yet?
Here pity lives when piety is dead.                     28
  Who shall be found more impious than he
  That passions at the doom by God decreed?
Raise up, raise up thy head and that one see            31
  For whom earth gaped before the Thebans' gaze,
  Whence cried they all: 'Now whither dost thou flee,
Amphiaraüs? Why leavest the war apace?'                 34
  Nor did he cease from plunging headlong down
  To Minos, who on all his clutches lays.
Mark how his shoulders now his chest have grown!        37
  Since he too far ahead his glance would dart,
  Backward he goes with look behind him thrown.
Observe Tiresias, who his form by art                   40
  Changed when from man a woman he became,
  His members altering in every part;
And had to smite the entangled serpents twain           43
  Yet later with his rod another blow

---

28. It is impious to pity those who suffer beneath the justice of God. Virgil has not disapproved of Dante's pity for individuals, such as Francesca da Rimini and Pier delle Vigne; but here it is the penalty itself that calls forth protesting tears.

31-36. The prophet Amphiaraüs was, like Capaneus in Canto xiv, one of the legendary seven Greek heroes who assailed Thebes. During the battle before the walls, the earth opened and swallowed him alive.

40. Tiresias was a legendary Theban soothsayer, roughly contemporaneous with Amphiaraüs. Ovid tells how he struck with his staff two snakes which he found twined together, and thereupon was transformed into a girl; and how, some years later, he discovered those snakes again, and again smiting them, was changed back into a man.

## CANTO XX

Before his manly beard he could regain.
He who with rear to that one's front doth go 46
 Is Aruns, who in Luna's mountain ways,
 Where grubs the Carrarese that lives below,
'Mid the white marbles had for dwelling place 49
 A cave, whence unobstructed was the scene
 If at the stars or at the sea his gaze.
And she who doth with loose-flung tresses screen 52
 And from thy vision thus conceal her breast,
 So that on that side all her hair is seen,
Was Manto, who through many lands made quest, 55
 Then settled in the place where I had birth,
 Whereof awhile I fain would have thee list.
When from this life her father was gone forth 58
 And Bacchus' city fallen to slavery,
 She for a long time wandered o'er the earth.
There lies a lake, high in fair Italy, 61
 By name Benaco, of those Alps at foot
 Which above Tyrol shut in Germany.

---

46-51. Aruns was an Etruscan soothsayer in Lucan's epic, *Pharsalia*. The ancient Luna was one of the chief Etruscan cities; the Carrarese kär'-rä-reez) mountains near by, where Aruns had his cave, are famous for the beautiful Carrara marble.

55 *ff*. Manto, the daughter of Tiresias, was the reputed founder of Mantua, the city of Virgil, into whose mouth Dante puts a story (somewhat different from Virgil's own in the *Aeneid*!) of its origin. This story is probably meant to relieve, with its idyllic beauty, the ingenious horrors with which the many cantos devoted to Malebolge abound. For the same purpose of relief, Dante later introduced the grotesqueries of Cantos xxi and xxii and the narratives of Ulysses and Guido da Montefeltro in Cantos xxvi and xxvii.

59. *Bacchus' city*. Thebes.

61 *ff*. The lake Benaco (bĕ-nä'-ko) is now called Lago di Garda. The town of Garda (gär'-dä) is on the east side of this lake; Val Camonica (väl kä-mo'-nee-kä) is a valley over fifty miles long on the west side. Apennino (ä-pĕn-nee'-no) is not the Apennine range, but a Mount Apennino of that locality.

| 'Twixt Garda and Val Camonica, I wot, | 64 |
|  More than a thousand springs bathe Apennino; | |
|  And in that lake their waters rest. A spot | |
| Is in its midst which pastors of the Trentino, | 67 |
|  Of Brescia, and Verona, all, no doubt, | |
|  Alike would bless if they should thither go. | |
| Peschiera's fortress, beautiful and stout, | 70 |
|  Brescians and Bergamese to hold at bay, | |
|  Stands where the shore is lowest round about. | |
| What in Benaco's bosom cannot stay | 73 |
|  Must thence descend, and doth a river grow | |
|  Which downward through green pastures makes its way. | |
| Soon as the water gathers head to flow, | 76 |
|  Mincio and not Benaco is its name | |
|  Even to Governo, where it joins the Po. | |
| Not long its course before it finds a plain | 79 |
|  On which it spreads and forms a marsh that may | |
|  At times in summer be a noisome bane. | |
| The tameless maiden, journeying that way, | 82 |
|  Was of dry land amid the fen aware; | |
|  Untilled and uninhabited it lay. | |
| To shun mankind she thither did repair— | 85 |
|  She with her servants;—there her arts she plied, | |
|  And lived and left her empty body there. | |
| Later, the men who round were scattered wide | 88 |
|  Collected in that place, whose strength was great | |

---

69. That is to say, the spot in question is a point in the lake at which the three dioceses of the Trentino (trĕn-tee′-no), Brescia (brä′-shä), and Verona meet.

70. Peschiera (pä-skyâ′-rä), a fortress at the northeastern extremity of the lake, was built by the Veronese as a defence against the Brescians and Bergamese (bĕr′-gä-meez).

73. That is, the overflow of the lake.

77. The river Mincio (meen′-cho) begins at Peschiera and ends at Governo (go-vĕr′-no), now Governola, about twelve miles beyond Mantua.

## CANTO XX

By reason of the morass on every side.
A town above those mouldering bones they set, 91
  Called, for her sake who first had chosen that soil,
  Mantua—no other name they asked of fate.
Its people numbered more in former while, 94
  Ere Casalodi through stupidity
  Had been deceived by Pinamonte's guile.
Hence if thou ever hearest (I caution thee) 97
  My city's origin was different
  From this, no fiction may cheat verity."
"Master, thy words are sure to such extent," 100
  I answered, "and they so my faith have won,
  All others are to me as embers spent.
But tell me of the folk now passing on, 103
  If any thou espy deserving note,
  Because my thoughts revert to that alone."
"He from the cheeks of whom the beard doth float 106
  O'er his dark shoulders was a seer when reft
  So of all males," he said, "was Greece throughout
That scarce were any for the cradles left; 109
  And he with Calchas did in Aulis show
  The time for the first cable to be cleft.
Eurypylus his name, and of him so 112
  My lofty Tragedy doth somewhere write,
  As well thou knowest, who the whole dost know.

---

94-96. In 1272, Pinamonte (pee-nä-mon'-tā) de' Buonaccorsi treacherously persuaded Count Alberto da Casalodi (kà-sä-lo'-dee), the master of Mantua, to expel many of the nobles from the city. He himself then headed the populace and drove out Casalodi, thus deprived of his chief support.

106 *ff*. Virgil now points out Eurypylus, who was like the seer Calchas associated with the expedition against Troy, when the mighty gathering of warriors from all Greece was mustered at Aulis, awaiting the signal for departure. He is mentioned in the *Aeneid*, which Virgil here calls a "tragedy" because of its elevated subject and style, just as Dante calls his own poem a "comedy."

That other one, about the flank so slight, 115
 Is Michael Scott, who of a certainty
 The game of magic frauds had mastered quite.
Guido Bonatti see; Asdente see, 118
 Who wishes now that he had kept at thread
 And leather, but too late repenteth he.
See the sad women who from the needle fled, 121
 From spool and spindle, sorcerers to grow;
 With herbs and images they witchcraft made.
But linger not; Cain with his thorns e'en now 124
 Doth hold of either hemisphere the bound
 And sinks into the wave, Seville below;
And only yesternight the moon was round;— 127
 Thou shouldst remember clearly, for no ill
 Sometimes she did thee in the wood profound."
He spake thus; we pursued our way, the while. 130

---

116. Michael Scott, a learned Scotchman who lived for many years at the court of Frederick II, was a noted student of the occult sciences.

118. Guido Bonatti (gwee'-do bo-nät'-tee) was a celebrated astrologer and soothsayer of Forli in the latter part of the thirteenth century. The shoemaker Asdente (äs-děn'-tā) of Parma was another renowned soothsayer of the same period.

123. *images.* That is, images of those persons on whom their witchcraft was practised. See D. G. Rossetti's poem *Sister Helen.*

124 *ff.* "Cain with his thorns" is the figure in the moon, which is here said to be at this moment bisected by the western horizon, beyond Seville. Therefore, since on the previous night (meaning the night before that through which they have just passed) the moon was full and helped Dante at times amid the dark wood in which he was lost, it is now about seven o'clock on the Saturday morning after Good Friday.

# CANTO XXI

*Eighth circle: Malebolge. The fifth chasm: the barrators in the burning pitch. The attending demons, or Malebranche. Parley and truce. The escort to find a new bridge.*

From bridge to bridge thus did we onward march
  With other talk, whereof to sing would irk
  My Comedy, till over the next arch
We halted, yet another gorge to mark     4
  Of Malebolge, and vain cries withal;

---

1. If Longfellow's comparison of the *Divine Comedy* to a great cathedral be allowed, Cantos xxi and xxii may be said to be its gargoyles. In these cantos Dante gives free rein to the grotesque; the language and incidents are ignoble and often coarse and semi-comic. Such treatment not only affords relief from the strain of the horrors which precede and follow, but suggests Dante's contempt for the sinners who are inmates of the fifth bolgia—the "other gorge" of line 4—with which these two cantos deal. These sinners are barrators, persons who trafficked in public offices or business, officials who took bribes or were guilty of other corrupt practices. They are punished by being immersed in boiling pitch, appropriate as a symbol of defiling corruption. Says Grandgent: "The peculiarity of swindlers is that they do dirty work in the dark; and unless they remain under cover, they are seized by the officers of the law. So Dante's barrators, or grafters, pursue their eternal career beneath the surface of a ditch full of boiling pitch, and demons stand ready to snatch them with hooks, if they attempt to 'air themselves.' Cunning as they were on earth, they still incessantly scheme to cheat and elude their watchers; and these, just as tricky and far more vile and mischievous, are as eager to catch the innocent as the guilty. Dante himself barely evades their wiles, even Reason being temporarily deceived, though human instinct is apprehensive." It is indeed notable that only here, during his journey through Hell, does Dante seem to be in any personal danger; in view of the fact that a charge of barratry was brought against him as the pretext for his banishment from Florence, it would seem that this episode of the narrative is a deliberate autobiographical reference.

And here I found it marvellously dark.
Even as in the Venetians' arsenal
  Boileth in winter the tenacious pitch
  To caulk the unsound ships they overhaul;
For then no sailing is—instead of which
  One builds at a new craft, and one a rib
  Rotted with many voyages doth patch;
At prow and stern hammers alike a tribe;
  Some fashion oars, and others cordage twine;
  And one the mainsail mends, and one the jib—
So, not by fire but by an art divine,
  Was boiling a dense pitch down there beneath,
  That did on every side the bank belime.
This I could see, but naught therein perceive
  Except the bubbles which the boiling raised
  And one great swell by turns subside and heave.
Now while I fixedly upon it gazed,
  My leader with a cry, "Beware, beware!"
  From where I stood drew me to him in haste.
Then wheeled I round like one who longs to share
  The sight of that which he hath need to shun,
  Yet who, because unmanned by sudden fear,
Although he looks, delays not to be gone;
  And a black devil behind us did I see,
  Who came along the bridgeway on the run.
Ah, in his aspect what ferocity!
  And with his outspread wings and step so fleet,
  How fell of purpose he appeared to me!
Upon his high and pointed shoulders set,
  Did both the haunches of a sinner ride,
  Of whom he gripped the sinews of the feet.
"Ye Malebranche of our bridge," he cried,

---

37. *Malebranche* (mä-lĕ-brän'-kä) means literally "Evil-claws." It is the name by which the demon guardians of this bolgia are known.

## CANTO XXI

"An Elder of Saint Zita! Down below
Thrust him, while to that town which doth provide
Me with so many, I for others go.     40
  There, save Bonturo, all are barrators;
  There for a bribe they make a 'Yes' of 'No.'"
He cast him headlong, and then wheeled his course     43
  Upon the flinty crag, nor mastiff freed
  To follow thief more swiftly ever scours.
The other sank and came up doubled; cried     46
  The demons whom the bridge hid from our eyes:
  "Here nothing doth the Sacred Face bestead!
Here is the swimming wholly otherwise     49
  Than in the Serchio! If thou wouldst not taste
  Our forks, do not above the surface rise!"
They caught him with a hundred prongs at least.     52
  "Here shouldst thou covered dance," went up their shout,
  "That if thou canst in secret filch, thou mayst!"
E'en thus into the middle of the pot     55
  Cooks have their scullions plunge the meat with keen
  Flesh-hooks in order that it may not float.
Said the good master: "Lest it should be seen     58
  That thou art here, behind a jag of stone
  Crouch down, and so make for thyself a screen.
And unto me whate'er despite be done,     61
  Fear not; for I am well advised, who once
  Before just such a bickering have known."

---

38. Saint Zita (dzee'-tä) was the patron saint of Lucca, which is, therefore, the city really meant.

41. The exception is ironical. Bonturo (bon-too'-ro) was the most notorious barrator of all!

48. *the Sacred Face.* An ancient wooden image of Christ, preserved at Lucca and greatly venerated there.

50. The Serchio (sĕr'-kyo) is a river near Lucca.

63. *such a bickering have known.* When sent down by Erichtho (Canto ix, 22 *ff.*).

| Then past the bridge's crest did he advance, | 64 |
| And when he gained the sixth bank, need was his | |
| To offer an unshaken countenance. | |
| With even the same storm and fury 'tis | 67 |
| That dogs rush forth upon a poor man, who | |
| Suddenly stops and begs from where he is, | |
| And that from 'neath the bridge the demon crew | 70 |
| Rushed, and their gaffs against him turned; but he | |
| Called out to them: "Be vicious none of you! | |
| Before your grapple ever toucheth me, | 73 |
| Send one to hear my words, and after that, | |
| About my seizure take good counsel, ye!" | |
| "Let Malacoda go!" they cried, whereat, | 76 |
| While the rest waited, one did nearer draw | |
| Unto us, muttering, "This shall gain him what?" | |
| "Malacoda," said my master, "thinkest thou | 79 |
| That I have come thus far, as thou dost see, | |
| Against your every hindrance safe till now, | |
| Except by Will Divine and destiny | 82 |
| Propitious? Let me pass, for this wild road | |
| I to another show; 'tis Heaven's decree." | |
| Then at his feet the demon dropped his goad, | 85 |
| So fallen was his arrogance, and cried | |
| Back to his mates: "To strike is not allowed!" | |
| "O thou that sittest cowering," spake my guide, | 88 |
| "Cowering among the splinters of the bridge, | |
| Return in safety now unto my side." | |
| Whereat I rose, and swift along the ledge | 91 |
| Came to him, and the fiends pressed forward so | |
| I was afraid they would not keep the pledge. | |
| Thus was it once I saw the soldiers who | 94 |

---

76. *Malacoda* (mä-lä-ko'-dä) means literally "Evil-tail."
88. Virgil now turns and, lifting his voice, addresses Dante.
94-96. The stronghold of Caprona (kä-pro'-nä), near Pisa, was taken

## CANTO XXI

Marched out by treaty from Caprona fear
At seeing themselves amid such numerous foe.
With my whole body to my leader near 97
 I crept, and did not turn mine eyes away
 From theirs, which had in sooth an evil leer.
They lowered their forks, and ever one would say 100
 To the others: "Shall I touch him up a bit
 Behind?" and: "Nick him well!" would answer they.
But that same demon who was speaking yet 103
 With my good master, quickly back did throw
 A glance, and cried: "Quiet, Scarmiglione, quiet!"
And then to us: "One can no farther go 106
 Along this bridge, because the sixth arch lies
 All shattered on the valley's floor below.
But would you still press onward otherwise, 109
 Proceed along the embankment wall, for near
 At hand another ridge a path supplies.
Five hours later yesterday, the year 112
 One thousand and two hundred and sixty-six

---

in 1289 by an army of Tuscan Guelfs, in which Dante, it appears, was serving. According to some accounts, the garrison, which capitulated on promise of safe-conduct, had so enraged the besiegers by their many cruelties that despite the compact they were eventually massacred. This, if true, would add a sinister note to the present comparison.

105. Scarmiglione (skär-meel-yo'-nā) may mean "Ruffler" or "Disheveled One."

106 ff. Malacoda makes three informative statements: (1) that the bridgeway is broken at the next bridge; (2) that another bridgeway close by is unbroken; and (3) that the wreckage was made at a time which, from his manner of stating it, was evidently that of the great earthquake during the Crucifixion—the same earthquake that caused the landslide guarded by the Minotaur. The first and third statements are true; the second false, as we learn in Canto xxiii. The time statement indicates to us that Malacoda is speaking at about 7 a.m. on the Saturday following Good Friday, for Dante misunderstood Luke to say that Christ died at the sixth hour, or twelve noon (see *Convito* iv, 23).

Was ended since the way was broken here.
To find if any soul an airing seeks, 115
   Thitherward send I some of these my men.
   Go with them; they will play no evil tricks.—
Come, Alichino, forth," began he then 118
   To say, "thou Calcabrina, and Cagnazzo;
   And Barbariccia, do thou lead the ten.
Let Libicocco come, and Draghignazzo, 121
   Mad Rubicante, Farfarello too,
   And Graffiacane, and tusked Ciriatto.
Search everywhere around the boiling glue; 124
   And to the next bridge that unbrokenly
   Crosses the dens, safely conduct these two."
"Oh, oh! my master, what is this I see?" 127
   Said I. "Ah, let us without escort go,
   If thou knowest how. I seek it not, for me.
If, as thy wont is, thou art wary, lo, 130
   Dost thou not notice how they grind their teeth,
   And how their brows are threatening us with woe?"
"I would not have thee be afraid," he saith, 133
   "And therefore at their fancy let them grind,
   For this they do at those who boil beneath."

---

118 *ff*. The names of the demons are at once grotesque and sinister. Some of them are easily interpreted: Alichino (ä-lee-kee′-no), Bentwing; Cagnazzo (kän-yäts′-so), Dog-face; Barbariccia (bar-bä-ree′-tchä), Curly-beard; Graffiacane (gräf-fyä-kä′-nä), Scratch-dog; Rubicante (roo-bee-kän′-tä), Rubicund. But Calcabrina (kal-kà-bree′-nä), Libicocco (lee-bee-kok′-ko), Draghignazzo (drä-geen-yäts′-so), Ciriatto (chee-ree-ät′-to), and Farfarello (fär-fä-rĕl′-lo) are less obvious. It has been plausibly argued that all are distortions of the names of certain political figures in Florence who were Dante's enemies.

125-126. This command appears ominous indeed when it is later discovered that no such bridge exists! The safe-conduct is treacherous and worthless.

## CANTO XXI

Along the left embankment wheeled their line,   136
  But each had first between his fangs displayed
  His tongue unto their leader for a sign,
And he had of his breech a trumpet made.   139

136. *Along the left embankment.* They have now crossed the causeway over the lake of pitch, and reaching the embankment wall between this bolgia of the barrators and the next inner one, proceed along that section of it which lies to the left of the bridgehead. Thus their course is, as usual, leftward.

139. The obscene signal for departure is only an extreme instance of the grotesque and ignoble vein which Dante deemed suitable for the two cantos concerning the vile barrators.

## CANTO XXII

*Eighth circle: Malebolge: fifth chasm. The demon
retinue sets out. A captured barrator. His ruse and
escape. The quarrel of the Malebranche. Their
disaster.*

Horsemen ere now my chance hath fallen to see
   Break camp or charge or hold review, and e'en
   Upon occasion for their safety flee;
Scouring your land, O people Aretine,                     4
   Scouts have I viewed and raiders go and come,
   And clashing tourneys, dashing jousts have seen,—
With trumpet now, and now with bell, with drum,       7
   Or beacon signal on a fortress set,
   And with familiar things and things unknown;
But never horse or foot or vessel yet                     10
   For sign of land or star until this day
   I saw move off to pipe so strange as that!
We went with the ten demons on our way.            13
   Ah, the fell escort! but in church with saint,
   In tavern with the gluttonous, they say.
Wholly upon the pitch was my intent,                 16
   To spy all features of that chasm black
   And them that were within its burning pent.

---

1-12. These opening lines are a brilliant bit of mock-heroic verse in reference to the astonishing obscenity which concluded the preceding canto. Thus the note of grotesqueness, which will persist throughout the twenty-second canto as it did through the twenty-first, is reintroduced and emphasized at outset. The military allusions are probably, as in the case of Caprona in Canto xxi, 94-96, to the campaign of 1289. Dante was present at the battle of Campaldino, in that year, when the forces of Florence and Lucca defeated those of Arezzo.

## CANTO XXII

As dolphins that by arching of the back 19
  Supply to mariners a warning sign
  That they to save their ship must counsel take,—
Thus, ever and anon, to ease the pain 22
  One of the wicked would his back reveal
  And swift as lightning cover it again.
And as at water's edge in ditch or swale 25
  Frogs sit with nothing but the muzzle showed,
  So that their feet and bodies they conceal,—
E'en thus on every side the sinners stood, 28
  But at the approach of Barbariccia they
  Withdrew at once beneath the boiling flood.
I saw—and still it shakes my heart to-day— 31
  A laggard, just as oft it will occur
  That one frog stays when others hop away;
And Graffiacane, of the fiends most near, 34
  Grappled his pitchy locks and from the slough
  Drew him aloft, an otter as it were.
(I knew the name of every one by now, 37
  So had I noted them when they were chose,
  And when they called each other, listened how.)
"O Rubicante, see thou fix thy claws 40
  Upon his back and flay that skin of his!"
  Shouted together all the accursed foes.
"Master, discover if thou canst who is 43
  That luckless wretch," I cried, "who thus forlorn
  Is in the clutches of his enemies."
My guide drew near and asked of him, ere torn, 46
  His origin, and thus did he accord
  An answer: "In Navarre was I born.

---

19-21. To see dolphins, as with arched backs they leaped through the water, was supposed to presage a storm.

48 ff. Nothing is known of this barrator beyond what is here told us. "Good King Thibault," of whom he was a retainer, is Thibault II, King of Navarre.

| My mother placed me servant to a lord, | 49 |
| For she had borne me to a ribald sire, | |
| Who both himself and all his means destroned. | |
| Later I served in good King Thibault's hire; | 52 |
| I set me there to practise barratry, | |
| For which I pay the reckoning in this fire." | |
| Here Ciriatto, from whose mouth rose high | 55 |
| On either side a tusk as of a boar, | |
| Made him to feel how one is ripped thereby. | |
| Of evil cats the mouse was in the power; | 58 |
| But Barbariccia arms about him cast, | |
| And cried: "Off! While I hold him thus, give o'er!" | |
| Then, having round unto my master faced: | 61 |
| "If thou desirest aught more from him to know, | |
| Ask it forthwith, ere some one lay him waste." | |
| "Of the other sinners," spake my leader now, | 64 |
| "Say if thou wottest of any Italian there | |
| Beneath the tar." And he: "Not long ago | |
| I left one who to such was neighbour near. | 67 |
| Would that his covering I still had worn, | |
| For then I should nor claw nor grapple fear." | |
| But Libicocco shouted: "We have borne | 70 |
| Too much!" and seized an arm so with his hook | |
| He carried off a sinew from it torn. | |
| And Draghignazzo, too, would fain have struck | 73 |
| Down at the legs; whereat around and around | |
| Wheeled their decurion with a glowering look. | |
| Without delay my leader importuned, | 76 |
| As soon as they were somewhat pacified, | |
| Of him who still kept gazing at his wound: | |
| "Who was that one thou sayest from whose side | 79 |
| Thou wentest in an evil hour abroad?" | |
| And: "It was Friar Gomita," he replied, | |

---

75. *their decurion.* The commander of the ten.

## CANTO XXII

"He of Gallura, vessel of every fraud,     82
  Who in his hands his master's enemies
  Held, and so dealt with them they sing his laud.
He took their money and let them go, he says,     85
  'Quietly'; and no mean barrator was he,
  But sovereign, in his other offices.
Don Michel Zanche keeps him company     88
  From Logodoro; and their tongues are ne'er
  With talking of Sardinia tired.—Oh me!
Look at that other who is grinning there!     91
  I would say more, if I were not afeared
  That now to scratch my scurf he doth prepare."
And their grand marshall, turning at his word     94
  On Farfarello, who with eyes of doom
  Leered as to strike, cried: "Off, thou villainous bird!"
Thereon the frightened creature did resume:     97
  "If you would see or hear, e'en face to face,
  Tuscans or Lombards, I will make them come.
But let the Evil-claws withdraw a space,     100
  That of their vengeance these may have no fear,
  And I, while sitting in this very place,
For one that I am, will make seven appear     103
  By whistling, as when one of us gets out,
  It is the custom that we follow here."
Cagnazzo, hearing this, upraised his snout,     106
  Shaking his head, and spake: "To leap below,
  That is the scheme. Hark to his treacherous thought."

---

81 *ff.* Gomita (go-mee'-tä) was a Sardinian friar in the employment of Nino Visconti of Pisa, who was judge of Gallura (gal-loo'-rä), one of the four districts into which the Pisans divided Sardinia when they conquered it. Logodoro (lo-go-do'-ro), where Michel Zanche (mī'-kĕl tsän'-kä) held office, was another of these districts. Gomita was hanged when it was discovered that he had released, for a bribe, certain prisoners in his keeping who were great enemies of Nino.

94. *their grand marshall.* A far-fetched title for Barbariccia.

| Then he that stratagems possessed in so | 109 |
|---|---|

Great store replied: "Too treacherous indeed,
When to my comrades I bring heavier woe."
No more held Alichino in, but said     112
  To him, quite counter to the others, thus:
  "Dive, and I shall not match on foot thy speed,
But beat my wings above the pitchy fosse.     115
  Leave we the crest and be the ridge our screen,
  To see if thou prevailest alone o'er us."
O Reader, thou shalt hear new sport, I ween!     118
  All to the other side now bent their glance,
  He first who had the most reluctant been.
The Navarrese selected well his chance,     121
  Gripped with his feet the ground, and instantly
  Sprang and released himself from their intents.
Then each was stung with guilt, but chiefly he     124
  That caused the loss, and therefore he in haste
  Launched forth while rang his shout: "Now have I thee!"
But this availed him nothing in the least,     127
  For wings could not outstrip the speed of fear.
  The other sank; he, skimming, raised his breast.
Not differently when draws the falcon near,     130
  The duck dives underneath the water quick,
  And baffled he returns with angry cheer.
But Calcabrina, furious at the trick,     133
  Came flying behind him, fain the sinner might
  Escape, that he a quarrel might better pick;
And when the barrator was gone from sight,     136

---

116. Alichino advised the demons to quit the summit of the bolgia wall where they could be seen by the barrators below, and to retire a little way down its opposite slope (that is, go down toward the next inner bolgia) so as to be screened from view by the crest of the embankment. The fiends no sooner even glanced in the direction indicated (the side of the ridge away from the pitch) than the Navarrese leaped to safety.

## CANTO XXII

Against his fellow turned his claws, and so
Was locked with him above the ditch in fight.
A sparrow-hawk, however, proved his foe, 139
   Doughty to rend him well, and both dropped down
   To the mid-boiling of the pond below.
The heat unclutched them promptly thereupon, 142
   But rising, ne'ertheless, was not to be,
   So sticky were the wings of either one.
Then Barbariccia, like his company 145
   Lamenting, made four fly to the other coast
   With all their drags, and each right speedily
This side and that descended to his post; 148
   They stretched their hooks toward the belimèd pair,
   Who were already baked inside the crust;
And even in such plight we left them there. 151

---

146. *the other coast.* The opposite shore of the pitch.

## CANTO XXIII

*Eighth circle: Malebolge. Escape from the demons.
The sixth chasm: hypocrites, clothed in leaden
mantles. Catalano de' Catalani and Loderingo degli
Andolo. Caiaphas. Malacoda's lie unmasked.*

Silent and unaccompanied we trod
  Our lonely way, one first and one behind,
  As Minor Friars go when on the road.
By reason of the present brawl my mind     4
  Was unto Aesop's fable (that wherein
  He telleth of the mouse and frog) inclined;
For "now" and "at this moment" are akin     7
  No closer than those cases, if with heed
  They are compared, both end and origin.
And as one thought doth from another lead,     10
  So out of this a second then was born
  Whereby redoubled fear was in me bred.
Thus I reflected: These are put to scorn     13
  Through us with injury and scoff so great
  That it must be to them a bitter thorn.
If rage should now their malice aggravate,     16
  They will more fiercely follow us than flies
  The dog that snappeth up the leveret.
I felt my hair with fright already rise,     19

---

3. *Minor Friars.* Franciscans.
5. *Aesop's fable.* The tale alluded to is not really in Aesop, but was then regarded as his. It tells of a frog which offered to carry a mouse across a stream, and then treacherously tried to drown his companion. A kite, seeing the struggle, swooped down and devoured the frog; the mouse, according to some versions, escaped. The obvious application is that the demons, intending evil to the captured barrator, had themselves come to grief.

## CANTO XXIII

And was intent behind me when I said:
"Master, unless thou speedily devise
Hiding for thee and me, I sorely dread 22
   The Evil-claws. They follow on behind.
   Meseemeth I hear them, so am I afraid!"
And he: "Thy aspect would not be defined 25
   In me, if I were leaded glass, more soon
   Than I receive the image of thy mind.
Just then thy thoughts were set before mine own, 28
   The same in object, wearing the same face,
   So from the two my counsel is but one.
If into the next gulch we go, in case 31
   The right bank slopes enough to be descended,
   We shall escape from the expected chase."
To speak of this resolve he scarce had ended 34
   When I beheld them, and not distantly,
   Eager to seize us, come with wings extended.
My leader then at once took hold of me 37
   (Even as a mother wakened by the stir,
   Who close at hand the climbing flames doth see,
Snatches her child and flies, and having more care 40
   For him than for herself, not even will bide
   Enough to cast a garment over her)
And from the summit of that steep to glide, 43
   Laid him supine, the sloping rock upon,
   Which bounds the neighbouring chasm on one side.
To turn a land-mill's wheel did never run 46
   The water through a sluice at such a speed,

---

25-29. "If I were leaded glass—that is, a mirror—I would not more clearly catch the image of your body than my mind now apprehends your idea, which is identical with my own."

31. *the next gulch.* The sixth bolgia, which, as they go leftward along the embankment between it and the fifth, lies to their right.

46. *a land-mill's wheel.* An overshot wheel of a mill on a river bank, to which the water is conveyed through a steepening sluice. In a river-mill the water flows underneath.

Even when nearest to the paddles come,
As down that border bank my master slid, 49
  Bearing me off with him upon his breast,
  Not as a comrade but a son indeed.
Scarce in that gorge his feet the bottom pressed 52
  When they were right above us on the scaur;
  But he was not made fearful in the least,
For the high Providence that ordained them o'er 55
  The fifth ditch for its ministers, e'en so
  To depart thence deprived them of all power.
We found a painted people there below, 58
  Who in appearance tired and quite fordone,
  Weeping went round with steps exceeding slow.
Mantles had they with hoods that came far down 61
  Before their eyes, and of a cut the same
  As for the monks they make them in Cologne.
Gilded outside, these dazzle like a flame; 64
  Within all lead and of such weight they be
  That those of Frederick were but straw to them.
O cloak that wearies through eternity! 67
  Again we leftward bent our course, along
  With them, while to their plainings listened we;
But being thus burdened, came the exhausted throng 70
  So slowly that at each new step we found
  That fresh companions we were now among.
Whence I addressed my guide: "Some one renowned 73
  By name or deed I fain would meet with here.
  While thus we go, cast thou thy glance around."

---

58 ff. In the sixth bolgia are the shades of the hypocrites. They trudge on for ever beneath the weight of huge cloaks, gilded outside and fair to see, but really made of lead. For the hypocrite wears a fair semblance, but goes through life oppressed by a burden of dissimulation.

66. *those of Frederick*. Frederick II is said to have wrapped traitors in lead and thrown them into a heated cauldron. This tradition is without authority.

## CANTO XXIII

| | |
|---|---:|
| And of the speech of Tuscany aware, | 76 |
|   One cried behind us: "Oh, your steps abate, | |
|   Ye who press onward through the dusky air. | |
| I can perchance fulfil thy wish." Thereat | 79 |
|   My leader turned about and bade me: "Stay; | |
|   And then proceed according to their gait." | |
| I stopped, and two I saw in look display | 82 |
|   Great haste of spirit to be with me at once, | |
|   But their loads hindered and the narrow way. | |
| When they had reached us, long with eye askance | 85 |
|   They gazed at me, nor any word spake out, | |
|   But held at last between them conference: | |
| "This one appears from action of his throat | 88 |
|   Alive; and by what privilege, if dead, | |
|   Go they divested of the heavy coat?" | |
| Then: "Tuscan who hast come unto the sad | 91 |
|   College of hypocrites, oh, do not scorn | |
|   To tell us who thou art," to me they said. | |
| And I: "In the great city was I born | 94 |
|   And bred by which fair Arno's stream doth flow. | |
|   I wear the body I have always worn. | |
| But who are ye from whom such bitter woe, | 97 |
|   As I perceive, distils adown your cheek? | |
|   What punishment doth glitter on you so?" | |
| "Our orange mantles are of lead so thick"— | 100 |
|   Thus one of them did answer make to me— | |
|   "Their weight compelleth us like scales to creak. | |

---

88. *action of his throat.* That is, breathing, with which the throat moves.

92. *College.* Used in the sense of "assemblage," "company." So do we say "electoral college."

99. Dante is not yet aware of the real nature of their mantles. He has seen only the brightness of these.

102. The lamentations of the wearers are grotesquely likened to the creakings of overloaded weighing-scales.

Jovial Friars and Bolognese were we, 103
And by thy city chosen together twain—
I Catalano, Loderingo he—
As one alone of wont is, to maintain 106
Its peace; and what we were may be descried
Round the Gardingo still by token plain."
"O friars, your deeds iniquitous," I cried— 109
And then broke off, because there met mine eyes
One on the ground, with three stakes crucified.
He writhed all over, blowing forth great sighs 112
Into his beard, on seeing me; then spoke
Friar Catalano, marking, in this wise:

---

103 ff. The members of the lay order of Beata Maria were called Jovial Friars, because they were not required to lead an ascetic life. Catalano (kä-tä-lä′no) and Loderingo (lo-dĕ-reen′-go) were men of great importance—the former a Guelf, the latter a Ghibelline—and were elected jointly to the office of Podesta of Florence in 1266 as a compromise measure by which it was hoped impartial government would be secured, since they were outsiders and of opposing factions. But they combined, under cover of hypocrisy, in promoting their own gain, and favoured the Guelfs. During the year of their administration the palaces of certain prominent Ghibellines were destroyed, notably those of the Uberti in the Gardingo (gär-deen′-go) neighbourhood. Gardingo was the name of an ancient fortress and later of a street, near the Palazzo Vecchio.

111 ff. Lying on the ground with arms outspread in the figure of a cross, nailed to earth with three stakes (one piercing each hand and one his two crossed feet), and right upon the path so that all the hypocrites that toil beneath the ponderous weight of their leaden mantles must trample on him in going around the circuit of the bolgia, is Caiaphas, the Jewish high priest when Jesus was put to death. See John xi, 49-50: ". . . Caiaphas, being the high priest that same year, said unto them, Ye know nothing at all, nor consider that it is expedient for us, that one man should die for the people, and that the whole nation perish not." The same fate is suffered by his father-in-law, Annas (see John xviii, 13, 14, 24) and the others who shared in condemning Jesus to death and so brought all subsequent retributive woes upon the Jewish race. Their crucifixion is contrasted with that of Christ, who was lifted up to draw all men unto him, whereas they lie on the ground and bear the weight, not of one leaden cloak, but of all the hypocrisy in Hell.

## CANTO XXIII

"That one transfixed, on whom doth rest thy look, 115
  Advised the Pharisees 'twas meet and good
  That one sole man should die for all the folk.
Traverse and naked lies he on the road 118
  As thou beholdest, and he is made to feel
  Of every one that passes by, the load.
Thus too his father-in-law fares in this vale— 121
  Yea, all who in that council had consent
  Which for the Jews hath been a seed of bale."
Then I saw Virgil, wondering, o'er him bent 124
  Who was in figure of a cross outspread
  So basely in the eternal banishment.
Afterwards to the friar these words he said: 127
  "If 'tis allowed, count it not onerous
  To tell if on the right there lies ahead
Some gap, that we may both find exit thus, 130
  And hence need none of the black angels call
  To come and from these depths deliver us."
He answered: "From the great encircling wall 133
  There springs a crag, nearer than thou hast hope,
  That spans the savage valleys one and all,
Save only this, where broken is the cope 136
  Nor covers it; but ye can mount upon
  The ruins, that lie piled along the slope."
My leader stood awhile with head bowed down, 139
  And finally said: "Hereof he told amiss

---

124. Virgil marvels because he is not acquainted with the details of Gospel history, and his own previous expedition into the depths of Hell was before the death of either Christ or Caiaphas.

138. *along the slope.* The inner bank of this bolgia, climbing which they will gain the embankment crest between it and the seventh chasm.

140. *he.* Malacoda, who had said there was an unbroken bridge close by. The plausibility of his falsehood lay in the circumstance that it was told between two other statements, both true.

Who forks the sinners." And the friar thereon:
"Once at Bologna heard I many a vice 142
  Laid to the devil, and this among their stock:
  He is a liar and the father of lies."
Then with great steps my guide went on, his look 145
  Somewhat disturbed by anger at the cheat;
  And I forthwith those burdened ones forsook,
Following the prints of his belovèd feet. 148

---

142. Bologna (bo-lon'-yä), the home of Catalano, was the seat of a great theological school.

## CANTO XXIV

*Eighth circle: Malebolge. Climb from the sixth bolgia. The seventh chasm: thieves amid serpents. A phoenix-like transformation. Vanni Fucci. His prophecy.*

When in the youthful season of the year
  The sun beneath Aquarius warms his rays
  And night and day to equal length draw near,—
And when the hoarfrost on the ground portrays 4
  The image of her sister fair and white,
  But of her pen the point is gone apace,—
The rustic, now his fodder faileth quite, 7
  Rises and looks, and sees as if with snow
  The fields o'erspread, and on his thigh doth smite,
Returning indoors, and grieveth to and fro 10
  Like a poor wretch at his wit's end indeed;
  Then he goes out again, and hope from woe
Recovers when he finds with how great speed 13
  The world is changed, and takes without delay
  His staff and drives the young sheep forth to feed.
Thus did the master fill me with dismay 16
  When I observed how troubled was his brow,
  But quickly on the wound the plaster lay.
For at the shattered bridge arriving now, 19
  My guide turned unto me with that sweet look

---

2. The sun is in the zodiacal sign of Aquarius from late January to late February, a period when warmth begins to return with the early Italian spring.

4-6. The white sister of the hoarfrost is snow. The hoarfrost copies it, but soon melts—literally, the pen soon loses its point so that the copying can no longer continue.

18. *the plaster.* "Balm" would be a more natural figure of speech to us.

| Which first beneath the mountain's foot I saw.
| Then, having on some plan within him struck, | 22
|   The ruins he regarded carefully,
|   Opened his arms, and hold upon me took;
| And even as one who works deliberately | 25
|   And seems always beforehand to provide,
|   So upward toward the summit lifting me
| Of one huge block, another next he eyed, | 28
|   Saying: "Now cling to this and climb atop;
|   But whether it will bear thee first be tried."
| No path was this for them that wore the cope, | 31
|   For scarcely we, he light and I pushed on,
|   Made shift from jag to jag to scramble up;
| And were the ascent not shorter than upon | 34
|   The boundary opposite, I answer not
|   For him, yet surely I had been fordone;
| But seeing that Malebolge slants throughout | 37
|   Down toward the opening of the lowest pit,
|   The site of every vale brings it about
| That less is one side's than the other's height;— | 40
|   And thus at length we reached the summit, where
|   The highest block doth from the embankment split.
| So from my lungs exhausted was the air | 43
|   When I was up, I could no farther go—
|   Nay, seated me on first arriving there.
| "From sloth," the master said, "thou needs must now | 46
|   Escape, for never into fame men come
|   Lying on down, or coverlet below;

---

21. The allusion is to Dante's first meeting with Virgil, at the foot of the mount of righteousness, when the three beasts blocked the way.

31. *the cope.* The leaden mantle of the hypocrites.

34 *ff.* See the Note on Canto xix, 35.

42. Where the highest fragment of the pile of ruins joins the solid rock of the embankment crest.

## CANTO XXIV

And who without it doth his life consume 49
   Leaves of himself on earth no greater trace
   Than smoke in air or in the water foam.
Therefore rise up! Conquer thy weariness 52
   With spirit that conquereth in every fight,
   If not too much the body's weight oppress.
A longer stairway must be climbed. This flight 55
   Is not enough. Now to thy profit put
   My words, if thou didst comprehend aright."
Then stood I as though not so destitute 58
   Of breath as I had felt myself. "Go on,"
   I cried, "for I am strong and resolute."
Our way we took, the rocky ridge upon, 61
   Which rugged proved and difficult and strait,
   And steeper far than was the former one.
I talked the while, not to seem faint, whereat 64
   Out of the seventh moat rose from beneath
   A voice ill suited to articulate.
I know not what it said, though on the path 67
   We now were come right o'er the arching span,
   Yet he that spake appeared inflamed with wrath.
I bent to look, but living eyes in vain 70
   Would seek the bottom through that murk withal;
   Whence I: "O master, haste we to attain
The girth beyond and there descend the wall; 73
   For here I look below and naught discern,
   E'en as I listen and catch no words at all."

---

55. *A longer stairway must be climbed.* Presently, from the centre of the earth to the summit of the Mount of Purgatory.

61. Along the new causeway they proceed up the steep arch of a bridge over the seventh bolgia.

72-73. Dante is eager to finish their passage of the bridgeway over the seventh bolgia so that he and Virgil may descend some distance down the side of the embankment wall beyond, and thus get a nearer, practicable view of the bottom of this chasm. They do so in lines 79-81.

"Answer," he said to me, "shall be forborn 76
  Except the deed, since to a fair request
  Silent performance maketh best return."
So from the bridgeway, where it joins the crest 79
  Of the eighth embankment, climbed we down and stood
  Whence unto me the chasm was manifest;
And there within I saw such fearful brood 82
  Of snakes, yea, such a strange and varied host
  That even now the memory chills my blood.
Let Libya of her sands no longer boast, 85
  For though chelydri, pharëae, jaculi,
  Cenchres, and amphisbaenae breeds that coast,
Never such dire and numerous plagues did she 88
  Display, with all the region Ethiope,
  Nor yet the land that lies by the Red Sea.
Amid this cruel and dismal swarm a troop 91
  Of people ran, naked and terrified,
  That could nor magic stone nor shelter hope.
Behind them were their hands with serpents tied, 94
  Which in their loins fixed head and tail and wound
  Themselves in knots upon the other side.
And lo, at one close to our vantage ground 97
  Darted a snake that pierced him with its bite

---

85-90. By Libya is meant the Roman province of Africa, immediately to the west of Egypt. In the ninth book of his *Pharsalia* Lucan tells of the many kinds of serpents found there, and Dante's list is a selection from these. The chelydri make their path smoke, the pharëae furrow the ground with their tails, the jaculi are swift as darts, the cenchres never follow a straight course, and the amphisbaenae have a head at each end. Ethiopia and Arabia, two other desert regions, are also cited for comparison.

91 *ff*. This is the bolgia of the thieves. The serpents hunt them and bite them, whereupon ensue amazing metamorphoses. For the thief is himself a sly, stealthy, creeping serpent, of many shifts and disguises.

93. *magic stone*. Heliotrope was a fabulous stone which conferred invisibility on its wearer.

## CANTO XXIV

Just where the neck is to the shoulders bound.
Nor *I* nor *O* might one so quickly write 100
  As he took fire and burned, and where he stood
  Must needs drop down, to ashes changèd quite;
And when he, thus dissolved, the earth bestrewed, 103
  Together drew that dust and instantly
  And of itself his former shape renewed.
So the most famous sages testify 106
  The phoenix dies and is reborn complete
  When to five hundred years her age draws nigh,—
She who in life no herb or grain doth eat, 109
  Only amomum and incense tears, and who
  Hath nard and myrrh for her last winding-sheet.
And even as one who fell, nor wherefore knew, 112
  By demon-force that dragged him to the ground,
  Or other seizure man is heir unto,
When he gets up, looks fixedly around, 115
  Wholly bewildered by the grievous throes
  He underwent, and heaveth sighs profound,—
Such was the sinner after he arose. 118
  Power of God, oh, how severe that so
  In retribution showereth down its blows!
My leader asked him who he was; whereto 121
  He answer made: "I rained from Tuscany

---

100. *I* and *O* are written with a single stroke.

107. The phoenix was a fabulous Arabian bird which burned itself, when it attained the age of five hundred years, on a funeral pyre of incense and was reborn from the ashes. It is mentioned in many authors accessible to Dante, but he drew his own account of it from Ovid's *Metamorphoses*.

110. Amomum is an aromatic shrub or vine. Tears of incense are solid tear-shaped drops of the gum of aromatic plants.

113. Epileptics were supposed to be possessed by devils.

122 *ff*. The speaker is Vanni Fucci (vän'-nee foo'-tchee) of Pistoia (pees-to'-yä), a bastard (that is what he means when he calls himself "mule") and a notorious ruffian. Dante is surprised to find him here

Into this savage pit not long ago.
Bestial, not human life—mule that I be!— 124
   Suited me. I am Vanni Fucci, beast.
   Pistoia was a fitting den for me."
"Bid him not stir," I did my guide request, 127
   "And ask what crime thrust *him* down to this place,
   For one of blood and rage I saw him last."
And the wretch heard, and feigned not, but his face 130
   And thoughts directed unto me; and then,
   With look of dismal shame for his disgrace:
"That thou hast come upon me in this pain 133
   In which thou seest me, grieves me more," said he,
   "Than when I from the former world was ta'en.
I needs must grant what thou requirest of me. 136
   I am put down so far because I stole
   The fair adornments of a sacristy,
Which once was of another falsely told. 139
   But lest thou, having seen, be made elate
   If ever thou escape from this dark hole,
Open thine ears while I foreshadow fate. 142
   Pistoia shall be stripped of Neri first.
   Florence shall folk and fashions renovate.
A bolt of lightning in thick clouds immersed 145

---

rather than among the violent in the river of boiling blood, but as Vanni Fucci himself explains, he on one occasion robbed the rich and beautiful sacristy of San Jacopo, in the church of San Zeno at Pistoia; his greatest crime took precedence in determining his fate. An innocent man was about to be punished for the theft, but Vanni Fucci saved both that individual and himself by revealing the name of the receiver of the plunder, who was forthwith hanged.

143 *ff*. This obscurely worded prophecy relates to the following events connected with Dante's exile. In 1301 the Neri (nā'-ree) were driven out of Pistoia; many of them took refuge in Florence, where, on the coming of Charles of Valois, most of the Florentine Whites, including Dante, were exiled. This "renovation" of the folk and fashions of Florence occurred in November, 1301. In 1302, war (Mars) drew into the field

## CANTO XXIV

Mars shall from Val di Magra draw, and when
With bitter and impetuous storm doth burst
The roar of battle on the Pescian plain,    148
That bolt shall suddenly rend the mist apart
So that each Bianco must thereby have pain.
And this I tell that it may pierce thy heart."    151

Moroello Malaspina (the lightning bolt), a nobleman of Val di Magra (väl dee mä'-grä) and captain of the Black forces (the "thick clouds" amid which he moved); and from the storm and welter of confused fighting which followed, his headlong prowess burst forth victorious, so that the result was disastrous to the hopes of Dante and of every other Bianco (byän'-ko).

## CANTO XXV

*Eighth circle: Malebolge: seventh chasm. Vanni Fucci's appalling blasphemy. His punishment. Other thieves. Weird metamorphoses: man and reptile merge into one; man and reptile exchange forms.*

The thief, when he had ended finally,
  Made with each hand on high the fig obscene,
  And shouted: "Take them, God! They are for thee!"
Thenceforth have I a friend of serpents been,     4
  For one of them coiled then about his neck
  As though to say: "No more shalt thou blaspheme."
And round his arms fastened another snake,     7
  Which now before him was so tightly tied
  That he could not have given those limbs a shake.
Oh why, Pistoia, hast thou not decreed     10
  To burn to ashes and no longer last,
  Since in ill-doing thou goest beyond thy seed?
Throughout all Hell's dark circles though I passed,     13
  Spirit toward God so impious found I none—
  Not him who from the walls of Thebes was cast.
He, speaking not another word, was gone;     16
  And I beheld a centaur, full of wrath,
  Come crying: "Where, where is that savage one?"

---

2. *the fig.* A grossly indecent and insulting gesture, made by holding up the fist with the thumb protruding between the fore and middle fingers.

12. Tradition had it that Pistoia was founded by the remnants of Cataline's army.

15. *him,* etc. Capaneus. See Canto xiv, 46-72, and Note.

18. *that savage one.* Vanni Fucci.

## CANTO XXV

Maremma not so many serpents hath,     19
  I do believe, as on his croup had he
  To where our human form uptowereth.
Behind his neck, upon his shoulders, lay     22
  A dragon with its wings wide open spread,
  That sets on fire whomever in the way
It meeteth. "He is Cacus, yonder," said     25
  My lord, "who oftentimes a lake of blood
  Beneath the rock of Aventine hath made.
He goes not with his brothers on one road     28
  By reason of his fraudulent thieving when
  The mighty herd was in his neighbourhood.
To all his tortuous deeds gave ending then     31
  The club of Hercules, smiting perchance
  A hundred blows, whereof he felt not ten."
During these words the centaur had gone thence,     34
  And there beneath us now were spirits three,
  On whom had fallen not yet my leader's glance
Nor mine, until they shouted: "Who are ye?"     37
  Whereat unto a halt our story came,
  And upon them alone intent were we.
I knew them not, but so it chanced with them,     40
  As oft by hap is such occasion made,
  That one had reason to call another's name,

---

19. Maremma (mä-rĕm′-mä), as a swampy region, abounded in serpents.

25. *Cacus*. Dante errs in making him a centaur. He was a half-human, fire-belching monster, who stole some of the oxen which Hercules had taken from Geryon and was carrying home.

28. That is, scouring the plain about the river of blood. See Canto xii. His theft places him among the thieves.

33. He was dead by the first ten, but Hercules continued to smite.

40-45. We know little or nothing of the five Florentine thieves with whom the rest of this canto is concerned. Hearing the name of Cianfa (chän′-fä), Dante recognized the group as his fellow citizens and made the customary sign for silence.

Saying: "Where can it be that Cianfa stayed?" 43
   Whence I, to hold my guide's attention, now
   Upward from chin to nose my finger laid.
No marvel, Reader, will it be if thou 46
   To credit what I shall describe art slow,
   For this can I who saw it scarce allow.
While with unswerving gaze I watched them, lo, 49
   In front of one a reptile with six feet
   Sprang up and grappled him and clung thereto.
Its mid legs round his belly tried to meet; 52
   The forward pair about his arms were twined,
   And in his either cheek its fangs were set.
The rearmost feet along his thighs inclined; 55
   And having thrust its tail between the two,
   It bent it up against his loins behind.
Ivy to tree so rooted never grew 58
   As did that monster hideous to be seen
   Its limbs to the members of the other glue.
Then they together stuck, as if they e'en 61
   Were of hot wax, mingling their hues; nor this
   Nor that now seemed what earlier it had been,
Just as on burning paper upward flies 64
   Before the flame a colour that is brown
   And not yet black, though ever the white dies.
The other two looked on, and each made moan: 67
   "Alas, Agnel', how swiftly changest thou!
   Already art thou neither two nor one."
The pair of heads became but one head now, 70
   When both their visages appeared to fade
   Into one face where this nor that we saw.
Two arms from the four several strips were made; 73

---

49-51. The reptile with six feet is Cianfa de' Donati. He fastens on Agnel' (än-yĕl'), or Agnello de' Brunelleschi; and their two forms are blended into one.

## CANTO XXV

Of thighs, of legs, of belly, and of chest,
  Such members as no eye hath e'er surveyed.
Every original aspect was effaced; 76
  Neither yet both that monstrous image showed;
  And thus with languid step it from us passed.
Even as a lizard 'neath the dog-days' goad, 79
  Darting from hedge to hedge, appears to view
  A flash of lightning, if it cross the road,—
So was it, toward the bowels of the other two, 82
  That now a fiery little reptile came,
  Livid and black like peppercorn in hue;
And this transfixed that part in one of them 85
  Whereat we first with nourishment are fed,
  Then fell and lay stretched out before him, tame.
The pierced one gazed thereon, but nothing said— 88
  Nay, stood with feet all motion had forsook,
  And yawned, as sleep or fever on him weighed.
He at the snake, the snake at him did look; 91
  The wound of one, the other's mouth as well,
  Smoked violently, and mingled was their smoke.
Henceforth be Lucan mute, nor longer tell 94
  Of poor Sabellus and Nasidius,
  But wait to hear the things I shall reveal.

---

*79 ff.* The fusion of Cianfa and Agnello being accomplished and the resulting monster having gone thence, a "fiery little reptile," swift as a darting lizard beneath the fiercest scourge of the summer sun, bites one of the others, and thereupon that man and the creature slowly exchange shapes.

*94 ff.* Lucan tells in his *Pharsalia* how Sabellus and Nasidius, Roman soldiers in Cato's army crossing the Libyan desert, were bitten by venomous serpents. The body of Sabellus melted away into liquid corruption. That of Nasidius swelled into a formless mass, bursting his armour. Ovid in his *Metamorphoses* tells of the transformation of the Greek hero Cadmus into a serpent, and of the nymph Arethusa, pursued by the river-god Alpheus, into a fountain. Dante boasts that he will outdo all these; for whereas Ovid describes only the change of

Be Ovid mute of Arethusa and Cadmus;  97
  If him into a serpent, her a fount,
  His fabling turns, I am not envious;
For never of two natures front to front  100
  Transformed so that both shapes were able to
  Exchange their substance, hath he given account.
Such correspondence did hereon ensue  103
  That while the reptile cleft its tail forkwise,
  The wounded man his feet together drew.
His legs to one another stuck—the thighs  106
  And all—so closely there was visible
  No mark of joining, soon, to any eyes.
The figure that he lost, the cloven tail  109
  Of the other was acquiring, and its skin
  Was growing soft, and his own hard like scale.
I saw his arms drawn through the armpits in,  112
  And to the same extent they were amended
  The creature's two short feet a lengthening win.
Its hinder legs did then, together blended,  115
  Become that member which a man conceals,
  Whereas from this the wretch had two extended.
And while the smoke with a new colour veils  118
  Them both, and causes hair to grow on one,
  And this from off another's body peels,
The one rose up and fell the other prone,  121
  Yet shifted not the glare of baleful eyes

---

a human being into something else, he himself will describe a double change, man and reptile assuming each other's shape. Note Dante's way of expressing this, different from our own: he does not say that the respective bodies change shape, but that the shapes change substance. And so they do: what has been the figure of a man becomes not merely the form but the substance—flesh—of a reptile, and *vice versa*.

## CANTO XXV

'Neath which the exchange of visages went on.
He that now stood drew toward the temples his; 124
   And from the excess of matter thither sent,
   On the flat cheeks of him did ears arise.
That which retained its place, nor backward went, 127
   Formed of the superfluity a nose
   And did the lips to proper size augment.
He that on earth lay prostrate, forward throws 130
   His muzzle, and his ears into his head,
   Even as doth the snail its horns, withdraws.
His tongue, which was united once and made 133
   For uttering speech, divides itself in twain.
   The cleft one closes. Now the smoke is laid.
The soul that had become a monster ran 136
   Hissing along the vale, and in its wake
   Sputtered his unaccustomed words the man.
Then he turned unto it his new-grown back, 139
   And said to him yet left: "Buoso shall range,
   Crawling, as I have done, along this track."
Thus I beheld the seventh ballast change 142
   And change again; and may I be excused
   If my pen falter, since the thing is strange.
And though mine eyes might somewhat be confused, 145
   And 'wildered was my mind, these could not flee
   So covertly but that I well perused

---

140. Here we learn that the man who was bitten and became a reptile was named Buoso (bwo'-so), but the old commentators do not agree whether he was Buoso degli Abati or the Buoso Donati who is mentioned in Canto xxx, 44.

142. *ballast.* An expressive word for the living *rubbish* (for ballast is usually stuff of no value) of this seventh bolgia. The perpetual shifting of the sinners' shapes is thus likened to the shifting of ballast to and fro in a ship's hold.

| | |
|---|---|
| Puccio Sciancato's features—of the three | 148 |
|   Companions who came first, the only one | |
|   Not metamorphosed; and his mate was he | |
| Whose death thy tears, Gaville, now atone. | 151 |

148-151. Puccio Sciancato (poo'-tcho shän-kä'-to)—that is, Puccio the Lame—is that one of the three first comers who has suffered no change himself but has only looked on at the transformation of the others. He who from being the "fiery little reptile" became a man by exchange of bodies with Buoso is a certain Francesco Guercio de' Cavalcanti, who was slain by the villagers of Gaville (gä-veel'-lä) in Valdarno, whereupon his kinsmen wreaked a cruel vengeance on that village.

## CANTO XXVI

*Eighth circle: Malebolge. The eighth chasm: evil
counsellors. The swathing flames. Ulysses and
Diomedes. Of the last voyage of Ulysses.*

Rejoice, O Florence, since thou are so great
   That over land and sea thy pinions ply
   And through all Hell thy name doth penetrate.
Five citizens of thine like these found I                     4
   Among the thieves, whence cometh shame o'er me,
   Nor to great honour risest thou thereby.
But if toward morn our dreams have verity,             7
   In no long time thou shalt become aware
   What Prato, if no other, craves for thee.
And it were not too soon if now it were.                 10
   So might it be, since it must needs betide,
   For as I age, 'twill grow the heavier!
Thence we set out; and up those stairs supplied      13
   By juts of rock to our descending tread,
   Mounted and drew me after him my guide.
And as our solitary way we made                       16
   Among the splinters of the crag, in vain
   Had feet unhelped by hands that path essayed.

---

4. *Five citizens of thine.* And all of prominent families!

7. The old belief was that dreams in the early morning were especially likely to be prophetic.

9. The Prato (prä'-to) that, not to go further and mention others, would delight in misfortune to Florence—misfortune which Dante feels is inevitable and will but weigh heavier on him if deferred till his old age—is perhaps the neighbouring town of Prato; or perhaps Cardinal Niccolo da Prato, papal legate to Florence in 1304.

13-14. *those stairs . . . tread.* See Canto xxiv, 79-81.

I sorrowed then and sorrow now again 19
  When unto what I saw is turned my thought,
  And curb my genius with a tighter rein
Lest it should run where virtue guides it not; 22
  So that I may not cheat myself if grace
  Of star or better thing that gift hath brought.
As many as the glowworms when the face 25
  Of him who lights the world is least concealed
  The peasant resting on the hill surveys
(That hour when to the gnat the fly doth yield) 28
  Below him in the valley where perchance
  He gathers in his grapes or plows his field,—
With flames so many the eighth chasm's expanse 31
  Gleamed, as I saw when I was come to where
  Its bottom was revealed unto my glance.
And even as he the bears avenged whilere 34
  Elias' departing chariot did espy
  When straight toward Heaven the horses rose through air
(Nor could he follow it so that to his eye 37
  Was other sight than of the fire vouchsafed,
  Ascending like a tiny cloud on high)—
Thus moved along the gullet of the cleft 40
  Those flames, and each of them doth closely cloak
  A sinner, and not one betrays the theft.
I stood upon the bridge, uprisen to look, 43

---

19 *ff.* The eighth bolgia is occupied by givers of evil counsel. Dante's sorrow is caused by his contemplation of men of great and noble faculties who had misused their Heaven-bestowed gifts. The poet, conscious of his own powers, takes the lesson of their fate to heart.

25-26. *when the face,* etc. That is, at the time of year when the sun is below the horizon for the shortest time.

28. In other words, at twilight.

34 *ff.* Elisha, having beheld Elijah (Elias) carried living to Heaven in a chariot of fire, was mocked by some children, who were thereupon devoured by bears. See Second Kings ii.

42. *betrays the theft.* Reveals the fact that it hides a sinner within.

## CANTO XXVI

And should have fallen beneath (so far I leant)
   Without being pushed, had I not clutched a rock.
My leader, who observed me thus attent,             46
   Explained: "Within those fires the sinners bide.
   All by the shrouds wherewith they burn are pent."
"Master, I feel more certain," I replied,               49
   "Through hearing thee; but I had deemed it so
   Already, and fain would ask who doth reside
In yonder flame which cometh cloven as though    52
   From off the pyre it were ascending where
   Eteocles lay with his brother-foe."
He answered me: "Ulysses suffers there             55
   His torture, and Diomed; and thus they speed
   Together in punishment as in wrath they were.
Amid that blaze the ambush of the steed            58
   They expiate by which the door was made
   Whence issued forth the Romans' noble seed.
The craft whereby Deïdamia dead                   61
   Still mourns Achilles, there do they deplore;
   And there is the Palladium repaid."
"If they within those sparks possess the power    64
   To speak," I said, "to thee I pray, dear lord,
   And pray again with prayers a thousand more,
Forbid me not to wait while hitherward            67

---

52-54. When Eteocles, King of Thebes, and his brother Polynices, who was leader of the legended expedition of the seven chiefs against him, were slain by each other's hands, they were placed on one funeral pyre together; but a divided flame rose from it.

55 ff. Ulysses suffers because of his many perfidious stratagems. Among these were the capture of Troy by means of the Wooden Horse (as a result of which the Trojan ancestors of the Romans went to Italy); the decoying of Achilles from Scyros to the Trojan War, whereupon Deïdamia, whose lover that hero was, died of grief; and the theft of the Palladium, a sacred image of Pallas, from Troy. Diomedes was the most frequent companion of Ulysses in his enterprises (see, for example, *Iliad* x).

Draweth the hornèd flame. Thou surely seest
How with desire do I incline theretoward."
And he: "Praiseworthy indeed is thy request, 70
 And hence I grant it; but hold thou in check
 Thy tongue, and since to me is manifest
What thou wouldst have, be it my part to speak; 73
 For they, mayhap, might be despiteous
 To words of thine, since they themselves were Greek."
After the fire had come so near to us 76
 That time and place were in my leader's view
 Now fit, I heard him make beginning thus:
"O ye that in a single blaze are two, 79
 If aught of you deserved, while living, I—
 If much or little I deserved of you
When in the world I wrote the verses high— 82
 Move not, but let one tell the tale he hath
 Of whither, being lost, he went to die."
The greater horn of ancient flame therewith 85
 Began to waver, murmuring, even like
 A struggling fire which the wind wearieth;
Then, swaying to and fro its very peak 88
 As though it were a tongue for utterance, threw
 Out voice and words, and thus began to speak:
"When I left Circe, who had near unto 91

---

74-75. As mighty figures of ancient Greece, Ulysses and Diomedes would respect Virgil, a poet of classical antiquity who wrote of affairs connected with their exploits, more than they would Dante, a modern.

82. *the verses high.* The *Aeneid*. It is written with Trojan sympathies, but celebrates in some measure the great deeds of these great men and helps to immortalize them.

85. *The greater horn.* That containing Ulysses, the more eminent of the two heroes.

91 *ff.* This famous and exquisite story of the last voyage of Ulysses seems to be Dante's own invention. Tennyson's poem *Ulysses* was obviously inspired by it, and a comparison of the two will show how great the indebtedness in both detail and spirit.

## CANTO XXVI

Caieta past a year sequestered me
  Before Aeneas gave the name thereto,
Nor fondness for my son, nor piety 94
  For my old father, nor to these combined
  The love that should have cheered Penelope,
Could conquer the desire in me to find 97
  Experience of the world, and verily
  To know the vice and virtues of mankind.
I put forth on the deep and open sea 100
  With but a single ship and that small band
  Which even till then had not deserted me.
Both sides as far as Spain I saw the land, 103
  Far as Morocco, and Sardinia so
  And many another wave-girt island scanned.
My company and I were old and slow 106
  When of that narrow strait we came in sight
  Where Hercules set up his bounds to show
That no man should essay a farther flight; 109
  And having already on my left hand passed
  Ceuta, I passed Seville upon my right.
'O brothers,' said I, 'who unto the West 112
  Have through a hundred thousand perils come,—
  In this brief waking-time, the very last
That for your senses yet remains to run, 115
  Be willing nowise to renounce the view
  Of the unpeopled world behind the sun.

---

92-93. Dante follows Virgil in placing the home of the enchantress Circe at Cape Circello, on the southeastern coast of Italy, near the town of Caieta (modern Gaeta), named by Aeneas for his nurse.

100. *the deep and open sea.* The Mediterranean.

107. *that narrow strait.* The Straits of Gibraltar, whose rock and the eminence opposite it on the African shore were called "the Pillars of Hercules," being fabled to have been set there by that hero to mark the western limits of the world of men.

111. *Ceuta.* In Africa, opposite Gibraltar. Ulysses had passed through the Straits and entered the Atlantic.

| | |
|---|---:|
| Think of the seed from which ye sprang; for you | 118 |
|   Were never born like brutes your ease to take, | |
|   But manliness and knowledge to pursue.' | |
| So eager for the voyage did I make | 121 |
|   My comrades with this utterance brief and burning, | |
|   That scarcely could I then have held them back; | |
| And having set our stern unto the morning, | 124 |
|   We sped with oars for wings on that mad flight, | |
|   Ever and ever more to leftward turning. | |
| Now all the stars of the other pole the night | 127 |
|   Beheld, and ours so low they never shone | |
|   Above the ocean floor. Five times the light | |
| Upon the under surface of the moon | 130 |
|   Had been rekindled, as many times to die, | |
|   Since we that arduous quest had entered on, | |
| When there appeared to us against the sky | 133 |
|   A mountain dim with distance, and methought | |
|   That never any had I seen so high. | |
| Then we rejoiced, but weeping soon were taught, | 136 |
|   Because a tempest came from that new shore | |
|   And on the forepart of the vessel smote. | |
| Three times it whirled her round with all the stour | 139 |
|   Of waters; the fourth time the poop exposed | |
|   And sank the prow, as willed a Higher Power, | |
| Until above our heads the sea had closed." | 142 |

---

124 *ff*. They started westward, but continually bent their course more and more to the south. Presently the night displayed all the stars of the southern hemisphere, and after voyaging for five full months they espied a mountain of enormous height. This was the Mount of Purgatory, which, according to the poet's geography, was the only land in the southern hemisphere.

141. *a Higher Power*. Unlike the blasphemous Vanni Fucci, Ulysses observes the taboo against the utterance of God's name in Hell.

## CANTO XXVII

*Eighth circle: Malebolge: eighth chasm. The flame of Guido da Montefeltro. He learns from Dante of conditions in Romagna. His story.*

Already was the flame erect and still,
  Speaking no further, and was passing on
  Through licence of the gentle poet's will,
When, following after, came another one          4
  And made us, by a sound confused which burst
  Out of its top, to look e'en thereupon.
As that Sicilian bull which bellowed first           7
  With the lament of him—and rightfully—
  Who with his file had shaped its form accurst,
Did so rebellow with the sufferer's cry           10
  That though of brass throughout its whole extent,
  Still it appeared transfixed with agony,—
Thus, having from the fire no path or vent         13
  At once, converted was its woeful speech
  Into the language of that element.
But when the words unto its point did reach,      16
  Giving it that vibration which before
  The tongue had given them in uttering each,
We heard: "O thou whom I would fain implore;    19
  Who didst but now in Lombard phrase exclaim,

---

4. The sinner within this new flame is Guido, Count of Montefeltro, the great Ghibelline general and one of the ablest Italians of the thirteenth century.

7-12. Phalaris, a Sicilian tyrant of the sixth century B.C., had a brazen bull so constructed that when victims were placed in it and burned to death, their cries sounded like a bull's bellowing. Its maker, Perillus of Athens, was the first to die in it.

20-21. That is, in dismissing the flame of Ulysses and Diomedes.

'Depart thou; I solicit thee no more'!
Albeit somewhat tardily I came,—  22
   To pause and talk, ah, let this irk not thee!
   Thou seest it irks not me, though burned in flame.
If thou from that sweet land of Italy  25
   Art fallen of late, whence I bring all my sin,
   Down into this blind world, declare to me
If peace or war Romagna dwelleth in;  28
   For I was of the mountains there, between
   Urbino and the chain where doth begin
The Tiber." Still attentive did I lean  31
   O'er, when my leader touched me upon the side,
   Saying: "Speak. This one is Italian."
And I thereon without delay replied,  34
   For of mine answer I had made prepare
   Already: "O spirit that below art hid,
In thy Romagna is not, and was ne'er,  37
   Within her tyrants' hearts a lack of feud;
   But open war just now was none whate'er.
Ravenna stands as she for years hath stood;  40
   O'ercovering Cervia with his pinions' span,
   The eagle of Polenta there doth brood.

---

28-30. Romagna (ro-män′-yä) is, roughly, the region between the Po, the Apennines, the Adriatic, and the Reno. The hill country of Montefeltro lies at the foot of the Apennines, between Urbino (oor-bee′-no) and Monte Coronaro, the chain where the Tiber begins.

33. *This one is Italian.* Not a person of classical antiquity like Ulysses, with whom Dante could not speak.

38. *tyrants.* The great families of the various cities, ever at strife with each other.

40-42. Ravenna was ruled at this time by Guido da Polenta (po-lĕn′-tä), the father of Francesca da Rimini. His shield bore the figure of an eagle. Cervia (chĕr′-vyä), a small town about twelve miles from Ravenna, was included in his domains. The figure of speech suggests that his rule was beneficent, in contrast to the next two.

## CANTO XXVII

Beneath the green paws finds itself again 43
The town that once endured a siege so long
And piled a bloody heap of Frenchmen slain.
The old mastiff of Verruchio and the young, 46
Because of whom Montagna foully died,
Where such hath been their wont still ply the fang.
The lion cub of the white lair doth guide 49
The cities of the Lamone and Santerno,
From summer unto winter changing side.
And she with flank washed by the Savio,— 52
As 'twixt the plain she lieth and the mount,
'Twixt freedom and tyranny lives she even so.
Now prithee give us of thyself account. 55
Be not more obdurate than another was,
So may thy name on earth hold high its front."
After the flame, according to its use, 58
Had roared awhile, it moved the point this way
And that, and presently gave forth its voice:
"If I believed that he to whom I say 61
These words could ever stand beneath the sky
Again, my blaze would shake no more for ay.
But since alive from this deep cavity 64

---

43-45. Forli was successfully defended against a French army in 1282 by Guido da Montefeltro himself. In 1300 it was ruled by the Ordelaffi, whose arms bore a green lion.

46-48. The castle of Verruchio (vĕr-rook′-kyo) was possessed by the cruel Malatesta and his son Malatestino, lords of Rimini, from which it was some ten miles distant. Malatestino, the "young mastiff," was a half-brother of Francesca da Rimini's husband, Gianciotto. Montagna (mon-tän′-yä) de' Parcitati, a Ghibelline leader, was defeated and captured by Malatesta and murdered by Malatestino.

49-51. Faenza on the Lamone (lä-mo′-nā) and Imola near the Santerno (sän-tĕr′-no) were governed by Maghinardo de' Pagani da Susinana, whose shield bore a blue lion on a white field. He alternately supported the Guelfs and the Ghibellines.

52. Cesena, on the Savio (sä′-vĭ-o), is meant.

None has returned if true be what I hear,
I answer without fear of infamy.
I was a man of arms, then Cordelier 67
Became in hope, thus girt, amends to make;
And verily my trust had failed not e'er,
But for the great High Priest, who brought me back 70
(May ruin seize him!) to my former sin;
And how and why, thereof I fain would speak.
While I that form of flesh and bones was in, 73
Had of my mother, a course did I pursue
Not to the lion but to the fox akin.
All stratagems and covert ways I knew, 76
And used of these so skilfully the art,
My fame went forth, the ends of earth unto.
When I beheld myself now at that part 79
Of life where every one should strike the sail
And coil away the ropes, my anxious heart
Found irksome what before had pleased it well. 82
Repentant and confessed, I turned from men
To God. Ah, woe! 'twould not have lacked avail!
The Prince of the new Pharisees, who then 85
Was waging war, the Lateran anear—
And it was not with Jew or Saracen;
Christian were all his enemies, nor e'er 88
Had any of them at Acre's conquest been

---

67. *Cordelier.* A member of the Franciscan brotherhood.

70. *the great High Priest.* The Pope, Boniface VIII.

85 *ff.* Boniface, who proclaimed a crusade against the Colonna family. They occupied the stronghold of Palestrina (pä-lĕs-tree'-nä), about twenty-four miles from Rome. It was surrendered to Boniface on his false promises, and then demolished.

88 *ff. nor e'er,* etc. A repetition of the statement that the enemies of Boniface were neither Jew nor Saracen. The Saracens fought against the crusaders at Acre; the Jews traded with the lands of the Sultan, a practice forbidden to Christians.

## CANTO XXVII

Or in the Soldan's land a trafficker—
Neither his holy orders nor supreme 91
  Office regarded, nor that cord about
  My waist which made those wearing it more lean.
As in Soracte Constantine besought 94
  Sylvester's aid to cure his leprosy,
  So me, as one adept, this man sought out
To cure the fever of his pride; of me 97
  Asked he advice, which I would not bestow
  For drunken seemed his words. At last said he:
'Let not thy heart be troubled. Even now, 100
  Lo, I absolve thee. Teach me so to do
  That Palestrina I can overthrow.
Mine is the power, as well thou knowest is true, 103
  To lock and unlock Heaven, for the keys
  My predecessor held not dear are two.'
Then by such weighty arguments as these 106
  Driven to believe the silent course less fit:
  'Father,' said I, 'since this thy cleansing frees
Me from the sin which I must now commit, 109
  Large promise unto small fulfilment wed
  Will make thee triumph on thy lofty seat.'
Saint Francis came for me when I was dead; 112
  But rose up one of the black cherubim:
  'Forbear thou. Wrong me not,' that demon said.
'He must go down among my servants grim 115
  Because he counselled fraud; yea, ever since

---

94. According to legend, Constantine the Great appealed to Pope Sylvester I, who during the previous persecution of the Christians had hidden himself in a cave on Mount Soracte, to be cured of leprosy. Being restored to health and converted, the Emperor made to Sylvester the famous "donation" (see Canto xix, 115-117, and Note).

105. *held not dear.* The reference is to the abdication of Pope Celestine V.

113. *one of the black cherubim.* That is, a devil.

That time have I been at the hair of him.
No power can absolve impenitence, 118
   Nor yet the contradiction this will grant:
   That any at once both wills and eke repents.'
O wretched, then he seized me (grown how faint!), 121
   Chuckling: 'Perhaps thou didst not think to find
   In logic so exact a disputant.'
He bore me unto Minos, who entwined 124
   His tail eight times around his stubborn back,
   And having bitten it in his fury blind:
'A sinner for the shrouding fire!' he spake. 127
   Hence am I lost, thou seest in what bourn,
   And sorrowing, thus robed, my way I take."
When he had ended all his words forlorn, 130
   The flame departed, as with sound of rue,
   Twisting and tossing high its pointed horn.
We onward passed, my leader and I too, 133
   Along the rock to the next arch beyond,
   Spanning the fosse where those receive their due
That win their load by severing a bond. 136

---

136. That is, that assume their burden of sin and punishment by sundering obligatory ties.

## CANTO XXVIII

*Eighth circle: Malebolge. The ninth chasm: schismatics and strife-begetters cloven by the sword. Mohammed. Pier da Medicina. Mosca. The headless horror: Bertrand de Born.*

Who, even in words not bound by verse, could e'er
  Though oft recounting, fully tell of all
  The blood and wounds that now I saw appear?
Yea, every tongue assuredly would fail;     4
  Our speech and mind have been alike endued
  With powers that are, for such a theme, too small.
If reassembled were that multitude     7
  Who on Apulia's fateful soil of yore
  Were made to grieve by reason of their blood
Shed by the Trojans, and in the long war     10
  Which heaped of rings together such a pile,
  Even as Livy writes, who doth not err;
With them that felt the pain of blows erewhile     13
  Opposing Robert Guiscard; and with all them
  Whose bones are heaped at Ceperano still,
Where each Apulian won a traitor's shame;     16
  And those who fell at Tagliacozzo, too,
  When without weapons old Erard o'ercame:—
And one of them displayed his limb pierced through,     19

---

7-21. The poet declares that the horrors of the ninth chasm would not be matched if all the killed and wounded of five different scenes of bloodshed, which he names, could be gathered together at one time and place. The first occasion of carnage to which he alludes is the conquest of Apulia (ä-pool'-yä), which then meant all southeastern Italy, by the Romans, here called Trojans for their ancestors. The next is the Second Punic War, in which from the dead Roman knights after the battle of Cannae alone more than three and a half bushels

One his cut off, beside the horrors pent
In the ninth chasm, 'twould be naught to view.
Never by loss of middle piece or cant 22
A cask doth gape so wide as saw I one
Split from the chin unto the lower vent.
Between his legs his entrails hung; anon 25
His vitals and that gruesome sack I spied
Which turns to dross whate'er is swallowed down.
While all my gaze was on him occupied, 28
He looked at me, and with his hands laid bare
His breast. "Behold how I am rent," he cried.
"Yea, mark how is Mohammed mangled. There 31
In front of me doth Ali weeping go,
Ripped through the face even from chin to hair.
And all the rest thou seest with us below 34
Were sowers of schism and dissension, too,
During their lives, and hence are cloven so.
There is a devil here behind us, who 37
Thus cruelly fashions us and puts to pain
Of the sword's edge each of our throng anew
When we have circled round this gloomy lane, 40

---

of rings are said to have been collected. The third is the wars of Robert Guiscard (gees-kär'), the Norman, in southern Italy and Sicily. The fourth is the battle of Benevento, in 1266, when Manfred's cause was lost by the disgraceful flight of the Apulian barons. There was no battle at Ceperano (chā-pā-rä'-no), but the betrayal of that pass by the Apulians paved the way for Benevento. Fifth and last is named Tagliacozzo (täl-yä-kots'-so), where Manfred's nephew, Conradin, was overthrown in 1268. This battle was won by a clever stratagem of the elderly Erard (ā-rär') de Valéry.

31-32. Dante looked upon Mohammed not as the founder of a new religion, but as the creator of a schism. It was then generally believed that he had been originally a Christian. Ali, his son-in-law, engaged in war over the succession to the Caliphate and thereby caused a schism within Islam itself.

34-36. Once more the punishment is appropriate. The author of division is himself divided.

## CANTO XXVIII

Because with healing do our gashes close
Ere any of us before him comes again.
But who art thou that on the cliff dost muse—  43
It may be to postpone the torture set
For thee when thou didst thine own self accuse?"
"Death," said my master, "hath not reached him yet,  46
Nor doth guilt lead him to receive his due;
But that a full experience he may get,
I who am dead must needs conduct him through  49
The nether Hell, from round to circling round;
And this, as that I speak to thee, is true."
More than a hundred, hearing such words resound,  52
Stopped in the trench that they might on me stare,
Through wonderment forgetting every wound.
"Then do thou word to Fra Dolcino bear—  55
Thou that perchance ere long shalt see the sun—
If speedily he would not follow here,
To lay up food, lest a great snow anon  58
Should to the Novarese bring victory
Which otherwise not easily would be won."
Such were the words Mohammed spake to me,  61
His foot already lifted; ending now,
He strode therewith, and so departed he.
Another then, whose throat was piercèd through,  64

---

45. *when thou didst thine own self accuse.* Before Minos. See Canto v, 7-8.

55-60. Fra Dolcino (dol-chee′-no) was a religious impostor and the head of a schism in Lombardy that gained such dimensions that a crusade was preached against it. The heretics defended themselves with great valour in the mountains between Novara and Vercelli, but were finally reduced by famine due to a heavy snowfall which made it impossible for them to replenish their store of provisions. Dolcino was horribly tortured and then burned to death in June, 1307. Therefore this canto, "foretelling" his end, must have been written after that date.

64. After the religious schismatics, Dante encounters authors of political discord.

Who had no longer but a single ear
And a nose cut off close beneath his brow,
Halted to marvel with the others there 67
   Gazing, stood forth from them, and open laid
   His windpipe, red of surface everywhere.
"O thou whom sin condemneth not," he said, 70
   "Whom once on Latian soil mine eyes did know
   Unless they by resemblance are misled,
Remember Pier da Medicina's woe, 73
   If ever thou revisit the sweet plain
   That from Vercelli slopes to Marcabo;
And make it known to Fano's two best men, 76
   Who Messer Guido and Angiolello be,
   That they, unless our foresight here is vain,
Shall from their ship be cast into the sea 79
   And drowned in sacks near La Cattolica
   Through a ferocious tyrant's perfidy.
A crime so heinous Neptune never saw— 82
   Not even by pirates or by Argives done—
   Between the isles of Cyprus and Majorca.
That traitor who of eyes hath only one, 85
   And holds the land a certain spirit here

---

73. Pier da Medicina (pyâr dä mä-dee-chee'-nä) sowed enmity between the Polenta of Ravenna and the Maletesta of Rimini, by fomenting their suspicions of each other.

74-75. The plain of Lombardy slopes from the town of Vercelli (vĕrchĕl'-lee) at its western extremity to the stronghold of Marcabo (mär'-kä-bo), situated near the mouth of the Po, in the territory of Ravenna.

76 ff. Malatestino, the one-eyed lord of Rimini, coveting the town of Fano (fä'-no), invited Guido (gwee'-do) del Cassero and Angiolello (än-jo-lĕl'-lo) da Cagnano, two of its chief citizens, to a conference at La Cattolica (kät-to'-lee-kä), a place on the Adriatic between Fano and Rimini, and then had them treacherously seized and drowned as they sailed thither.

83. *Argives*. The Greeks were famous as free-booters.

84. From one end of the Mediterranean to the other.

## CANTO XXVIII

Would fain his gaze had never fed upon,
Shall bid them come, as with him to confer, 88
 And then so do that need for them shall be
 Against Focara's wind, of vow nor prayer."
And I to him: "Show and explain to me, 91
 If tidings of thee thou wouldst have me take
 To earth, which is it rues that sight." Then he
Laid hand on one of his companions' cheek, 94
 And oped the mouth of him to our survey,
 Exclaiming: "This is he, nor doth he speak.
This man, when banished, swept the doubt away 97
 In Caesar's mind, by saying that one prepared
 Can only with detriment sustain delay."
Ah, how affrighted Curio appeared 100
 With tongue cut from his throat—how in a daze—
 ·He that erewhile in speech so greatly dared!
Now one whose hands were both lopped off, did raise 103
 The stumps on high, there in the murky gloom,
 So that the blood from them befouled his face,
And cried: "Recall that Mosca, too, by whom— 106
 Alas!—'A thing done hath an end,' was said,
 Which to the Tuscans proved a seed of doom."

---

89-90. The headland of Focara (fo-kä´-rä), near La Cattolica, was so notorious for its gales that sailors used to supplicate Heaven for a safe passage of it. Guido and Angiolello, being already drowned, did not need to do so.

93. *which is it rues that sight.* That is, which spirit wishes, as Pier said in lines 86-87, that he had never seen Rimini.

97-99. The tribune Curio, banished from Rome by the party of Pompey, advised Caesar to lead his army across the river Rubicon, the boundary of his province, and thus begin the Roman Civil War. The Rubicon flows near Rimini.

106. Mosca (*mo´*-skä) de' Lamberti, by instigating the Ameidi family to murder Buondelmonte, who had broken troth with a daughter of their house, inaugurated the feud between the Guelf and Ghibelline factions of Florence.

| | |
|---|---:|
| "And to thy kindred, death," 'twas mine to add; | 109 |
|   And he, by woe thus heaped on woe constrained, | |
|   Went on his way like one through sorrow mad. | |
| But I to watch the changing throng remained, | 112 |
|   And saw a thing anon that I should be | |
|   Afraid to tell of, by no proof sustained, | |
| Were it not that conscience reassureth me, | 115 |
|   That good companion which emboldens one | |
|   Beneath the breastplate of his purity. | |
| Truly I saw, and seem to look upon | 118 |
|   It still, a headless body onward tread | |
|   As the others of that dismal herd went on. | |
| And by the hair it held the severed head, | 121 |
|   Swung from its hand as 'twere a lantern lit; | |
|   And this did eye us, and "Ah me!" it said. | |
| It made itself a lamp for its own feet, | 124 |
|   And they were two in one and one in two; | |
|   How this may be, he knows who ordereth it. | |
| When close beneath our bridge the monster drew, | 127 |
|   It lifted high its arm, with the whole head, | |
|   Nearer to bring its words of bitter rue. | |
| "Thou who dost breathing go to scan the dead," | 130 |
|   It spake, "behold this grievous penalty. | |
|   Consider if any great as mine be had. | |
| And learn, that tidings thou mayst bear of me: | 133 |
|   Bertrand de Born, who gave the counsels fell | |
|   Unto the youthful king—lo, I am he. | |
| Against the sire I made the son rebel. | 136 |
|   With wicked goadings did no more than this, | |

---

134-136. Bertrand de Born, one of the great Provençal troubadours and a doughty knight, set the young Prince Henry at strife with his father, Henry II of England. The prince is called "king" because he was crowned during the lifetime of his father; he did not actually live to succeed to the throne.

## CANTO XXVIII

By David and Absalom, Ahithophel.
Since persons joined so closely I amiss 139
  Severed, I bear my brain—oh, misery!—
  Severed from its source, which in this body is.
Thus retribution may be seen in me." 142

## CANTO XXIX

*Eighth circle: Malebolge: ninth chasm. Of Dante's
kinsman, Geri del Bello. The tenth and last chasm:
falsifiers. The pestilence-smitten multitude. The
two lepers: Griffolino and Capocchio, alchemists.*

The many folk with wounds diverse and deep
  Had made mine eyes so drunk with tears that fain
  They were to linger there awhile and weep.
But Virgil said: "Why dost thou still remain,     4
  Watching? Why is thy glance still bent upon
  The woeful, mutilated shades in pain?
Thus at no other chasm hast thou done.     7
  Consider, if thou thinkest to count them, that
  The vale for two and twenty miles winds on.
Already is the moon beneath our feet;     10
  Short is the time now left us for our way,
  And things there are thou hast not looked on yet."
"If thou," in answer I began to say,     13
  "Hadst but divined the reason of my gaze,
  Thou mightest have granted me a longer stay."
Meantime my guide was going on apace;     16
  And I behind him came, while this reply
  Was spoken, and added: "In that hollow place
Whereon mine eyes were held so fixedly,     19
  Wails for that sin which there hath payment sore
  A spirit, methinks, of mine own family."

---

9. That twenty-two miles is the circumference of the ninth bolgia, is the first specific measurement given in the *Inferno*. But see Note on Canto xxx, 86-87.

10. If the moon, just past the full, is under foot, the sun must be almost overhead; it is nearly noon of Saturday, the day before Easter.

## CANTO XXIX

Then said the master: "Let thy mind no more 22
With him be troubled. Elsewhere turn thy thought,
And let him even abide as heretofore;
For 'neath the bridge I saw him point thee out 25
And make with finger threats most vehement;—
Geri del Bello then his name I caught.
So wholly wast thyself on him intent 28
Who formerly possessed Hautefort that thou
Didst not look thither; and he onward went."
"O guide, his violent death, which standeth now 31
Yet unavenged," I said, "by any of them
Who are partakers of the shame, I trow
Made him indignant; therefore, as I deem, 34
He strode away without a word to me;
And hence my pity is greater still for him."
Conversing thus, to the first point came we 37
From which the next vale, had there been more light,
Even to its very bottom one might see.
Now when at last we stood upon the height 40
O'er Malebolge's final cloister, whence
Its brethren were revealed unto our sight,
Then was I pierced by manifold laments, 43

---

27. Geri del Bello (jā'-ree dĕl bĕl'-lo) was a first cousin of Dante's father. He sowed discord among the members of the Sacchetti family of Florence, and was therefore killed by one of them.

29. Bertrand de Born was lord of Hautefort (ot-fŏr').

37 ff. Dante and Virgil come within view of the tenth and last bolgia, in which are punished falsifiers of all kinds. These include alchemists (falsifiers of metals), fraudulent impersonators, counterfeiters, and liars. They are afflicted with various diseases, which alter their appearance as they on earth falsely altered the appearance of things. The poet compares them to the inmates of the hospitals of three notoriously unhealthy regions at the worst season for heat and malaria. Valdichiana (väl-dee-kyä'-nä) and Maremma (mä-rĕm'-mä), in eastern and western Tuscany respectively, and the lowlands of Sardinia alike were swampy and pestilential.

Which had their shafts with pity barbed, so I
Covered mine ears against them with my hands.
Such suffering as if every malady 46
From Valdichiana's hospitals, and from
Maremma and Sardinia, 'twixt July
And late September, should together come 49
All in one chasm, was there, over whose lip
Rose, as from mortifying limbs, the fume.
From the long bridge to the last embankment steep 52
Descended we, the left hand still towárd,
And then more clearly I beheld that deep
Wherein the servant of the Most High Lord, 55
Justice infallible, sets, their dooms to dree,
The falsifiers she doth here record.
I do not think it was more sad to see 58
The people of Aegina all infirm,
With the air full of such malignity
That every creature, even to the tiniest worm 61
Fell dying, whereon was the ancient stock
(So do the poets verily affirm)
Restored from seed of ants, than 'twas to look 64
Upon the spirits through that valley black
Languishing in great heaps of mingled folk.
One on another's belly lay, or back; 67
Still others on their hands and knees did creep,
Dragging themselves along the dolorous track.
We without speech moved onward step by step, 70
Gazing upon and listening to the sick

---

52 ff. Having crossed the bridge over the tenth bolgia, they see into its depths better from the top of the embankment which forms the inner wall of that chasm. They proceeded leftward along the embankment, looking down into the bolgia as they go.

59. It is told in classical mythology that Juno sent a pestilence which killed all the inhabitants of the island of Aegina save King Aeacus, at whose prayers Jove repopulated it by turning ants into men.

## CANTO XXIX

Who could not lift their bodies. In that deep
I saw two sit, leaning together, like 73
  Pans that against each other warming lean,
  From head to foot with scabs o'erspotted thick;
And never currycomb I yet have seen 76
  Plied by a groom the while his lord doth wait,
  Neither by one who is for slumber fain,
As each plied fast upon himself the bite 79
  Of claws, for rage of itching that assails
  These twain, who have no other help for it.
And so they drew the scurf down with their nails 82
  As with a knife one scrapeth flake by flake
  A bream or other fish with larger scales.
"O thou," to one my guide began to speak, 85
  "Who with thy fingers art dismailing thee
  And sometimes, too, dost pincers of them make,
Tell us if an Italian chance to be 88
  Among those here confined; so may suffice
  Thy nails unto their work eternally."
"Italian are we both, on whom thine eyes 91
  Now look, disfigured so," that one replied,
  Weeping, "but who art thou inquiring this?"
And: "I am one," answered thereto my guide, 94
  "Who with a living man from round to round
  Descend, that I may show him Hell." Then wide
The mutual prop was broken at such sound, 97
  And trembling turned they toward me instantly,
  As others did who heard him by rebound.
The master good beside me drew quite nigh, 100
  And: "Ask whate'er thou wilt," to me did say;
  And since it was his pleasure, began I:
"So from the minds of men may fade away 103
  Never upon the earth your memory,
  But live beneath the suns of many a day,—

Tell who ye are and of what folk are ye. 106
    Let not your foul and loathsome doom forbid
    Your revelation of yourselves to me."
"I of Arezzo was," did the one confide, 109
    "By Albert of Siena burned; but it
    Brings me not here—the thing for which I died.
'Tis true I told him, jesting, that in flight 112
    I could through air upraise myself, whereon
    He, that had vain desire and little wit,
Willed that the art I show him, and alone 115
    Because no Daedalus I made him then,
    He had me burned by one who called him 'son';
But unto the last pocket of the ten, 118
    Minos condemned me, he that cannot err,
    For the alchemy I practised among men."
And to the poet I said: "Now was there e'er 121
    A race so frivolous as the Sienese be?
    Surely with them the French cannot compare."
Whereat the other leper, hearing me, 124
    Responded to my words: "Leave Stricca out,
    He who was wont to spend so moderately;
And Niccolo, the first to institute 127

---

109. This alchemist of Arezzo (ä-rĕt'-so) is identified by early commentators as one Griffolino; but nothing is known of him.

116. That is, because he was not able to fly like Daedalus, the fabled artificer of Crete (see Canto xvii, 109, Note).

117. *one who called him 'son.'* The Bishop of Siena (see-ĕn'-a). Albert, who belonged to a prominent Sienese (see'-ĕn-eez) family, was reputed to be his illegitimate son.

125 *ff*. The exceptions are ironical. Stricca (streek'-kä), Niccolo (neek'-ko-lo), Caccia (kä'-tchä) of Ascian' (ä-shän'), and the Abbagliato (äb-bäl-yä'-to) were all members of a group of gay young men of Siena who were known as the "spendthrift brigade." It is not certain what was the expensive use of cloves referred to. By "the garden where such seed takes root" is meant Siena, where such folly, once introduced, takes a firm hold.

That use of cloves which is extravagance,
   Within the garden where such seed takes root;
And the brigade where Caccia of Ascian's          130
   Vineyards were squandered and his many a tree,
   And the Abbagliato's wit found utterance.
But that thou mayest learn who seconds thee       133
   Against the Sienese, keenly look, that so
   My face will meet thy gaze, and thou shalt see
I am the shadow of Capocchio,                       136
   Whose alchemy did metals falsify.
   Thou must recall, if thee I rightly know,
How good an ape of nature once was I."           139

---

136. Capocchio (kä-pok'-kĭ-o) was an alchemist who was burned at Siena in 1293.

## CANTO XXX

*Eighth circle: Malebolge: tenth chasm. The rending maniacs. Master Adam. Sinon and Potiphar's wife. The quarrel of the arch-knaves. Dante's unworthy curiosity. His shame and penitence.*

When Juno was against the Theban blood
   Incensed with rage because of Semele,
   As she on more than one occasion showed,
On Athamas fell such insanity                                                            4
   That, seeing his wife with double burden pass
   Of her two sons on either hand, cried he:
"Let us spread out the nets, the lioness                                              7
   And cubs that I may take, in transit found";
   And then stretched forth his talons pitiless,
Seized upon one, Learchus, whirled him round,                10
   And on a great rock dashed him, shattering;—
   Whereat herself and other charge she drowned.
And at the time when Fortune's downward swing        13
   Brought low the Trojans' overweening pride,
   So with his kingdom was undone the king,
Sad Hecuba, when she had seen how died                         16
   Polyxena, and now in misery
   A captive friendless and forlorn, descried
Upon the sand her Polydorus, she,                                       19

---

1-21. This canto opens with two examples of madness, from classical mythology, which serve as comparisons with that of the maniacs whom Dante next beholds. The first is the insanity which Juno, implacable in her wrath against the family of Semele because of Jupiter's love for that Theban princess, visited upon Athamas, the husband or lover of Semele's sister. The second example is that of Hecuba, Queen of Troy. Her city taken by the Greeks, her husband Priam dead, her daughter Polyxena sacrificed on Achilles' tomb, and herself an old woman and a slave, she

## CANTO XXX

Bereft of reason, like a dog did bark,
   Sorrow had wrung her soul to such degree.
But ne'er of Thebes or Troy might any mark      22
   Such furious frenzies with a cruelty,
   For goading beasts or human limbs, so stark
As in two pale and naked shapes which I      25
   Beheld run biting even as a boar
   Runneth when he is loosed from out his sty.
The one came to Capocchio, and tore      28
   His neck, and thereby dragged him so it made
   His belly scrape along the rocky floor.
And the Aretine, who stayed there trembling, said      31
   To me: "'Tis Gianni Schicchi—that fierce sprite—
   And harrying others thus he rangeth, mad."
"Oh," I replied, "as thou wouldst shun the bite      34
   Of the other's teeth, forbear not to unfold
   Who it may be, before departeth it."
And he thereto: "That is the ancient soul      37
   Of wicked Myrrha, who her father e'en
   In other than a rightful love did hold.
And thus it was she came with him to sin,      40
   By counterfeiting of another's form;
   Just so did that one, to obtain the queen

---

found washed up on the beach the body of her last remaining son, Polydorus, who had been murdered by Polymestor, the Thracian king in whose safe keeping she had placed him. Forthwith she was bereft of reason, and barked like a dog.

31. *the Aretine.* Capocchio's fellow leper of the preceding canto.

32. Gianni Schicchi (jän'-nee skeek'-kee) was a member of the Cavalcanti family and a famous mimic. On the death of Buoso Donati (bwo'-so do-nä'-tee), Gianni was induced to impersonate the dead man in bed and dictate a will in favour of Buoso's son. He took advantage of this opportunity to insert some bequests to himself, Gianni, among which was that of a very fine mare.

38. The story of the incestuous love of Myrrha for her father Cinyras, King of Cyprus, is told in Ovid's *Metamorphoses* x.

42-43. *that one ... going now herefrom.* Gianni Schicchi.

Of all the herds—he going now herefrom— 43
 Dare as Buoso Donati to disguise
 Himself and make a will most duly drawn."
After those ravening two, on whom mine eyes 46
 Had fixed themselves, were passed, I turned about
 To mark the other wretches born amiss.
I saw one shaped in fashion of a lute 49
 If only had his groin at the place
 Been severed where a man doth forkèd sprout.
The heavy dropsy, which proportionless 52
 By ill-digested humours makes each part,
 So the paunch corresponds not with the face,
Was causing him to hold his lips apart, 55
 As doth for thirst the patient feverous
 One toward the chin and upward one contort.
"O ye, who in this world of woe are thus 58
 Exempt from every punishment (I have
 No knowledge why), look," he exhorted us,
"On Master Adam's misery! When alive, 61
 I had such plenty as all desires fulfils,
 And now, alas, one drop of water crave.
The little brooks that from the verdant hills 64
 Of Casentine into the Arno drain,
 Making their channels cool and moist—those rills
Ever before me stand, and not in vain; 67

---

61 *ff.* Master Adam was a famous coiner of the thirteenth century. He was induced by Guido (gwee'-do) and Alessandro (ä-lĕs-sän'-dro) and their brother, the counts of Romena (ro-mā'-nä), to make florins of only twenty-one instead of twenty-four carats of gold, and for this was burned by the Florentines. The florin bore on one side the figure of John the Baptist.

65. The Casentino (here rendered in the trisyllabic Anglicized form "Casentine," like "Aretine" and "Aventine") is a district in the mountains at the head of the valley of the Arno. The castle of Romena was situated in that locality.

## CANTO XXX

Far more their vision parches me and dries
   Than doth the disease that strips my face so lean.
For Justice, always faithful to chastise, 70
   Taketh occasion from the place I sinned
   Still more to speed the passage of my sighs.
There is Romena, where I falsely coined 73
   The money with the Baptist's image dight,
   And therefore my burnt body left behind.
But could I see vile Guido in such plight 76
   Or Alessandro or their brother, ne'er
   For Branda's fount would I exchange the sight.
One is already come, if they who here 79
   Run raving speak the truth, but what of good
   Is that to me whose limbs are fettered? Were
I only still so light that I but could 82
   Move in a hundred years one inch's space,
   I even now would be upon the road
In search of him among this loathly race, 85
   Although eleven winding miles it be
   Around, and half a mile across—no less.

---

78. Branda (brän'-dä) was the name of a spring near Romena, as well as of the famous fountain in Siena.

79. Guido died before 1300.

86-87. Here again are exact measurements. On the basis of them and of the previous specific information given in xxix, 9, much labour has been uselessly expended in trying to compute the dimensions of Dante's Hell. The fact is that the poet wished only to convey the general impression of its enormous extent and rapid narrowing toward the bottom; for since the journey of Dante and Virgil through it in twenty-four hours was incapable of rationalization, details as to the distance they traversed had to be avoided. The circumference of eleven miles assigned to the last bolgia does not even harmonize with what follows. For "eleven miles around" means a diameter of three and one-half miles, and there is a considerable distance between the top of this bolgia's inner wall and the edge of the precipice guarded by the giants, that descends to the lowest circle, the floor of which must, then, be little more than two miles across—its radius scarce more than a mile from the precipice foot to

| | |
|---|---|
| Through them I dwell in such a family; | 88 |
|   Those florins they persuaded me to strike | |
|   Which had three carats of impurity." | |
| "Who are the two poor wretches, smoking like | 91 |
|   Wet hands in winter," I asked him, "lying e'en | |
|   Close to thy right side?"—"When into this dike | |
| I rained," he answered, "here I found them then; | 94 |
|   And since that time they have not turned, and eke | |
|   Will not to all eternity, I ween. | |
| The man is Sinon, Troy's deceitful Greek; | 97 |
|   The woman unto Joseph's wrong deceived. | |
|   From raging fever send they forth such reek." | |
| And one of them, who felt perchance aggrieved | 100 |
|   At being named thus darkly, on that pot | |
|   Of rigid belly a great buffet heaved. | |
| It sounded like a drum; and thereon smote | 103 |
|   Him Master Adam full across the face | |
|   With limb which any whit less hard was not, | |
| Saying to him: "Although my body is | 106 |
|   Deprived of motion and thus weighted sore, | |
|   I have an arm free for such need as this." | |

---

where Lucifer stands at its centre, reared "from his mid-breast forth above the ice." Now, Dante says that Lucifer's arms are greater in comparison with a giant's whole figure than a giant is in comparison with Dante; and the giants are certainly not less than fifty-five feet tall—are perhaps much taller. This makes Lucifer have a stature of one thousand feet or more; the visible part of him must have towered up two or three hundred feet, at least. Yet when Dante and Virgil first behold him, *after they have crossed three of the four concentric zones into which the bottom of the pit is divided*, he is still so distant that he appears like a windmill seen far off. Obviously, then, it must be very much more than a mile—rather, it must be several miles—from the outer edge of the ninth circle to its centre.

97 ff. The fever-stricken pair are Sinon, the Greek who with a lying tale persuaded the Trojans to take the Wooden Horse within their city walls, and Potiphar's wife, who slandered Joseph to her husband (Genesis xxxix).

## CANTO XXX

The other answered: "When thou wentest of yore 109
 Unto the fire, 'twas not so ready, in truth;
 But for thy coining quite as free, and more."
The dropsical: "In this thou sayest sooth. 112
 A less veracious witness formerly
 Wast thou at Troy when put upon thine oath."
"If I spake falsely, thou didst falsify 115
 The coin," said Sinon. "For one crime I groan,
 But thou for more than any fiend comes nigh."
"Think of the horse, thou perjurer!" thereon 118
 He of the swollen paunch gave answer back.
 "Be this thy torture: o'er the world 'tis known."
"Thy torture be the thirst which maketh crack 121
 Thy tongue, and the foul water which doth now
 Puff up thy belly before thine eyes," the Greek
Replied.—"As ever, to speak ill thy jaw 124
 Thus open gapes," the counterfeiter said.
 "If I have thirst, though sodden, yet hast thou
The burning fever and the aching head. 127
 To lap Narcissus' mirror greedily,
 Thou wouldst no lengthy invitation need."
I hung intent on listening, when to me 130
 The master said: "Aye, look, forsooth, thy fill!
 It wants but little that I quarrel with thee."
And when I heard him speak with accents chill 133
 Of anger, I turned toward him with such shame
 That through my memory it swirleth still.
Now as a man who dreams of his own bane, 136
 And dreaming wishes that he dreamt, and so
 For what is real, as it were false, is fain,—
Even thus did I, bereft of utterance, grow; 139

---

117. The coinage of each debased florin is reckoned a separate sin.
128. *Narcissus' mirror.* Water. Narcissus, in classical mythology, became enamoured of himself on beholding his image in a pool.

I would excuse myself, and could not guess
That I was doing it the while;—but lo:
"A greater fault than thine hath been, by less 142
Of shame," my leader said, "is washed away.
Therefore unburden thee of all distress;
And reckon that I am beside thee ay, 145
Should it again fall out that Fortune place
Thee where are people in like wrangling fray,
For the desire to hear such things is base." 148

---

141. *That I was doing it the while.* By so evident contrition.

## CANTO XXXI

*On the edge of the central well. The giants in the darkness. Nimrod. Ephialtes. Antaeus. The descent into the pit.*

One and the selfsame tongue first wounded me
  So that it reddened all my countenance,
  And then supplied me with the remedy.
Thus do I hear it of Achilles' lance—                         4
  His and his father's: first the source of bale
  'Twas wont to be, and then came healing thence.
We turned our backs upon the wretched vale              7
  And overpassed the bank that girds it round.
  While crossing, neither spoke a syllable.
There less than night and less than day we found,       10
  And now my vision very little went
  Before me; but I heard a horn to sound,
So loud it would have made all thunder faint,            13
  Whence wholly were mine eyes, that countertraced
  The course thereof, in one direction bent.
After the dolorous rout which brought to waste         16
  Charlemagne's sacred army, never blew

---

4-6. The spear which Achilles inherited from his father Peleus possessed the magic power of healing, especially in the case of wounds it had itself inflicted.

7. *the wretched vale.* The last bolgia, of the plague-smitten falsifiers.

10. *less than night and less than day.* The dimmest twilight.

14-15. *countertraced The course thereof.* Sought the direction of the sound.

16-18. When, through the treachery of Ganelon (xxxii, 123, and Note on xxxii, 113 *ff.*), the rear-guard of Charlemagne's army (called "sacred" because it had been engaged in a campaign against the Saracens in Spain —a holy war) was surprised and annihilated in the pass of Roncesvalles,

Roland on his so terrible a blast.
Not long that quarter my attention drew, 19
  When many lofty towers beheld I there,
  Methought. "What city cometh into view,
Master?" said I. And he: "Thy gaze doth peer 22
  Too deep into the darkness, and therefore
  It is that thine imagining doth err.
When thou approachest, how the sight is sore 25
  Deceived by distance, clearly shalt thou see;
  Hence onward spur thyself a little more."
Then by the hand he took me lovingly, 28
  And said: "Before we any closer go,
  That the reality may seem to thee
Less strange, they are not towers, thou must know, 31
  But giants; and from the navel downward they
  Stand in the pit, all round its bank, a-row."
As, when a fog is vanishing away, 34
  Whate'er the vapours hide which crowd the air
  Little by little doth its shape display,—
So, while I pierced the dense, dark atmosphere 37
  As more and more we neared the chasm's bound,
  Fled error from me, greater grew my fear.
For even as on its circling rampart's round, 40
  Montereggione wears a coronal
  Of turrets, so the horrible giants crowned
With half their bodies the embankment wall 43

---

Roland, their leader and chief hero, blew in the moment of death so mighty a blast on his horn that Charlemagne, many miles away, heard it.

33. *the pit*. The last abyss of Hell, which Dante and Virgil now approach. The giants, as rebels against God (here again the distinction between Jehovah and Jove is blurred), border the mouth of the central well, which constitutes the ninth circle, the place of traitors.

41. Montereggione (mon'-tā-rĕj-jo'-nā) was a strong castle near Siena.

## CANTO XXXI

That hems the abyss, whom Jove, when from his throne
   He thunders, still is threatening, withal.
And now I could discern the face of one,                 46
   The shoulders, breast, his belly's greater part,
   And both his arms that hung beside him down.
Certainly Nature, when she left the art                   49
   Of their creation, did most well, that hence
   She took from Mars such ministers of hurt.
If she repenteth not of elephants                       52
   And whales, whoever subtly looks will find
   Therein her justice and her providence;
'Tis when are joined the faculties of mind              55
   With evil will and power, that shield is none
   Against them for our race, of any kind.
In length and width like to Saint Peter's cone         58
   At Rome, methought his visage to appear,
   And in the same proportion every bone;
Wherefore the bank, which from the waist as 'twere   61
   An apron clothed his body, left thereof
   So much yet visible that to reach his hair

---

44. The use of the name "Jove" here for "God" prepares the mind for accepting the rebellious giants of classical mythology as enemies of the Almighty.

49-57. Nature showed rare discrimination when she ceased to produce giants; for they combined strength with intelligence, and hence man was helpless against them. She still brings forth whales and elephants; but these, lacking reason, are not so destructive.

58. *Saint Peter's cone.* A pine cone of gilt bronze, which once crowned the Mausoleum of Hadrian (the Castle of Saint Angelo) and is now, somewhat mutilated, in the Vatican gardens, stood in Dante's time in the fore-court of Saint Peter's. Its height then has been variously estimated at anywhere between six and eleven feet; so we can be no more specific about the size of the giants than to say that the poet conceived of them as ten or twelve times as tall as men. That is also the size of Gulliver's Brobdingnags.

| | |
|---|---:|
| Three vaunting Frisians would have vainly strove: | 64 |
|   Thirty great spans adown him I could spy | |
|   From where one buckles on his cloak above. | |
| *"Rafel mai amech zabi almi"*— | 67 |
|   So did the savage mouth, for which was fit | |
|   No sweeter psalmody, begin to cry. | |
| At him my leader: "Thou insensate spirit, | 70 |
|   Keep to thy horn, and vent thy heart therewith | |
|   When rage or other passion seizeth it. | |
| Search round thy neck; 'tis there the baldric lieth, | 73 |
|   As thou wilt find; and see, O soul confused, | |
|   The horn across thy mighty breast beneath." | |
| And then to me: "This one is self-accused. | 76 |
|   Nimrod is he, but for whose evil plans | |
|   One language in the world would still be used. | |
| Let us not speak in vain, but where he stands | 79 |
|   Leave him, for every tongue to him appears | |
|   As his to us, which no one understands." | |
| Hence, turning now to leftward, did we traverse | 82 |
|   The distance of a crossbow-shot and find | |
|   The next in order, far more large and fierce. | |
| Who and what master was it that could bind | 85 |
|   Him thus, I cannot tell; yet he was bound— | |
|   The left hand fast in front, the right behind— | |
| From the neck downward with a chain that wound | 88 |

---

64. That is, standing one on top of the other. The Frisians were reputed to be the tallest men in Europe.

66. From neck to waist. The span is another measure of uncertain length, but the "thirty great spans" probably represents upwards of twenty feet.

67. This fragmentary line is meant to be gibberish.

77. Nimrod, the "mighty hunter" of Genesis, was commonly thought to have been a giant and the builder of the Tower of Babel. Having caused the confusion of tongues, he is now himself confused of mind and can neither understand the speech of any other people nor be understood by them.

## CANTO XXXI

About him so that on the part which rose
To view, five times the coils wrapped him round.
"This proud one willed, of his own power gross,     91
Trial to make against all-highest Jove,"
My leader said, "and is rewarded thus.
His name is Ephialtes, and he strove     94
Mightily when the giants taught gods to fear;
The arms he wielded, nevermore can move."
And I to him: "If possible it were,     97
I would that of immense Briareüs
Mine eyes might have the sight."—"Not far from here,"
To this he answered, "thou shalt see Antaeus,     100
Who speaks and is not chained, and who will on
The lowest depth of sin deposit us.
A great way off, and even like this one     103
Fashioned and bound, is he whom thou wouldst see,
But more ferocious still to look upon."—
No mighty earthquake shook so violently     106
Ever a tower, as himself therewith
Shook the huge Ephialtes suddenly.
Then was it, most of all, I dreaded death;     109
And save my fear there needed naught for it,

---

94 *ff*. Ephialtes and his brother Otus attempted to scale Olympus by piling one mountain on another. Dante doubtless considered this episode a distorted pagan recollection of the story of the Tower of Babel, and the rest of the fabled war between gods and giants, in which Briareüs also took part, as a similar distortion of the revolt of the rebel angels; hence he could the more easily assimilate these myths with his own theology.

100. Antaeus was a giant whom Hercules slew—by lifting and crushing him, because he magically multiplied his strength whenever felled to earth. He is permitted more freedom than his fellows, being less guilty, for he did not take part in their impious war, but only opposed a Heaven-favoured hero.

102. *The lowest depth of sin.* The floor of the lowest circle.

108. With rage, because Virgil had said Briareüs was of more ferocious aspect.

Had I not seen the shackles of his girth.
So kept we on our way, until we met 112
  Antaeus, who at least five times an ell,
  Besides his head, protruded from the pit.
"O thou, who even in that fateful vale 115
  Which Scipio the heir of glory made,
  When with his host was routed Hannibal,
Of yore a thousand lions, thy prey, didst lead; 118
  By whom, hadst thou but shared that warfare bold
  Thy brethren waged, the sons of Earth had had
The victory, it appeareth some yet hold:— 121
  Disdain not thou, but set us there below
  Where fast is bound Cocytus by the cold.
To Tityos nor Typhon make us go; 124
  This man can give what here is hungered for.
  Bend therefore down, nor curl thy muzzle so.
Still in the world thy fame he can restore. 127
  He lives, and hopeth long on earth to bide,
  If Grace doth call him to her not before
His time." The master thus;—and that one hied 130
  To stretch those hands whose mighty grasp was laid
  Once upon Hercules, unto my guide.
When Virgil felt himself thus taken, he said 133
  To me: "Come hither, that I may take thee, too";
  Then of himself and me one bundle made.

---

113. The length of an "ell," too, is doubtful, but it was evidently greater than the English ell.

115 *ff.* The cave of Antaeus was said to have been near Zama, where Scipio defeated Hannibal. Virgil first flatters Antaeus, then plays upon his jealousy of his fellow giants Tityos and Typhon, and finally holds out the almost unfailing inducement that his fame will be celebrated in the world unless Dante should die unexpectedly soon.

120. *the sons of Earth.* The giants.

## CANTO XXXI

As seems the Carisenda to the view 136
  Beneath its leaning side, when goes a cloud
  Above it so the tower inclines thereto,—
Such did Antaeus seem to me who stood 139
  Watching to see him stoop; that moment's fear
  Made me right fain to use another road.
But in the abyss that whelmeth Lucifer 142
  With Judas, both of us he gently placed;
  Nor thus bent over did he linger there,
But raised himself as in a ship the mast. 145

136 ff. The Carisenda (kä-ree-sĕn'-dä) is a leaning tower in Bologna. When one stands beneath its overhanging wall and looks up at it, the passage of a cloud overhead in the opposite direction to the inclination makes the tower seem to begin to fall.

## CANTO XXXII

*The lowest hell: ninth circle. The frozen pool of Cocytus. The first ring: Caina: traitors against relatives. Camicion de' Pazzi. The second ring: Antenora: traitors against country. Bocca degli Abati. Ugolino and his prey.*

If I had rhymes that were as hoarse and rough
  As would befit the dismal hole whereon
  All other rocks thrust downward from above,
I would the juice of my conceptiön     4
  Press out more fully; but since 'tis otherwise,
  Not without fear, to utterance thereupon
I bring myself. Aye, no light enterprise     7
  Is this, the bottom of all the universe
  To picture, nor for tongue that "Mamma!" cries
And "Papa!" May those Ladies help my verse     10
  Who helped Amphion the great walls to heap
  Of Thebes, that word and fact be not diverse.
O rabble the most miscreate, who keep     13
  Within that place hard to describe, on earth
  Better had ye been only goats or sheep!
When we were down in the dark pit, beneath     16
  The giant's feet, but lower far, and I
  Was scanning still its lofty sides, there saith

---

2-3. All the rocky walls and declivities of the other circles converge upon the pit of Hell, for it lies at the centre of the earth.

10. *those Ladies.* The Muses, who gave such power to the lyre of Amphion that by playing upon it he made great stones move from their places on Mount Cithaeron and build of themselves the walls of Thebes.

17. *lower far.* Apparently the giants did not stand on the floor of the pit, which was far deeper than their height, but only just below its rim, upon a shelf above which the sides became perpendicular.

## CANTO XXXII

A voice to me: "See thou walk carefully, 19
 Nor trample with thy soles, as thou dost pass,
 Thy weary, wretched brothers' heads, so nigh."
And then I turned and saw before me was, 22
 And underfoot, a lake whose frozen glare
 Had semblance not of water but of glass.
Never in Austria did the Danube wear 25
 Over his wintry course a veil so thick,
 Nor Don beneath the frigid sky afar,
As here was spread, for even if Tambernic 28
 Or Pietrapana had fallen thereon, 'twould not
 Have given so much as at the edge a creak.
And as a frog sits croaking with its snout 31
 Thrust from the water, what time the peasantess
 Dreams often of her gleaning,—so, all about,
The woeful shades, livid, up to the place 34
 Where shows the blush of shame, were in the ice.
 Like storks they chattered with their teeth. His face
Each of them downward held. The mouth supplies, 37
 Itself, unto their cold a witness clear,
 And to the sadness of their hearts the eyes.
When round me I had gazed awhile, more near 40
 My feet I looked, and two beheld so close

---

23. *a lake.* Cocytus. It occupies the entire ninth and last circle.

28-29. The mountain Tambernic cannot be positively identified. Pietrapana (pyâ-trä-pä′-nä) is a peak of the Tuscan Apennines.

32-33. *what time,* etc. In summer.

34 *ff.* The ice in which the sinners of the ninth circle are fixed symbolizes the utter coldness of the traitor's heart. This circle is divided into four parts, situated concentrically one inside another. The first and outermost ring, in which Dante and Virgil now are, is for those who were traitors against their kindred, and is called Caina, for Cain, who slew his brother. Its inhabitants were found to be in the ice up to their faces, which they held downward, while their chattering teeth made a noise like the chattering of a stork's bill, thus testifying to the cold, as their weeping eyes did to their sadness.

That on their heads was intermixed the hair.
"Ye who together press your bosoms thus, 43
   Tell me," I said, "who are ye?" Back did strain
   Their necks, and when their faces toward me rose,
Their eyes, which wept but inwardly till then, 46
   Gushed at the lids, and straight the frost congealed
   The tears between and locked them up again.
Board against board by clamp was never held 49
   So fast; whereon they butted like a pair
   Of he-goats, over them such rage prevailed.
And one, who by the cold had lost each ear, 52
   Said, looking downward still: "Why without tire
   Dost thou so fixedly upon us stare?
To know who these two are, if thou desire, 55
   The valley whence Bisenzio descends
   Was theirs and was Alberto's—he their sire.
They issued from one body; searching hence, 58
   Thou shalt not find a spirit, all Caina through,
   For whom the ice were worthier recompense:
Not him whose breast and shadow at one blow 61

---

53 ff. Whereas in most of the other circles the lost souls have been eager for earthly renown, in this last abyss they wish rather to hide their shame. But as they were traitors on earth, so here, still true to their nature, *they betray each other* to Dante, revealing their own identity only to win credence for their words, or for other ulterior purposes.

55. The two in whom Dante was interested are Napoleone and Alessandro, sons of Alberto (äl-bĕr′-to), Count of Mangona. A Ghibelline and a Guelf respectively, they quarrelled over their inheritance and slew each other. The little river Bisenzio (bee-sĕnt′-sĭ-o) empties into the Arno near Florence.

59. "Caina" is to be read as a dissyllable (kā′-nä). Most authorities pronounce "kä-ee′-nä," as in the Italian; but it means "the place of Cain," and "Cain" with us is one syllable—not "kä-een"!

61. Modred, the traitorous nephew (or son) of King Arthur, was killed by that monarch with a thrust which "let daylight through him." Focaccia (fo-kä′-tchä) de' Cancellieri of Pistoia and Sassol Mascheroni (säs′-sol mäs-kä-ro′-nee) of Florence were murderers of kinsmen, as

## CANTO XXXII

Were piercèd both alike by Arthur's hand,
   Focaccia not, nor him who screens me so
That for his head I see no farther, and             64
   Was Sassol Mascheroni named;—if thou
   Art Tuscan, well of him dost understand.
And to be done with speech, I will avow          67
   Me Camicion de' Pazzi; to have ease
   Of blame, I do await Carlino now."
Later I saw a thousand visages                      70
   Grown doggish with the cold, whence I am led
   To shudder, evermore remembering these,
At frozen pools. But as our way we made        73
   On toward the centre of all gravity,
   And I was shivering in the eternal shade,—
Whether 'twere will or chance or destiny,        76
   Now as among the heads I walked, my foot
   Against the face of one struck violently.
"Why treadest on me," weeping, it cried out,    79
   "Unless thou come the vengeance to increase,
   Molesting me, for Montaperti's rout?"

---

was the speaker himself, Camicion de' Pazzi (kä'-mee-chon dā päts'-see), who feels that when his relative Carlino (kär-lee'-no) dies and is placed in the next inner ring for betraying the castle of Piantravigne to the Neri, his own guilt will appear less black by comparison.

71. *doggish.* Their lips drawn back by the cold, as if snarling.

74. Toward the centre of the earth. The plain of ice was not horizontal, but sloped downward.

77 *ff.* The poets have come to the second ring, containing traitors against their country and called Antenora after Antenor of Troy, who was supposed to have revealed to the Greeks what measures were necessary for the capture of that city.

79 *ff.* The speaker is Bocca (bok'-kä) degli Abati, most infamous of Florentine traitors, who at a critical moment of the battle of Montaperti (mon-tä-pĕr'-tee) cut off the hand of the Florentine standard-bearer and thus brought on the rout and terrible slaughter of his comrades. (See Canto x, 32, Note.) Hearing the name of that fatal field, Dante suspects the sinner's identity and stops to make sure of it.

"Master, now tarry here that so may cease 82
  A doubt I have, respecting him," I said;
  "Then make me haste however much thou please."
My leader stood, and I unto that shade, 85
  Who still kept bitterly reviling: "Who
  Art thou, that dost another thus upbraid?"
"Nay, who art thou," he said, "that goest through 88
  The Antenora, smiting cheeks amain?
  Wert thou alive, too much were this to do."
"I *am* alive, and if thou seekest fame," 91
  Was my response, "it may advantage thee
  That I upon my tablets set thy name."
But he thereto: "I want the contrary. 94
  Away with thee! Vex me no more. 'Tis clear
  Thou knowest not what to us is flattery."
Then on his hinder scalp I seized, and sware: 97
  "Either thou shalt reveal thy name withal,
  Or not a hair shall bide upon thee here."
And he to me: "Even if thou strip it all, 100
  I will not tell nor show thee who am I,
  Though on my head a thousand times thou fall."
Already amid his locks my hand did ply, 103
  And had pulled out more tufts than one, the whiles he
  Was barking, with his eyes bent downwardly,
When here another cried: "Bocca, what ails thee? 106
  Is it not enough to chatter with thy jaws,
  But thou must yelp besides? What devil assails thee?"
"Now," said I, "for thy speech there is no cause 109
  To wish, accursed traitor. Truthfully
  Of thee shall I report the shameful news."
"Begone!" he answered; "tell what pleases thee, 112

---

96. Promise of fame is no inducement to the traitors.

## CANTO XXXII

But keep not silent, if thou gettest hence,
Of that one who spake up so readily.
The silver of the French he here laments.  115
'Him of Duera,' canst thou say, 'e'en where
The wicked stand a-cold for their offence,
I saw.' Shouldst thou be asked who else was there,  118
Thou of the Beccheria hast that one
Whose gullet Florence cut, beside thee near.
Gianni de' Soldanier is farther on,  121
I think, with Tribaldello, who unlocked
Faenza while it slept, and Ganelon."
When we had left him, I behold two yoked  124
Within a single hole, so close one head,
As though it were a hood, the other cloaked.
And he above, as hunger eateth bread,  127
Made of his fellow for his teeth a prey,
Where to the nape the brain is fastenèd.
Not otherwise gnawed Tydeus furiously  130
On Melanippus' temples than upon

---

113 ff. His own identity betrayed, Bocca takes a fiendish delight in betraying that of all his neighbours, who like himself would fain have remained unrecognized. The spirit who called him by name, he reveals, is Buoso da Duera (doo-ā'-rä) of Cremona, who in 1265 was bribed by the French to allow the troops of Charles of Anjou, on their way to the conquest of Naples, to pass unmolested by the Ghibelline army with which he had been sent to oppose them. Another traitor near by is Tesauro de' Beccheria (bĕk-kā-ree'-ä) of Pavia, who was beheaded by the Florentine Guelfs in 1258 for conducting secret negotiations with the Ghibelline exiles. Others named are two perfidious Ghibellines, Gianni de' Soldanier (jàn'-nee dā sŏl'-dà-nyâr) and that Tribaldello (tree-bäl-dĕl'-lo) who opened Faenza (fä-ĕnt'-sä) to her enemies, together with Ganelon, the traitor in the Charlemagne romances, who brought about the destruction of the rear-guard of the great king's army at Roncesvalles, where Roland and Oliver and their heroic comrades were slain.

130. Tydeus was one of the chieftains in the expedition of "the Seven against Thebes." Mortally wounded by Melanippus in battle, he yet slew his adversary, whose severed head he gnawed in a frenzy of rage as he lay dying.

The skull and other parts contiguous, he.
"O thou whose hate so bestially is shown 133
  Toward him whom thou devourest, tell me why
  'Tis so," I said, "on this conditiön:
If thou of him complainest rightfully, 136
  Knowing who ye are and what his sin, I may
  Yet in the world requite thee presently,
Unless my tongue be withered, then, away." 139

## CANTO XXXIII

*Ninth circle: second ring. Ugolino's story. The third ring: Ptolomea: traitors against friends and guests. Fra Alberigo. Of damnation before death. The traitor tricked.*

His mouth uplifting from his fell repast,
   The sinner wiped it first upon the hair
   Of that same head which he behind laid waste.
Then he began: "Thou willest an added share     4
   I take of grief which even in thought o'erweighs
   My heart, ere speech doth make it heavier.
But if my tale may be a seed to raise     7
   Infamy to the traitor whom I gnaw,
   Words shalt thou have and weeping, both apace.
I know not who thou art, nor how hast thou     10
   Come hither down, but Florentine to me
   Thou seemest verily when I hear thee. Know,
I was on earth Count Ugolino, he     13
   Ruggieri the Archbishop; wherefore I
   Am such a neighbour, I will declare to thee.
That by effect of his malignancy     16

---

13. Ugolino (oo-go-lee'-no) della Gherardesca, Count of Donoratico, was long the head of the Guelfs in Pisa. He displayed great talents of statecraft, but his policies were not always above suspicion. Finally, in 1288, being at variance with his nephew, Nino Visconti, who was associated with him in the leadership of their party, he intrigued with the Archbishop Ruggieri (rood-jâ'-ree) degli Ubaldini, head of the Pisan Ghibellines, to expel this kinsman adversary and his adherents from the city. But when the Guelf faction was thus weakened, the Archbishop betrayed Ugolino in turn, and imprisoned him in a tower with two of his sons and two grandsons, where they were presently starved to death. Ugolino's piteous story is, with the possible exception of Francesca da Rimini's, the most famous episode in the *Divine Comedy*.

I, trusting him, was made a prisoner
And later murdered, it needs not that I say;
But what it is impossible thou didst hear— 19
  That is, how cruel was my death, I mean—
  Thou shalt hear now; then judge if wronged I were.
A narrow window, that hawk's cage within 22
  Which for my sake as Hunger Tower is known
  (And others, too, hereafter it will pen!)
Had shown me through its opening many a moon 25
  Already, when I had the evil dream
  That pierced for me the future's veil. This one,
Lord of the hunt, did on the mountains seem 28
  Which betwixt Lucca and the Pisans stand,
  To track the old wolf and his whelps. With lean,
Eager, and well trained hounds, Gualandi and 31
  Lanfranchi and Sismondi he had sent
  Forward in front of him. After they ran
A short course only, sire and sons were spent, 34
  Meseemed, with running and (so to me appeared
  The dream) their flanks by the sharp fangs were rent.
When I awoke before the dawn, I heard 37
  My children, who were with me, in their sleep
  Moaning aloud for bread. My every word
Proves thee unpitying if now thou keep 40
  From tears to think whereof my heart was seer.

---

25. Their imprisonment had, in fact, lasted from July to March.

27 *ff*. Ugolino's dream is that Ruggieri hunted down an old wolf and its whelps (which symbolize Ugolino and his progeny) on Monte San Giuliano, an eminence which hides Lucca (look'-ka) from the view of the Pisans. The Archbishop sent ahead of him (that is, made his agents) three of the chief Ghibelline families of Pisa, Gualandi (gwä-län'-dee) and Lanfranchi (län-frän'-kee) and Sismondi (sees-mon'-dee), with their hounds (the Pisan mob); and the quarry were soon overtaken and slain.

37-39. The others were dreaming of starvation, a more literal augury.

## CANTO XXXIII

Nay, if thou weep not, what can make thee weep?
They had awakened, and the hour drew near 43
   When it was wont our food should there be placed;
   But each debated o'er his dream in fear.
And then I heard the outer door made fast 46
   Of the horrible tower; at which all silently
   Upon the faces of my sons I gazed.
I wept not, so to stone within grew I; 49
   *They* wept; and darling little Anselm cried:
   'Thou lookest so! Father! what aileth thee?'
Yet still I shed no tear, nor word replied 52
   All that day or the next night, till the sun
   Once more came forth upon the world outside.
But when into the prison shadows wan 55
   A little glimmer found its way, and lit
   Four faces wherein I might read my own,
Both of my hands in agony I bit; 58
   And they, supposing it through hunger's stress,
   Rose suddenly up and said: 'If thou wilt eat
Of us, O Father, we should suffer less. 61
   'Twas thou thyself didst clothe us with this poor
   Flesh; do thou strip it off.' To quietness
I forced me then, not to afflict them more. 64
   That day we all stayed dumb, and all next day.
   O obdurate earth, thou didst not gape—wherefore?
The fourth day Gaddo threw him down and lay 67
   Stretched out before my feet, crying: 'Hast thou
   No help, no help for me, my father?'—yea,
And died there; and as thou seest me, I saw 70
   The three fall one by one between the fifth

---

46-75. These thirty lines were pronounced by Landor to be "unequalled by any other continuous thirty in the whole dominions of poetry."
67. Gaddo (gäd'-do).

And sixth days, whereon I betook me, now
Already blind, to groping over each, 73
And two days called them after they were dead.
Then fasting was more powerful than grief."
Rolling his eyes askance, when he had said, 76
He fastened upon the wretched skull with strong
Teeth like a dog's, which on the bare bone fed.
Ah, Pisa! shame of all men who belong 79
In that fair land where tongue-of-*si* doth sound,
Since ne'er to vengeance do thy neighbours throng,
Let Cáprar' and Gorgona shift their ground 82
And at its mouth dam up the Arno's stream,
That every living soul in thee be drowned!
For though Count Ugolino thou didst deem 85
Betrayed thy castles, thou shouldest not have set
His sons on such a cross. Thou couldst not ween
Either Brigata, Uguccione, or yet 88
The other two I named were guilty—these,
Thou second Thebes, their tender years acquit.

---

75. Does this line mean merely that Ugolino, who had not died of grief already, now died of hunger? Or (ghastly alternative) that the intolerable pangs of hunger drove him, in desecration of his grief and love, to feed upon the bodies of his children? "Pity and terror" reach their climax in this dread ambiguity.

80. In Italy. *Sì* is Italian for "yes." So was the Provençal tongue, in which "yes" is *oc*, called the *langue d'oc* (language of *oc*).

82. Caprara and Gorgona (gor-go'-nä) are two small islands in the Mediterranean not far from where the Arno empties; and the poet calls on them to change their position and block up the mouth of that river so as to drown all the accursed people of Pisa. For "Caprara" the translation uses the poetic abbreviation "Caprar'," Anglicized to be accented on the first syllable.

88 *ff*. Uguccione (oo-goo-tcho'-nä) and Gaddo alone were Ugolino's sons; Brigata (bree-gä'-tä) and little Anselm were his grandsons; but the poet conceives of them all as too young to engage in any possible treachery. He calls Pisa a second Thebes because of all ancient cities Thebes was stained with the most horrible episodes, such as the parricide and incest of Oedipus and the fratricidal strife of his sons.

## CANTO XXXIII

Thence we passed on, to where the ice doth seize 91
With rugged clasp a different folk, who lie
Not downward bent—upon their backs they freeze.
Their very weeping, weeping doth deny, 94
And grief, which from their eyes no longer flows,
Turns inward to increase the agony.
For the first tears become a knot which grows 97
Till like a mask of crystal fixed it stays,
Filling the cavity beneath their brows.
And though, as if it were a callous place, 100
By reason of the cold all feeling now
Completely had departed from my face,
Meseemed that I perceived some wind to blow; 103
Whence I: "Who, master, moveth this? Are not
All exhalations quenchèd here below?"
But he to me: "Thou soon shalt reach a spot 106
Where, seeing the cause which raineth down the blast,
Thine eye shall answer thee concerning that."
Then one among those wretches frozen fast 109
Cried out to us: "O ye so criminal
That for your station is assigned the last,
Lift from before mine eyes the rigid veil 112

---

91. Dante and Virgil now come to the third division of the frozen lake of Cocytus. Here traitors against friends and guests lie outstretched on their backs, with only their upturned faces uncovered, whereas in Caina they had been fixed in the ice upright, with down-bent heads emerging, and similarly in Antenora except that there apparently their heads were not inclined. This third ring is called Ptolemea, either from Ptolemeus, the captain of Jericho, of whom it is told in the First Book of Maccabees that he invited Simon and two of his sons into his castle and there treacherously murdered them, or from Ptolemy, King of Egypt, who murdered Pompey the Great.

105. Dante believed all winds the result of exhalations raised by heat, and hence could not understand the presence of a blast across the ice-field of Cocytus.

110-111. The frozen, blinded spirit thinks Dante and Virgil are two traitors on their way to the next and last division of this lowest circle.

And let me vent the grief which swells my heart,
A little, ere again the tears congeal."
"If thou wouldst have mine aid, say who thou art,"          115
I answered, craftily, "and if I do
Not loose thee, may it even be my part
To go unto the bottom." He thereto:                          118
"I am Fra Alberigo, of the bad
Fruit, who receive here dates for figs, my due."
"What," I exclaimed, "art thou already dead?"                121
"How, in the world above, my body fares,
I have no knowledge," unto me he said;
"For such a privilege is Ptolomea's                          124
That oft a spirit falleth to this place
Ere Atropos impel it with the shears.
And that thou mayest more willingly my face                  127
Rid of the drops incrusted thereupon,
Know that, immediately the soul betrays
As I did, straight a demon seizes on                         130
Her body, and thereafter governs it
Till its appointed time is wholly run.
Herself down rushes to our cistern pit.—                     133
Perchance his form yet among men doth show

---

116. *craftily.* As a penalty upon himself if he does not relieve the sinner, Dante's words invoke precisely what he is going to do in any case!

119. Alberigo (äl-bā-ree'-go) de' Manfredi, of Faenza, was one of the order of Jovial Friars. Having been struck by his younger brother, Manfred, he feigned a reconciliation and invited him and his son to a banquet. At the signal of his command, "Bring in the fruit!" assassins entered and killed both guests. "The bad fruit of Fra Alberigo" became proverbial.

126. Atropos was that one of the three Fates in classical mythology who cut the thread of life.

131-133. *Her . . . Herself.* To avoid ambiguity, "soul" is here considered as feminine, as it is in Italian, for such personification is not unknown in English—for example, "with Psyche, my Soul" (Poe's *Ulalume*).

## CANTO XXXIII

Who here behind me wintereth; howbeit,
If thou art come but lately, thou shouldst know.    136
This is Ser Branca D'Oria; many years
Have passed since he was first imprisoned so."
"I deem thy words are only lying snares,"    139
I answered him, "for by no means is Branca
D'Oria dead, but eats, drinks, sleeps, and wears
His clothes."—"The chasm of the Malebranche    142
Above, where boils the sticky pitch," he said,
"Had not received the soul of Michel Zanche
When this man left a devil in his stead    145
Within his own flesh, as did one, likewise,
Akin to him, who shared the treacherous deed.
Now hither reach thy hand; open mine eyes."    148
But I—I did not ope them! Verily,
Despites to him were fittest courtesies.
Ye Genoese! from all morality    151
Estranged, in whom all foulness doth abound,
Wherefore not scattered from the world are ye?
For with Romagna's vilest spirit I found    154
One of you such as for his crimes hath been
In soul already in Cocytus drowned,
While still on earth his living body is seen!    157

---

137 *ff.* Branca D'Oria (brän'-kä do'-ree-ä), of the great Genoese family of Doria, with the aid of a relative murdered that Michel Zanche (mī'-kĕl tsän'-kä) who was mentioned in Canto xxii as being one of the barrators in the lake of pitch guarded by the Malebranche (mä-lĕ-brän'-kä). Branca D'Oria actually reached his place of punishment sooner than his victim did his, though his body, inhabited by a devil, still moved among men in 1300.

154. *Romagna's vilest spirit.* Fra Alberigo.

## CANTO XXXIV

*Ninth circle. The fourth ring: Judecca: traitors to benefactors. Lucifer, or Dis. Judas, Brutus, Cassius. Past the earth's centre. The hidden way. The return to the upper world.*

"'*Vexilla regis prodeunt*' inferni
   Against us. If his shape thou canst discern,"
My master said, "behold in front of thee."
And as a mill appears the wind doth turn,     4
   Seen from afar, when breathes a heavy mist
Or night upon our hemisphere is born,
Methought I saw a structure such as this—     7
   And then, by reason of the wind, I drew
Behind my guide; no shelter was but his.
Now had I come (and 'tis with fear I do     10
   These verses) unto where the shades were quite
Beneath the ice, and only glimmered through
Like straws in glass: some prone, and some upright,     13
   This one upon its soles, that on its head,
And feet-to-crown, bow-bent, another's plight.
When we, advancing still, our way had made     16
   To where it pleased my master I be showed
That creature who so fair was fashionèd,

---

1. "The banners of the King of Hell advance." *Vexilla regis prodeunt* ("The banners of the King advance") were the first words of an old Latin hymn, which Virgil now adapts to the situation by adding *inferni*. The banners here are the wings of Lucifer, which "come into view."

10. The poets have reached the fourth and last ring, Judécca, named for Judas Iscariot. Here are the traitors against their lords or benefactors. They are entirely covered with ice.

18. Lucifer was one of the fairest of the angels before his fall from Heaven.

## CANTO XXXIV

He stayed my steps, and from before me stood,    19
   Saying: "Lo, here is Dis, and here the place
   Where thou must arm thyself with fortitude."
How frozen I then became and powerless,    22
   Ask me not, Reader; I could ne'er contrive
   To tell what words are helpless to express.
I did not die, and yet I did not live.    25
   Judge, if thou hast of wit the slightest share,
   My state, deprived of each alternative.
He of the realm of pain the Emperor    28
   Stood from his mid-breast forth above the ice,
   And better with a giant I compare
Than do the giants with those arms of his;    31
   Wherefore consider how great must be that whole
   Which doth to such a part conform in size.
If once he were as fair as he is foul,    34
   And 'gainst his Maker lifted up his brows,
   From him may well proceed the sum of dole.
And oh, it seemed to me how marvellous    37
   When I beheld three faces on his head:
   The one in front—and that vermilion was—
While o'er the middle of each shoulder-blade    40
   The others rose, beside it, to his extreme
   Crest, where all met and were together wed.
Yellow and white the right one was between;    43
   In hue like them who dwell where valleyward
   The Nile flows down, that on the left did seem.

---

20. *Dis.* Lucifer. See Note on Canto viii, 68.

27. *each alternative.* Death and life.

38 *ff.* The three faces form a sort of infernal Trinity. They may be understood to represent respectively Hate, Impotence, and Ignorance, as opposed to Wisdom, Power, and Love (see Canto iii, 5-6). Unlike Milton's Satan, there is nothing sublime about the arch-fiend of Dante; he is wholly horrible and hideous.

44-45. That is, black.

Beneath each face two mighty wings out-soared, 46
  Such as were fitting for a bird thus great:
  Sails of the sea I never saw so broad.
They had no feathers, but as of a bat 49
  Were fashioned. These continually he flapped,
  Whereby three winds went forth from him; and that
It was which all Cocytus froze. He wept 52
  Out of his six eyes, and down every chin
  The trickling tears and bloody slaver dripped.
A sinner in each mouth he champed between 55
  His teeth, as with a brake, so three there were
  In all whom thus he racked with torment keen.
For him in front, the biting in compare 58
  Unto the clawing seemed a thing of naught;
  Often his spine was flayed completely bare.
"That soul aloft is Judas Iscariot," 61
  The master said, "who pain the sorest hath.
  With head inside, he plies his legs without.
And of the two whose heads drop down beneath, 64
  Brutus is he that hangs from the black jowl—
  See how he writhes himself and nothing saith;
The other Cassius, in limb so full. 67
  But night is reascending; now must we

---

55 *ff*. In Lucifer's mouths are punished three sinners, selected by the poet as guilty beyond all others. "Judas, Brutus, and Cassius are the worst of traitors, having not only betrayed their benefactors, but also, in doing so, having done violence to the divinely ordered scheme for the well-being of mankind. Christ, betrayed by Judas, was the head of the Church, the supreme spiritual authority. Caesar, betrayed by Brutus and Cassius, was regarded by Dante as the founder of the Empire, the supreme authority in temporal affairs. Church and Empire were in Dante's scheme equally divine institutions for the government of the world."—Norton. Brutus by his silence preserves some dignity even in his torture. It is not known why Cassius is conceived as large of limb.

68. It is the nightfall of Easter-eve.

## CANTO XXXIV

Depart, for truly we have seen the whole."
I clasped his neck as he commanded me, 70
And he advantage took of time and place,
And when the wings were opened wide and free,
Unto the shaggy sides did he address 73
Himself, and tuft by tuft descended, down
Between the matted hair and crusts of ice.
When we had come where turns the thigh upon 76
Its socket and the haunches thickest swell,
My guide with labour and with breath hard-drawn
Brought round his head where were his legs erewhile, 79
And like one mounting, grappled on the hair;—
Methought we were returning into Hell.
"Hold fast to me, for 'tis by such a stair," 82
The master said, panting as one forspent,
"That out of so great evil we must fare."
Then through the opening where a rock was rent 85
He passed, upon whose brim he seated me
And thither climbed with footstep vigilant.
I lifted up mine eyes, and thought to see 88
Lucifer even as I had left him placed;
But now with legs turned upward, lo, was he;
And if in mind I grew not sore bedazed, 91
Let those dull folk decide who wit have none
To see what point it was which I had passed.

---

73 *ff.* In at least some places there is space between the shaggy body of Lucifer and the ice which he pierces. By clinging to the hair, Virgil clambers down him, bearing Dante, until far below the surface of the ice they reach the haunches of the gigantic fiend. Here, at the point midway his total length, is the centre of the earth and hence of gravity; so here Virgil reverses his body and thenceforth climbs upward instead of descending, though he travels in the same direction as before. Presently they find a resting place on a ledge, where Dante, who lost his sense of direction when the centre of the earth was passed, raises his eyes and sees not the body but the enormous legs of Lucifer towering above him.

"Rise up," my leader said, "thy feet upon. 94
  The way is long and difficult the road,
  And now to middle tierce returns the sun."
No palace hall it was in which we stood, 97
  But natural dungeon, and ill paven this
  And wanting light. "O thou my master good,
Before I pluck myself from the abyss," 100
  I said on rising, "that I may be drawn
  From error, briefly speak to me. The ice?—
Where is it? How is this one upside down 103
  Thus fixèd? How in so short time is whirled
  The sun through all his course from eve to morn?"
And he: "Thou thinkest thee still where I took hold, 106
  The other side the centre, on the hair
  Of that fell worm who pierces through the world.
While I descended, thou indeed wast there; 109
  But when I turned, we past the point achieved
  Which draws all gravities from everywhere.
Under the hemisphere thou art arrived 112

---

96. Middle tierce is 7:30 a.m. Dante is bewildered to learn it is morning when only a few minutes earlier (line 68) Virgil said night was at hand. He is told that on passing the centre of the earth and consequently entering the opposite hemisphere there was a change of twelve hours; it is now morning again of that same Saturday which was just drawing to a close.

108. *worm.* An opprobrious epithet (meaning literally "dragon") here used loosely of Lucifer as in Canto vi of Cerberus.

112. Standing on a little sphere or disk that is the reverse or "under" surface of the block of ice and stone which is pierced by Lucifer's body (on the other side it is of ice and is called Judecca; here it is of stone), they have reached, Virgil explains, the side of the earth's centre beneath the hemisphere of water, and opposite to the familiar one of land beneath the zenith of which (Jerusalem being regarded as the central point of the northern hemisphere) Christ was crucified. The southern hemisphere, now covered with water except for the Mountain of Purgatory, was formerly the place where the land was which now covers the northern. This land fled to the northern hemisphere when Lucifer fell from Heaven upon the southern, piercing to the centre of the globe;

## CANTO XXXIV

Opposed to that of the great land, beneath
Whose heaven's cope He who was born and lived
Wholly devoid of sin was put to death;   115
  And now thy feet are on a little sphere
  Which for its hinder side Judecca hath.
Here it is morn when it is evening there;   118
  And as before, so is he fixèd still
  Who made for us a ladder with his hair.
On this half world from Heaven down he fell,   121
  And the broad land upon it formerly
  Through fear of him made of the sea a veil
And came to our half; and perchance to fly   124
  His presence, the earth now upon this side
  Left thus a chasm and rushed toward the sky."
A place there is below, that leads as wide   127
  From Beelzebub as e'er his tomb extends,
  Unknown to sight, where but the sound doth guide
Of a small rivulet which here descends,   130
  With slow declivity and tortuous wind,
  The cleft rock-channel it hath eaten thence.
And now upon that hidden road and blind   133
  My guide and I did enter, to return
  To the fair world; he first and I behind,
Unresting, mounted till I could discern   136

---

and in no less revulsion the earth and rock which formerly occupied the space that is now the cavity of Hell rushed to the surface of the southern hemisphere and there formed the Mountain of Purgatory.

127-128. A narrow chasm leading from the legs of Beelzebub ("the prince of devils," Matthew xii, 24—here used as another name for Lucifer) as far as the cavity of Hell extended upward from his body —that is, to the surface of the globe.

136. *Unresting.* The ascent to the upper world occupied the entire space of that Saturday through which the poets were passing a second time; they emerged only a little before dawn on the morning of Easter Sunday.

Through a round opening those bright luminars
So beautiful, that in the heavens burn.
We issued, and once more beheld the stars.

---

137. *luminars.* Luminaries. The coinage seems legitimate to gain a rhyme word which will enable the poem to end with "stars" in imitation of the original. The same word, *stelle,* with its suggestion of light and hope, concludes each of the three parts of the *Divine Comedy.*